Exemplary Science in Grades 5–8

Standards-Based Success Stories

Exemplary Science in Grades 5–8

Standards-Based Success Stories

Robert E. Yager, Editor

NATIONAL SCIENCE TEACHERS ASSOCIATION
Arlington, Virginia

NATIONAL SCIENCE TEACHERS ASSOCIATION

Claire Reinburg, Director
Judy Cusick, Senior Editor
J. Andrew Cocke, Associate Editor
Betty Smith, Associate Editor
Robin Allan, Book Acquisitions Coordinator

PRINTING AND PRODUCTION, Catherine Lorrain-Hale, Director
   Nguyet Tran, Assistant Production Manager
   Jack Parker, Electronic Prepress Technician

NATIONAL SCIENCE TEACHERS ASSOCIATION
Gerald F. Wheeler, Executive Director
David Beacom, Publisher

Library of Congress Cataloging-in-Publication Data
Exemplary science in grades 5-8 : standards-based success stories / [edited] by Robert Yager.
   p. cm.
 Includes bibliographical references and index.
 ISBN 0-87355-262-8
1. Science--Study and teaching (Middle school) I. Yager, Robert Eugene, 1930-
Q181.E94 2006
507'.1'273--dc22

                    2005016739

Contents

Implementing the Changes in Middle School Programs Envisioned in the National Science Education Standards:

Where Are We Nine Years Later?

Robert E. Yager
Science Education Center
University of Iowa

How This Book Came About

Nine years have elapsed since the 1996 publication of the National Science Education Standards (NSES) (NRC 1996). The critical issues in science education now are these: How far have we progressed in putting the vision of the NSES into practice? What remains to be done? What new visions are worthy of new trials?

The four monographs in the NSTA Exemplary Science Monograph series seek to answer these questions. The monographs are *Exemplary Science: Best Practices in Professional Development*; *Exemplary Science in Grades 9–12*; *Exemplary Science in Grades 5–8* (the book you are reading); and *Exemplary Science in Grades K–4*.

The series was conceived in 2001 by an advisory board of science educators, many of whom had participated in the development of the National Science Education Standards. The advisory board members (who are all active and involved NSTA members; see p. xiii for their names) decided to seek exemplars of the NSES' *More Emphasis* conditions as a way to evaluate progress toward the visions of the NSES. The *More Emphasis* conditions provide summaries of the NSES recommendations in science teaching, professional development, assessment, science content, and science education programs and systems. (See Appendix 1 for the six *Less Emphasis/More Emphasis* lists.) The board sent information about the projected series to the NSTA leadership team and to all the NSTA affiliates, chapters, and associated groups. A call for papers on exemplary programs also appeared in all NSTA publications. In addition, more than a thousand letters inviting nominations were sent to leaders identified in the *2001–2002 NSTA Handbook*, and personal letters were sent to leaders of all science education organizations.

After preliminary responses were received, the advisory board identified teachers and programs that it felt should be encouraged to prepare formal drafts for further review and evaluation. The goal was to identify 15 of the best situations in each of the four areas—professional development and grades 9–12, 5–8, and K–4—where facets of the teaching, professional development, assessment, and content standards were being met in an exemplary manner.

The most important aspect of the selection process was the evidence the authors of each article could provide regarding the effect of their programs on student learning. This aspect proved the most elusive. Most of us "know" when something is going well, but we are not well equipped to provide real evidence for this "knowing." Many exciting program descriptions were not among the final titles—simply because little or no evidence other than personal testimony was available in the materials forwarded. The 15 middle school models that make up this monograph were chosen by the advisory board as the best examples of programs that fulfill the *More Emphasis* conditions; each has had a clear, positive impact on student science learning.

The History of the National Science Education Standards

Before discussing the contents of this book at greater length, I would like to offer a brief history of how the National Science Education Standards came to be.

Most educators credit the National Council of Teachers of Mathematics (NCTM) with initiating the many efforts to produce national standards for programs in U.S. schools. In 1986 (10 years before the publication of the National Science Education Standards), the board of directors of NCTM established a Commission on Standards for School Mathematics with the aim of improving the quality of school mathematics. An initial draft of these standards was developed during the summer of 1987, revised during the summer of 1988 after much discussion among NCTM members, and finally published as the *Curriculum and Evaluation Standards for School Mathematics* in 1989.

The NCTM standards did much for mathematics education by providing a consensus for what mathematics should be. The National Science Foundation (NSF) and other funding groups had not been involved in developing the math standards, but these groups quickly funded research and training to move schools and teachers in the direction of those standards. Having such a "national" statement regarding needed reforms resulted in funding from private and government foundations to produce school standards in other disciplines, including science.

NSF encouraged the science education community to develop standards modeled after the NCTM document (1989). Interestingly, both the American Association for the Advancement of Science (AAAS) and the National Science Teachers Association (NSTA) expressed interest in preparing science standards. Both organizations indicated that they each had made a significant start on such national standards—AAAS with its Project 2061 and NSTA with its Scope, Sequence, and

Coordination project. Both of these national projects had support from NSF, private foundations, and industries. The compromise on this "competition" between AAAS and NSTA leaders led to the recommendation that the National Research Council (NRC) of the National Academy of Sciences be funded to develop the National Science Education Standards. With NSF funding provided in 1992, both NSTA and AAAS helped to select the science leaders who would prepare the NSES. Several early drafts were circulated among hundreds of people with invitations to comment, suggest, debate, and assist with a consensus document. A full-time director of consensus provided leadership and assistance as final drafts were assembled. Eventually, it took $7 million and four years of debate to produce the 262-page NSES publication in 1996.

There was never any intention that the Standards would indicate minimum competencies that would be required of all. Instead, the focus was on visions of how teaching, assessment, and content should be changed. Early on, programs and systems were added as follow-ups to teaching, assessment, and content.

NSES and the Middle School Science Classroom

The philosophy of the middle school in the United States matches the *More Emphasis* conditions of teaching. In many respects, the middle school teachers have found it easy to be more "student centered," to be more collegial with other teachers, and to work on common projects across the curriculum. The mix of teachers with secondary school endorsements and the nearly one-half with elementary school licenses and teaching focus provides for more cross-pollination in terms of discipline/curriculum focus or focus upon current, local, and relevant problems.

On one hand, it would be good if school systems could uniformly designate the five though eight grade levels as middle school grades. However, with the more typical K–5 elementary school, 6–8 (and sometimes 9) junior high, and (either 10–12 or 9–12) high school, the middle schools have the advantage of being less rigidly defined, with fewer problems related to immediate means for fulfilling the four goals for science in the NSES. These goals are basic to middle schools; they focus on the production of students who

1. experience the richness and excitement of knowing about and understanding the natural world;
2. use appropriate scientific processes and principles in making personal decisions;
3. engage intelligently in public discourse and debate about matters of scientific and technological concern; and
4. increase their economic productivity through the use of the knowledge, understanding, and skills of the scientifically literate person in their careers.

(NRC 1996, p. 13)

The 14 *More Emphasis* conditions for continuing staff development more closely resemble what is done in middle schools—where there is less concern for an inadequate preparation in science found in teachers in elementary schools—and less emphasis on life, physical, and Earth science with few opportunities to build ideas and approaches across the high school grades.

Assessment, too, is more likely in the middle school to focus on the ways assessment practices should change as advocated in the NSES. The Standards call for more emphasis on:

1. Assessing what is most highly valued
2. Assessing rich, well-structured knowledge
3. Assessing scientific understanding and reasoning
4. Assessing to learn what students do understand
5. Assessing achievement and opportunity to learn
6. Students engaged in ongoing assessment of their work and that of others
7. Teachers involved in the development of external assessments

Reforms in the middle school provide many good reasons for optimism. First of all there is a focus on all the basic disciplines with specialists—unlike the situation in elementary schools where a single teacher is in charge of nearly the total curriculum—sometimes excepting music, art, and physical education. Middle schools basically include teachers with secondary school credentials and elementary school credentials— many times with equal numbers of each. Secondary teachers are often subject matter-bound, where elementary teachers are more focused on students, their unique problems and their struggle to learn. Getting professional teams with both interests and expertise is a worthwhile combination in terms of both a focus upon science as well as student learning.

Middle schools are also excellent places for reform since, unlike high schools, there is less singular focus on college preparation. Administrators and parents are often more willing to deal with student learning and the problems of early adolescents as opposed to a major focus on academic preparation for high school and later college.

Middle school teachers typically are organized with grade level groups and discuss and plan for the total curriculum. It is not uncommon for science teachers to work only tangentially with other science teachers and instead focus on the whole program for students in one grade level. With such a focus it is easy to organize projects around issues and problems where the concepts and skills from all areas of the curriculum come into play.

Middle schools have become more common and more philosophically attuned to standards, problem-based learning, and all four goals of the National Science Education Standards. Most prefer the name "middle school" opposed to the typical designation some decades ago as "junior high schools." Such a term usually meant trying to keep the same discipline format as the high school—but with concern for the appropriateness of the content for 12–14-year-old students. Many more had secondary school licensure and often organized science around the same high school disciplines: life science, physical science, and Earth science.

An interesting development has occurred since the publication of the NSES with respect to the middle school designation, specifically in terms of defining "middle school" as grades 5 through 8. Although few schools have moved formally to include all four grade levels in a single building unit, many are considering the advantages. The mix of teacher preparation and interests is ideal. It is easier to focus on the goals, on assessment strategies to determine how well goals have been met, on how professional development should become part of the plan for the entire professional life of a teacher, and on local community-based problems that are both personally

Errata

Table of Contents

Chapter 6

P. 85: The author order should read Ann M. Novak, Chris Gleason, Jay Mahoney, and Joseph S. Krajcik.

The citation for this chapter should be:

Novak, A. M., C. Gleason, J. Mahoney, and J. S. Krajcik. 2006. Creating a classroom culture of science practices. In *Exemplary science in grades 5–8: Standards-based success stories*, ed. R. E. Yager, 85–98. Arlington: National Science Teachers Association Press.

Chapter 7

P. 99: The author order should read LeeAnn M. Sutherland, Elizabeth Birr Moje, Alycia Meriweather, Sheryl Rucker, Paula Sarratt, Yulonda Hines-Hale, and Joseph S. Krajcik.

The citation for this chapter should be:

Sutherland, L. M., E. B. Moje, A. Meriweather, S. Rucker, P. Sarratt, Y. Hines-Hale, and J. S. Krajcik. 2006. More emphasis on scientific explanation: Developing conceptual understanding and science literacy. In *Exemplary science in grades 5–8: Standards-based success stories*, ed. R. E. Yager, 99–114. Arlington: National Science Teachers Association Press.

relevant to students' lives and current in terms of news reports and community concerns. It is easier to involve local experts, parents, administrators, and business and industrial leaders.

Conclusion

The 15 middle school exemplars all show great progress for implementing the Standards and the stated goals for science in grades 5–8. Each author team was asked to reflect on the *More Emphasis* conditions that were recommended for teaching, assessment, and content (and to some degree those concerned with the continuing education of teachers). To what extent these conditions were met by the exemplars is discussed in the final chapter.

This monograph indicates where we are with respect to meeting the visions for reforms in science for middle schools. It is important to know how our efforts during the four-year development of the NSES have impacted science classrooms. We feel that an exhaustive search has occurred during the past three years, and are impressed with what the search has revealed. We hope others reading about these exciting programs will find new ideas to try and that they will want to share more stories of their successes, especially in terms of similar experiences with their own students. We trust that this volume is an accurate record of what can be done to meet the Standards while also pinpointing some continuing challenges and needs. The exemplary programs described in this monograph give inspiration while also providing evidence that the new directions are feasible and worth the energy and effort needed for others to implement changes.

We also hope that the exemplars included will bring new meaning and life to the *More Emphasis* conditions. In many respects, the *Less Emphasis* conditions are not bad, but they do not usually result in as much learning or in ways the four goals for science teaching can be exemplified.

Hopefully the 15 examples in this monograph will serve as generators for new questions and new ideas for developing even more impressive programs so that the decade following the publication of the NSES results in even more exciting advances by 2006.

References

National Council for Teachers of Mathematics.1989. *Curriculum and evaluation standards for school mathematics*. Reston, VA: Author.

National Research Council (NRC). 1996. *National science education standards*. Washington, DC: National Academy Press.

Acknowledgments

Members of the National Advisory Board for the Exemplary Science Series

Hans O. Andersen
Past President of NSTA
Professor, Science Education
Indiana University-Bloomington
Bloomington, IN

Charles R. Barman
Professor
Science and Environmental Education
Indiana University School of Education
Bloomington, IN

Bonnie Brunkhorst
Past President of NSTA
Professor
California State University-San Bernardino
San Bernardino, CA

Rodger Bybee
Executive Director
Biological Sciences Curriculum Study
Colorado Springs, CO

Audrey Champagne
Professor
State University of New York
Albany, NY

Fred Johnson
Past President of NSTA
Consultant
McKenzie Group
Memphis, TN

Roger Johnson
Professor
University of Minnesota
Minneapolis, MN

Mozell Lang
Science Consultant
Pontiac Northern High School
Pontiac, MI

LeRoy R. Lee
Past President of NSTA
Executive Director
Wisconsin Science Network
DeForest, WI

Shelley A. Lee
Past President of NSTA
Science Education Consultant
Wisconsin Dept. of Public Instruction
Madison, WI

Gerry Madrazo
Past President of NSTA
Clinical Professor—Science Education
University of North Carolina
Chapel Hill, NC

Dick Merrill
Past President of NSTA
University of California, Berkeley
Berkeley, CA

Nick Micozzi
K–12 Science Coordinator
Plymouth Public Schools
Plymouth, MA

Edward P. Ortleb
Past President of NSTA
Science Consultant/Author
St. Louis, MO

Jack Rhoton
President of NSELA
Professor of Science Education
East Tennessee State University
Johnson, TN

Gerald Skoog
Past President of NSTA
Professor and Dean
Texas Tech University
Lubbock, TX

Emma Walton
Past President of NSTA
Science Consultant
Anchorage, AK

Sandra West
Associate Professor
Science Education
Southwest Texas University
Canyon Lake, TX

Karen Worth
Senior Scientist
Education Development Center
Newton, MA

Assistant Editors at the University of Iowa

Suzanne Butz
Kris Dolgos
Brian J. Flanagan
Nancy C. Rather Mayfield

About the Editor

Robert E. Yager—an active contributor to the development of the National Science Education Standards—has devoted his life to teaching, writing, and advocating on behalf of science education worldwide. Having started his career as a high school science teacher, he has been a professor of science education at the University of Iowa since 1956. He has also served as president of seven national organizations, including NSTA, and been involved in teacher education in Japan, Korea, Taiwan, and Europe. Among his many publications are several NSTA books, including *Focus on Excellence* and *What Research Says to the Science Teacher.* Yager earned a bachelor's degree in biology from the University of Northern Iowa and master's and doctoral degrees in plant physiology from the University of Iowa.

Teaching Science With Student Thinking in Mind

Jacqueline Grennon Brooks
Hofstra University

Setting

This chapter describes the Discover Lab Concept (DLC), a project that began in a teaching/learning laboratory at Stony Brook University over ten years ago, and today is a foundation of science instruction in classrooms on Long Island and regions beyond. Thousands of students and hundreds of teachers from diverse districts have participated in DLC interdisciplinary programs based on the National Science Education Standards. Originated through a National Science Foundation grant (DUE # 9353460), the Discover Lab Concept situates both teaching *and* learning within a tradition that demands conceptualization, data collection and theory building for both teachers *and* students. Discover Lab was created as a working research lab, designed for the young scientist. It served kindergarten through adult learners from private and public schools, diverse organizations, sectarian and nonsectarian groups, with teachers ranging from novice to master, from new bachelor's degree graduates to Ph.D. career professionals. It hosted national and international visitors. However, its primary participants were students from school districts on Long Island and the Borough of Queens, representing the full range of socioeconomic, racial, and ethnic diversity, with many classes using the Discover Lab visit as a "jumpstart" for new lines of inquiry. Discover Lab was also an intellectual home for 60 teacher leaders from New York State participating in an extensive five-year program funded by the National Science Foundation grant (ESI # 9618962) to integrate mathematical, scientific, and technological studies in the classroom. It is from within this setting that the stories of this chapter unfold.

This chapter describes the nature of programs for students in grades 5–8 and highlights Oceanside School District, one of the many school districts whose present work has changed as a result of participation. Two of the 60 teacher leaders participating in the NSF program mentioned above are Kathy Chapman and Donna Migdol. Ms. Chapman now serves as science supervisor, grades 6–8, and Ms. Migdol serves as mathematics supervisor, grades K–6, for the Oceanside School District, located on the south shore of Long Island, approximately 30 miles east of New York City. It has 5,000 students, housed within one kindergarten center, six elementary schools of grades 1–6, one middle school and one high school. Grades 5 and 6 are organized departmentally with common prep periods for teachers to collegially determine the best support structures for the academic, social, and emotional needs of their students. For example, teachers recently mapped curriculum links among subjects in order to offer a program that maximizes opportunities for students to consolidate understandings of the big ideas that transfer to new applications. In grades 7 and 8, students are grouped within teams, within a middle school structure. Seventh-grade students "move up" with their academic teachers to the eighth grade for a two-year continuum, a practice called "looping."

The Discover Lab Concept considers both science teaching and science learning as investigatory endeavors. Curriculum is based on themes that embed mathematical, scientific and technological principles into problems of emerging relevance for students, themes such as "Keeping Our Planet in Balance," "The Changes We Make," or "Science at the Amusement Park." Each theme includes a number of separate but related challenges for students to consider. For example, "Science at the Amusement Park" was set up for students to use equipment and materials and to interact with teachers and peers to help them answer the following sample questions:

- Why do many new rides require shoulder harnesses?
- On a carousel, do some horses move faster than others?
- How does a roller coaster move so fast without any engines or motors to propel it?
- What makes that tasty popcorn at the concession stand pop?
- What can explain why some people enjoy the scary and thrilling experiences of amusement park rides while others avoid them?
- Why are roller coaster "loops" always placed at the beginning of the ride and not at the end of the ride?
- How do engineers "slow down" riders on free-fall attractions?
- What causes the feeling of "weightlessness" on pendulum rides?

Each year teachers refine these curricula, based on findings from their action research studies. Donna Migdol and Kathy Chapman have established professional learning communities within their district, a structure recommended in *How People Learn* (Bransfrod, Brown, and Cocking 2000). These learning communities establish curriculum studies that re-frame teaching practice based on data derived from teachers' own action research projects, and they create instructional programs that fuse science and mathematics with their societal and technological links.

The *More Emphases* Conditions

The committee that forged the National Education Science Standards (NSES) envisioned changes throughout the educational system and detailed that vision in a series of tables entitled "Changing Emphases" (NRC 1996, pgs. 52, 72, 100, 113, 224, 239). This chapter examines how the content and inquiry standards of these Changing Emphases has informed the Discover Lab Concept and how the teaching standards have intellectually supported the educational practices that have emerged from that concept. All of the standards complement one another, set the stage for learning, and are represented within the Discover Lab Concept. This chapter will focus on

- The second condition within the Content and Inquiry Standards: *More Emphasis* on subject matter disciplines in technological, social, and historical contexts, with less emphasis on subject matter disciplines for their own sake.
- The third condition within the Teaching Standards: *More Emphasis* on student understanding and use of scientific knowledge, ideas and inquiry processes, with less emphasis on student acquisition of information.

The conditions described in the Teaching Standards can improve student performance in meaning-making activities only when teachers understand how to extract basic, organizing principles and content from student inquiries (Hawkins 1992; Brooks 2002). Presented in the following pages are examples of the processes and interactions by which teachers and learners construct meaning from the technological, social and historical contexts in which we all live every day. Teacher facility in identifying unifying pedagogical ideas and unifying science concepts in specific teaching/learning situations must be in place before an increase in student learning and complex thinking can occur (Mintzes, Wandersee, and Novak 1997; Wiske, Hammerness, and Wilson 1998). The remainder of this chapter provides illustrations of how developing teacher facility and developing student learning proceed hand in hand.

The Nature of Science and the Nature of the Classroom

The NSES committee advocates that students study the technology that guides scientific inquiry, the personal and social perspectives on scientific progress, and the history and nature of science. Discover Lab advocates the same. It operates not only as a science learning center for youngsters and adults, but also as science *of* learning center for educators and parents. Situated at a major research university, Discover Lab is a microcosm of the university's larger culture that, by its definition as a research center, embodies the quests and attributes of science research. Research centers have personal and social components, use technology to solve problems, contribute milestones to the history of science, and define the nature of today's leading edge science. Likewise, Discover Lab fosters students' use of technology to solve problems and contributes milestones to the personal learning history and the leading edge of the thinking of thousands of students and teachers.

Donna Migdol and Kathy Chapman bring that concept to life in their work with practicing teachers at Oceanside School District and in their work as adjunct faculty at Hofstra University, where they begin the cycle all over again, introducing new teachers to these powerful ideas. Teachers and students are involved in ongoing inquiry process as they do the work of scientists, mathematicians, and engineers. Donna and Kathy plan investigations with teachers that incorporate standards driven instruction; then, working with teachers in their classrooms, they model ways to provide opportunities for student theory-building as they pose questions, problem solve, and seek solutions to the various problems each class is investigating. Ongoing professional development is an integral part of the learning process. Weekly meetings that include ways to utilize big ideas in math and science, questioning for understanding, uncovering student misconceptions, linking science inquiry skills into math instruction, and incorporating embedded assessment into teaching practices support teachers as learners.

The MST Institute at Hofstra University, a 2–3 week summer institute designed to foster curriculum integration of mathematical, scientific, and technological concepts, is another venue in which teachers become part of an intensive learning community. In this setting, teachers can deepen their knowledge and understanding of content and process skills of math and science. As members of this institute, teachers incorporate instructional strategies learned in a Discover Lab setting with children. Follow-up sessions in teachers' classrooms continue to provide an avenue for support and reflection on practices.

Unique Features, Unique Learning, Unique Successes

We have found that in order for all learners—students or teachers—to deepen their understandings of general science concepts, they need heightened exposure to the science embedded in the artistic, musical, literary, and otherwise beautifully complex world around us. The National Center for Improving Science Education, after considerable debate many years ago over "what are the important concepts to teach?" generated a list of "conceptual themes" (Bybee et al. 1990). These themes are

1. Cause and effect,
2. change and conservation,
3. diversity and variation,
4. energy and matter,
5. evolution and equilibrium,
6. models and theories,
7. probability and prediction,
8. structure and function,
9. systems and interactions, and
10. time and scale.

The current National Science Education Standards have collapsed these original conceptual themes into five broad unifying concepts and processes that represent ways of thinking about the natural and human-made world:

1. systems, order, and organization;
2. evidence, models, and explanation;
3. constancy, change, and measurement;
4. evolution and equilibrium; and
5. form and function.

We have found that not only do young students rarely describe their thinking in the ways just described above, but that most adults with degrees in the sciences have difficulty describing their specialty science area in these terms. Students have limited chances of discerning unifying concepts within their investigations without teachers who can discern them themselves, highlight them, and structure lessons to address them explicitly. Thus, we have found that "Big Ideas" seminars that address these unifying themes at explicit levels can help teachers create age-appropriate intermediate-level lessons for their young students.

During one seminar series, Professor Emeritus Cliff Swartz invited the adult participants on a journey through probability and prediction by asking the classical problem of predicting the number of piano tuners in New York City. Professor Tom Liao highlighted the intricacies of the structure/function dynamic through an inquiry into technological design. Could the physics and the mathematics of how bar codes route letters to their destinations really have an analog in biological DNA processes? Professor David Hanson challenged members of the class to define the elusive, chameleon-like terms of energy and matter, without using terms that have energy in *their* definitions! Professor Don Lindsley provoked intellectual skepticism of models and theories with a history of plate tectonics and Professor Robert Kerber took us on a journey through the history of alchemy. Why do we think we know what we think we know?

The seminars described above address the pedagogical challenge of creating an instructional design based on unifying concepts that also supports understandings of the nature of science. What type of teaching fosters student understanding of the broad, inclusive concepts that define scientific thinking? Kathy and Donna at Oceanside School District focus both professional development for teachers and curriculum for students around the essential questions: What is true and how do we know it is true? A number of examples follow of curriculum approaches that invite Ocean side School District students to answer that same question in various domains.

In grade 5 mathematics classes, students respond to the question: How do algorithms serve as models for mathematicians to understand number relationships? Students are involved in an in-depth study and analysis of different multiplication systems: the Russian Peasant, Egyptian, and Lattice methods. They compare and contrast the patterns and relationships in each. They are asked: What is the "best" method for multiplying? Students defend their thinking. In Grade 5 science classes, students investigate the development of landforms. They utilize stream tables to simulate the erosion and deposition of land and to respond to the question, "Is change always positive?"

An astronomy unit in grade 6 asks students to create models to account for phenomena and use them to make predictions. Students develop models of movement of the Earth and Moon to justify their thinking about why the Moon has different phases and the reason for the seasons on our Earth.

Life science classes in grade 6 focus on models, simplified representations of objects, structures, systems used in analysis, explanation, interpretation, and design. Students analyze, construct, and operate models of two ecosystems in order to discover attributes of the "real thing" and to answer the essential question, "What is the relationship between living and nonliving factors in an ecosystem?" Students are initially challenged to construct their ideas from simple land and water ecosystems that they build in bottles. Over the course of several weeks, they observe interactions in these ecosystems. Students collect data by measuring temperature, humidity, salinity, and pH, and by making observations.

In mathematics classes, these students explore measures of central tendency and grapple with the question, "How does a change in sample size affect the analysis of the data?" Their needs for larger sampling serve as a model of what scientists do in order to extrapolate data and make predictions about the world. Back in the science classroom, students use the internet to compare data from different locations and interpret how changing one physical factor affects the living things in different environments.

Living in Oceanside, New York, on or near canals and large bodies of water, students frequently hear about how human interactions impact ecosystems. Recently, it became clear to a group of students that comparisons between the real world and their model ecosystems would be more valid and relevant if they found out how changes in salinity, increased algae, or increased acidity affected their ecosystems. They began to ask "what if" questions such as, "What would happen if the pH were more acidic? What would happen if the salinity were increased? What would happen if new organisms were introduced or removed from the systems?" Once students analyzed the effects of pollution or overpopulation, sample questions that emerged were, "What caused this unbalance?" and "Are the benefits worth the disadvantages?" Opportunities to see relevance among their studies with their bottles and their everyday lives were not necessarily limited to science and mathematics classes. Students generated insights into the complexity of the issues and the need for discourse among concerned people, and their teachers established role-playing scenarios to allow this complexity to develop within the policy-making and social science realm.

To begin a study of evolution in grade 8 life science classes, students are often given a series of cartoon cells and asked to sequence them in order so that they tell a story. Through this activity, students explore and debate the idea that inferences make up most scientific arguments and that inferences are based on data (observations) and prior knowledge. This foundation leads into comparing and contrasting the evolutionary models of Darwin and Lamarck by judging how well they explain the data, how consistent they are with other knowledge, and how well they could be used to predict new data.

Let's examine two "big ideas" in depth, one from a fifth-grade class and one from an eight-grade class at Discover Lab, in order to illustrate, on a more detailed level, the NSES' Content and Inquiry Standards and Teaching Standards.

The Problem of Finding North

Understanding magnetic forces is a common science topic taught in elementary and middle schools. To tie this topic to the four goals of science education delineated by the NSES committee, we posed the problem of finding north to groups of students in grades 5–8. We contended that the problem of finding north was an example of the four science education goals of

1. inviting students to experience the richness and excitement of understanding the natural world;
2. illustrating the necessity to use appropriate processes and principles in deciding what factors were important to include in generating a solution set;
3. engaging in intelligent discourse over matters of technological appropriateness; and,
4. in general, becoming a scientifically literate person.

The majority of students in grades 5–8 could not independently use a compass to find geographic headings, although most self-reported that they knew how to use a compass. Thus, the curriculum challenge of finding north was a problem of emerging relevance and of instructional value. The student responses presented here are from a fifth-grade class. This class made their own compasses using magnets hung from thread. The novice teacher introduced the Earth as one very large magnet with two poles that share the same characteristics as the smaller magnets on the Earth. That is, the magnets the students had in their hands, would, if given the opportunity to move freely without being handled, orient themselves along the Earth's north/south alignment. The teacher asked students to prove that statement, and then, to distinguish north from south.

The lesson began with the teacher asking students to investigate the magnets in order to generate some findings that might be helpful in making an informed selection of one of the magnets for their compass. Several students suggested that some magnets are stronger than others. The teacher asked the students if there was any way to prove that such is true. She asked the students to design their own experiments to determine if different magnets did, indeed, have different strengths. The teacher's role at the beginning of the lesson was to guide students in determining ways of measuring strength, a sophisticated concept for any age.

A classic experimental tool to measure magnetic strength used in many published curricula for young people is a set of paper clips. The greater the number of paper clips a magnet can hold, the greater its strength. These curricula instruct students in the use of the paper clips. This young teacher read these curricular guides, marveled at the clever idea of using paper clips to measure magnetic strength, but decided to make the paper clips available for the students on the supply table, along with an array of other objects that are magnetic. She asked the specific question as to whether or not any of the materials on the table could be used as a tool to measure strength. The teacher did not take the cognitive relationship between the paper clips and the measure of magnetic strength as a given and did not instruct students in the use of the paper clips, or other objects, until she established that the students viewed the paper clips as a proxy measurement for strength. The teacher changed the investigation differentially and evaluated the logic of her students' present understandings, relying on students' logic to guide her professional judgment for appropriate next steps. Student voices were critical to all that followed.

The students in the class described above, did, indeed, explore the force of different magnets by testing their relative strengths using metal washers, nails, small hooks, and most of all, paper clips. However, they used these materials only after they articulated what they were doing and why they were doing it. After sorting magnets in terms of strength, students then chose one of their magnets to make a compass in order to find north. Most students established alignment of the north/south axis, but at that point, distinguishing between north and south became a problem for all of the students. The teacher focused classroom discussion and investigation on north and south, mediating discussion concerning what other variables could be included to distinguish north from south. Opportunities to investigate many skills, concepts, and processes emerged: map making and map reading; magnetic forces; navigation and orienteering; geometry of circles or angle measurements, etc. Students suggested the moss on trees, height of the Sun, location of the Sun, length of the shadows, traffic patterns, and temperature—all as potential evidence for directionality.

Performance assessment occurred in a number of ways. Students kept a portfolio from the start in which they noted experimental design, newly emerging hypotheses, equipment and supplies used, collegial partners, and so forth. They tracked and shared their thinking through field notes, journals, reports, and presentations. This documentation served not only as a guide to assessment of the student's present thinking and skills, but as a planning tool for future lessons.

The Chinook Winds and Adiabatic Pressure

With an eighth-grade Earth Science class, another teacher began the lesson by asking the students what they knew about heat. Almost instantaneously and in chorus, they offered: "Heat rises." The teacher responded with, "I've heard that before and it's written in a lot of textbooks. That's why those really warm winds in Colorado that can shoot so strongly down the mountains are so puzzling to me. It can be 30 degrees Fahrenheit outside and the breezes can be 75 degrees. They seem to hug the mountain. So, in the valley, there's a warm breeze with cold air above it!"

The teacher put big sheets of paper on the tables and groups of four to five students tried to draw diagrams or write explanations that might bring about some understanding of this phenomenon. They had many questions: What actually happens when the winds blow? How fast do they blow? How often do they blow? The teacher gave details. Several groups decided to draw diagrams using arrows for the winds. Some students restated the dilemma: "That *does* seem strange that warm winds are coming *down*!" One student removed her textbook from her backpack and flipped through pages. Several other students followed suit. One student, with great animation, said: "Maybe we could look in the glossary." "Oh, yeah" was heard around the room. Another student asked: "But, what word would we look up?" Someone suggested, "heat." A student with the glossary opened declared that the definition "Thermal energy that is transferred from a warmer object to a cooler object" is no help. A student looked to the instructor and asked if there was any other word that they could look up. The instructor said, "Try adiabatic pressure." Another student asked, "How do you spell that?" Someone had already found it and said, "Look on page 567." By that time, almost all the students had taken out their textbooks and were searching for page 567.

The above description of a common classroom event illustrates the third condition within the Teaching Standards: *More Emphasis* on student understanding and use of scientific knowledge, ideas, and inquiry processes, with *Less Emphasis* on student acquisition of information. Accurate information is critical to conceptual development, but it is not synonymous. Students acquire and use information in the quest to build understanding and knowledge.

Let us revisit the above scenario from this perspective. The class looked somewhat casual. Some students had diagrams on their papers. Others did not. Earlier in the lesson, some students had their textbooks open. Some did not. Some were talking to each other and some were reading. The teacher responded to students more often than she directed them. However, there was nothing casual at all about this scenario. The teacher started the lesson with a prompt used to accomplish two goals. First, she wanted to validate that being confused is okay and actually may be the very best starting point for learning. Trying to resolve a perceived discrepancy is a well-researched pathway to new concept formation. Second, she wanted to scaffold the opportunity for students to deal with this apparent discrepancy: heat is "supposed" to rise and we see examples of that around us, but in that class, we heard of an example that did not fit in with what we knew. When a student asked for specific guidance, she offered a specific response: "Try adiabatic pressure."

There was nothing casual or random about the selection of the word "adiabatic" to research. Just as it was neither casual, nor random for the instructor to choose the winds coming off the eastern side of the Rocky Mountains, called the Chinook winds, as a prompt to start the lesson. The "big idea" of the lesson in the teacher's mind was that when air is compressed or expanded very quickly, with no energy leaving or entering the system, the air will heat or cool, respectively. Trying to visualize and explain those pressure/temperature/energy relationships in a variety of settings is part of the process in which the learner must engage in order to generate understandings of those concepts. It is not easy and it takes time.

Under what conditions does a gas compress with no energy change? Is the increased temperature an indicator of no energy change? How can energy not change if the temperature is rising? What do I need to know about pressure? Many related questions must be answered in numerous contexts in order for the learner to come to appreciate the many variables of this complex system and how they influence the others. This opening segment of one lesson is one small piece of a learner's quest to understand this complex array of variables, all exercising an influence on one another.

Evidence of Success

I just described some of the unique features of the teaching/learning dynamic with the Discover Lab Concept, the learning behaviors of some fifth- to eighth-grade students and the instructional practices of some of their teachers. Analysis of these commonly occurring dynamics suggests three issues related to competent teaching and effective learning in NSES-based classroom environments:

Valuing the Self-Regulating Process of Becoming Educated

Becoming educated is a self-regulating process. Therefore, behavior in the classroom that provides evidence that the learner is making decisions about his or her own learning was coded as successful in the scenarios described previously. The students showed evidence of coming to understand essential scientific concepts rather than repeating scientific information. The teacher provided scaffolding for students' emerging abilities in systematic inquiry and this inquiry provided the basis of enhanced concept formation. The questions the students asked and the manner in which the teacher fostered learning provide examples of success. We find that greater numbers of students engage in such behavior after they perceive the unspoken "permission" that intellectual differences can be voiced and accepted, and after they understand that voicing and accepting intellectual differences is a pathway to one's own intellectual growth.

Determining the What/How Distinction

Students make connections between what they are learning and how they are learning, and they establish that the "something" they are learning is either a good thing to learn, or not. Students must value what they are doing in order to put the necessary energy into important learning. Value emerges in contexts that are problem based. Many students say: "Just show me what to do." Therefore, when the students posed their own specific questions, created a mechanism for answering their own questions, sought guidance from appropriate sources on how to proceed, and documented their findings in literate and logical media, we coded such behaviors as evidence of success that teaching practices and program features were meeting the learning objectives embedded in the national standards.

Recognizing the Paradigm Shift

The Discover Lab Concept encourages a view that NSES-based schooling is a web of iterative events in which the learner is constantly reconstructing and reformulating his or her knowledge with teachers responding to the challenges of mentoring students who are grappling with ill-defined problems. One of the most difficult shifts in thinking for students—and their teachers—occurs within the domain of assessment. There exists a great distinction between assessing what is most highly valued and assessing what is most easily measured. The methods of assessing student learning occur within the context of the learning setting and focus on what is most highly valued. The curriculum and the assessment are inextricably interwoven and success is documented with narrative reports on students' conceptual change, as illustrated through the nature of the concepts investigated, the materials used, the nature of questions posed, and the nature of the concepts generated.

Summary

The self-regulated nature of learning is often invisible, but its significance is well documented in the literature (Ausubel 1963; Piaget 1970.) The National Science Education Standards for teaching are based on this premise. These standards can only become standards in the minds of students when teachers fully model the values in which the standards are embedded. Specifically, the focus on student understanding and use of scientific knowledge, ideas and inquiry processes—as opposed to student acquisition of information—becomes a real standard, which students strive to meet, when their teachers recognize that student understanding is self-regulated and, thus, demands differentiated instruction.

In the Oceanside School District, Kathy and Donna engage every day in the process of making this happen on a widespread and consistent basis. Using the work of Wiggins and McTighe (1998), Donna and Kathy help teachers question students for understanding according to six facets—explanation, application, interpretation, empathy, self-understanding, and perspective—beginning with opening up alternate theories and addressing them through instruction.

Another important issue is the "what/how" distinction. Students learn the "what" of the Content Standards through the "how." Learning the unifying concepts and the supporting, substantive content flourishes and continues along the life span when concepts and content are learned in a manner in which the disposition to want to learn more and an attitude toward scholarship and genuine inquiry are valued and fostered. Teachers who value intellectual freedom afford it to their students. Teachers in the Oceanside School District are currently determining student understanding of the big ideas through written responses to essential questions.

A third issue that emerged as relevant for us is the recognition of the paradigm shift. A dominant public and professional view is that schooling is a series of well-defined steps carefully monitored with praise dispensed to students as a motivator. In encouraging a view that schooling can be a series of iterative events in which the learner's own internal mechanisms for resolving cognitive conflict is the driving force to learn, both students and teachers often find themselves in intellectual turmoil. Paradigm shifts do not come easily!

References

Ausubel, D. B. 1963. *The psychology of meaningful verbal learning*. New York: Grune and Stratton.

Bransford, J. D., A. L. Brown, and R. R. Cocking, Eds. 2000. *How people learn: Brain, mind, experience, and school.* Washington, DC: National Academy Press.

Brooks, J. G. 2002. *Schooling for life: Reclaiming the essence of learning.* Alexandria, VA: ASCD.

Bybee, R.W., C. E. Buchwald, S. Crissman, D. R. Heil, P. J. Kuerbis, C. Matsumoto, and J. McInerney. 1990. *Science and technology education for the middle years: Frameworks for curriculum and instruction.* Washington, DC: National Center for Improving Science Education.

Hawkins, D. 1992. Investigative arts: Science and teaching. An opening chairman's address to the second International Conference on the History and Philosophy of Science and Science Teaching, Kingston, Ontario, Canada.

Mintzes, J., J. Wandersee, and J. Novak. 1997. *Teaching science for understanding: A human constructivist view.* New York: Academic Press.

National Research Council. (NRC). 1996. *National science education standard*s. Washington, DC: National Academy Press.

Piaget, J. 1970. *Structuralism.* New York: Basic Books.

Wiggins, G., and J. McTighe. 1998. *Understanding by design.* Alexandria, VA: Association for Supervision and Curriculum Development (ASCD).

Wiske, M. S., K. Hammerness, and D. G. Wilson. 1998. How do teachers learn to teach for understanding?, in *Teaching for understanding: Linking research with practice,* ed. M. S. Wiske, 87–121. San Francisco, CA: Jossey-Bass.

Do You See What I See?

The Relationship Between a Professional Development Model and Student Achievement

Charlene M. Czerniak, Svetlana Beltyukova, Janet Struble
The University of Toledo

Jodi J. Haney
Bowling Green State University

Andrew T. Lumpe
Southern Illinois University

Teacher Effectiveness

The current federal educational legislation in the United States, called No Child Left Behind, sets the stage for gauging the impact of schools on student success. It is becoming increasingly clear that teachers, one major factor in school improvements, are important to the success of education reforms; experts contend that teachers play a key role in system-wide school change processes (Fullan and Miles 1992). According to the National Science Education Standards (NSES), "The most important resource is professional teachers" when evaluating science education programs (NRC 1996, p. 218).

The role of the teacher in systemic reform is multifaceted. Over the last several decades, researchers have examined a number of factors to determine their relationship to students' achievement: (a) teachers' years of education and teaching experience, (b) subject matter knowledge, (c) pedagogical knowledge, (d) certification or licensure status, and (e) teachers' classroom behaviors (Darling-Hammond 1999; Jones 1998). Several studies show that better prepared teachers are able to positively affect student learning. Research in Tennessee (Sanders 1998; Sanders and Horn 1998, 1994; Wright, Horn, and Sanders 1997; Meyer 2000) indicates that teacher effectiveness is the major factor predicting students' academic progress. "Teacher effects on student achievement have been found to be both additive and cumulative with little evidence that subsequent effective teachers can offset the effects of ineffective ones" (Sanders and Horn 1998, p. 247).

Some studies show that a teacher's participation in professional development that focused on content-specific pedagogy is associated with higher student achievement (Cohen and Hill 1997; Langer 2000; Wiley and Yoon 1995; Brown, Smith, and Steihn 1995). The National Board for Professional Teaching Standards (2000), the National Commission on Teaching and America's Future (1996), and the National Commission on Mathematics and Science Teaching for the 21st Century (2000) show that teachers need to know their subject matter and also be knowledgeable about pedagogy of teaching. Teachers in exemplary science programs usually have had more recent (and higher levels of) professional development (Penick and Yager 1983). States such as North Carolina, Kentucky, and Connecticut—which have poured funding into improving teacher preparation and teacher quality—have seen increases in student achievement on NEAP scores (Darling-Hammond 1999). Conversely, few student achievement gains were shown in states where reforms focused on student testing rather than improved teaching or higher-quality teachers.

In light of the increasing emphasis placed on the importance of teachers and their actions and the reality that we have an inadequate pool of qualified science and mathematics teachers to meet our needs (American Council on Education 1999; Hussar 1999; Kelly 2000), many reform efforts and funding initiatives focus on teacher professional development. To enlarge the pool of qualified teachers and improve the quality of inservice teachers, the National Science Foundation has funded numerous undergraduate and Teacher Enhancement Initiatives. A large sum of government money is being spent in the United States to provide inservice for science teachers and many of these funded programs rely upon (possibly ineffective) professional development strategies (Luft 1999). Thus, it is important to examine research-based professional development models. This chapter reviews a professional development model implemented in a National Science Foundation-funded program and presents data regarding the relationship between the model and student achievement.

The Professional Development Model

A model of science teacher professional development was developed in an effort to address the critical role of the teacher. Haney and Lumpe's (1995) model, based on an extensive review of professional development literature, integrated various aspects of planning, training, and follow-up (Figure 1). All of these aspects of professional development are focused on commonly accepted goals based on academic standards. Science teachers' beliefs regarding standards must be identified and clarified prior to, and during, professional development activities. In addition to teachers' beliefs, the supportiveness of the teaching context may play a critical role in success (Lumpe, Haney, and Czerniak 2000). To ensure successful classroom implementation of innovative curriculum materials, support structures for teachers should also be implemented (Valencia and Killion 1988; Shroyer 1990).

Setting

The Haney-Lumpe professional development model served as the basis for the design of a National Science Foundation (NSF) funded Local Systemic Change (LSC) program entitled the Toledo

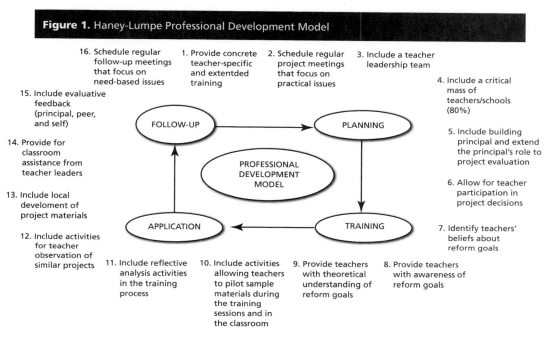

Figure 1. Haney-Lumpe Professional Development Model

16. Schedule regular follow-up meetings that focus on need-based issues

15. Include evaluative feedback (principal, peer, and self)

14. Provide for classroom assistance from teacher leaders

13. Include local develoment of project materials

12. Include activities for teacher observation of similar projects

11. Include reflective analysis activities in the training process

10. Include activities allowing teachers to pilot sample materials during the training sessions and in the classroom

1. Provide concrete teacher-specific and extentded training

2. Schedule regular project meetings that focus on practical issues

3. Include a teacher leadership team

4. Include a critical mass of teachers/schools (80%)

5. Include building principal and extend the principal's role to project evaluation

6. Allow for teacher participation in project decisions

7. Identify teachers' beliefs about reform goals

8. Provide teachers with awareness of reform goals

9. Provide teachers with theoretical understanding of reform goals

FOLLOW-UP

PLANNING

PROFESSIONAL DEVELOPMENT MODEL

APPLICATION

TRAINING

Haney, J.J. & Lumpe, A. T. (1995). A teacher professional development framework guided by science education reform policies, teacher's needs, and research. *Journal of Science Teacher Education, 6*(4), 187–196.

Area Partnership in Education: Support Teachers as Resources to Improve Elementary Science (TAPESTRIES). This is a collaborative partnership between the fourth largest urban school district in Ohio—Toledo Public Schools (TPS), a suburban district— Springfield Local Schools (SLS), and the Colleges of Education and Arts and Sciences at two universities: The University of Toledo (UT) and Bowling Green State University (BGSU). TAPESTRIES is designed to achieve a comprehensive, system-wide transformation of K–6 science education and to improve science teaching and learning through sustained professional development of all K–6 teachers.

Both the TPS and SLS schools face severe challenges in raising student achievement in science, and TPS is ranked as an "academic emergency" school district by the state's standards. TPS has a student enrollment of 37,315, including 46.73% qualifying for free or reduced lunch. Nearly a third of its students are from single-parent homes and/or living below the poverty level. Of the system's nearly 40,000 students (K–12), 45.1% are Caucasians, 46.0% African American, 6.7% Hispanic, 1.3% multiracial, and .01% other cultural groups.

The TAPESTRIES project (funded for five years by the NSF and now funded with local district monies) has goals that aim to improve science teaching and learning. The following are the key organizational components of the TAPESTRIES program; they play a critical role in the implementation of systematic science reform and providing a support system.

Support Teacher Development: Sixteen Support Teachers (elementary teachers who are given full-time release from teaching responsibilities) provide assistance to classroom teachers implementing science inquiry, help teachers with district assessments, and execute their district action plans for improving science literacy. Support Teachers receive more than 200 contact hours of leadership training in the form of a two-week Summer Institute, two three-semester-hour courses, a staff retreat, and a spring conference.

Project Staff Retreat: To establish a cohesive project staff with shared philosophies, expectations, and true collaborative decision making, the entire project staff (science educators, scientists, elementary Support Teachers, and graduate assistants) attends a two-day retreat each spring. This retreat prepares the staff for the Summer Institute by informing them of the latest research on science teaching and learning, by reflecting on comments made by teachers' evaluations from previous years, and by developing a plan of action in content and pedagogy for the upcoming Summer Institute and the following academic year.

Summer Institutes: Six two-week-long Summer Institutes have been conducted each year for the last five years at UT and BGSU. Teachers participate in sessions aligned with the National Science Education Standards, which focus on inquiry-based instruction, science content knowledge, and science process; these are culled from the districts' K-6 scope and sequence and adopted curriculum (FOSS, STC, and Scholastic kits). The Institutes run eight hours a day for two weeks (80 contact hours). The Summer Institutes are co-taught by science educators, Support Teachers from TPS and SLS, and scientists from UT and BGSU. The classroom sessions followed the constructivist 5E model while introducing pedagogy and science content.

Local Academic Year Activities: Professional development is sustained during the academic year by focusing on the implementation of the curriculum and assessments. The Support Teachers visit an assigned cohort of teachers biweekly. They provide assistance with science curriculum preparation, give strategies for teaching science, supply science content background information (if necessary, with the help of the university scientists), assist with classroom and district science performance-based assessments, model science lessons, and offer peer coaching for the classroom teacher. Each teacher conducts a "research lesson"—a Japanese-style lesson study that involves the teacher writing a lesson in the inquiry style 5E learning cycle model (Bybee 1997). The teacher's assigned Support Teacher views the lesson, critiques its effectiveness using the NSF-Horizon Research Institute "Classroom Observation Protocol," and provides written feedback to the teacher. Subsequently, the teacher writes a two-page reflective analysis of the lesson identifying specific strengths and weaknesses. The research lesson assignment gives each teacher an opportunity to analyze his or her teaching and receive constructive feedback from a peer in a nurturing environment. These academic year activities provide 24 additional hours of professional development. Nearly 1,000 classroom teachers (approximately 72% of all of the district's elementary teachers) have received 104 hours of staff development in science content, pedagogy, and assessment as they implement their curriculum.

Annual Science Symposium: A symposium is held each year for TAPESTRIES teachers. The symposium provides professional development and support for implementing science inquiry. Topics focus on science teaching ideas, activities, and resources than can improve teaching and student learning. These sessions are facilitated by the entire project staff as well as invited speakers (e.g., community leaders and experts from the Center of Science and Industry, Toledo Zoo, and Metro Parks).

Retreat for Principals: All principals participate in a one-day retreat and follow-up sessions throughout the academic year. Model lessons are presented, and principals are made aware of science education reform research. Additionally, the TAPESTRIES leaders solicit their support for the project and their input on the challenges of implementing science reforms.

Community Involvement: Support Teachers schedule two local community meetings to involve city leaders, parents, and local principals in this science reform effort. These meetings take many forms—e.g., family science days, PTO meetings, and proficiency test information sessions.

Newsletter: TAPESTRIES has a presence throughout the district in the form of a newsletter published fall and spring. The newsletters contain information about the program, research articles, data concerning the program's effectiveness, teaching tips, and anecdotal field accounts.

Online: A website *(www.tapestries.ut-bgsu.utoledo.edu)* serves as a networking and information platform. The "Ask a Scientist" feature, for example, gives classroom teachers the opportunity to ask questions of the university scientists. Under "Resources," a variety of tools are provided, such as lesson plans, sample assessments, teacher-tested tips for implementing the science kits, and other useful websites related to the kit topics.

Application of the Professional Development Model

The TAPESTRIES project described in this chapter is a direct application of the Haney and Lumpe science teacher professional development model. The TAPESTRIES professional development program was also matched with the National Science Education Standards (NSES) and, as such, can be compared with the NSES Changing Emphasis (NRC 1996). The table in the chapter appendix (pages 33–43) makes these comparisons.

Testing the Effectiveness of the Professional Development

To test the effectiveness of the professional development model, we researched the program's relationship to science achievement scores. The primary research question was:

What evidence is there that the TAPESTRIES program had a positive impact on K–12 student learning in the Toledo Public Schools? Related research questions included (1) Did science proficiency scores improve significantly after the implementation of the TAPESTRIES program in Toledo Public Schools? (2) Does student achievement (fourth and sixth grade) differ significantly between the schools with the highest percentage of teachers' professional development (PD) hours and lowest percentage of professional development (PD) hours? (3) What is the cumulative effect of TAPESTRIES-trained teachers on student achievement?

Methodology

We measured the impact of the TAPESTRIES program by following and comparing gains for each fourth and sixth grade cohort's Ohio science proficiency score over five years. One of the most substantial measurement challenges we overcame consisted in collecting data over multiple years that tracked students to the teachers they had over the course of their elementary experience. Because students in urban districts move frequently, this oftentimes meant tracing transient students through one or more teachers in a given year and linking them through complex databases to their teachers and the records we kept regarding the teacher's accumulated TAPESTRIES professional development hours, classroom or school location, and classroom observation ratings.

Table 1. Fourth-Grade Proficiency Scores Before and After Implementation of TAPESTRIES Program (1996–2003)

Code	School	Before TAPESTRIES, 1996–1998		During TAPESTRIES, 1999–2003			
		M	SD	M	SD	df	t
100	Arlington	208.09	29.93	213.32	35.54	594	-1.883
111	Elmhurst	215.89	31.84	219.12	30.07	359	-0.825
110	Edgewater	212.93	31.78	207.88	30.53	267	1.093
130	Larchmont	198.42	33.41	203.01	31.02	356	-1.271
150	Riverside	189.09	28.65	189.24	33.17	655	-0.009
156	Spring	166.67	30.41	171.17	30.55	696	-1.891
112	Fall Meyer	218.76	28.26	216.32	28.53	295	0.825
104	Burroughs	202.23	33.10	219.83	30.87	512	-6.058***
159	Walbridge	199.98	28.90	202.79	31.17	513	-0.810
162	Westfield	178.20	28.23	179.35	30.79	403	-0.303
160	Warren	161.01	26.82	168.98	28.89	249	-2.024*
131	Lincoln	189.52	27.02	174.44	30.97	344	4.212***
134	McKinley	195.19	29.18	192.40	30.55	658	1.203
132	Longfellow	205.27	30.60	213.48	34.20	949	-3.736***
149	Reynolds	190.10	30.69	187.96	28.92	531	0.725
163	Whittier	203.14	32.94	195.76	32.98	960	3.415**
102	Beverly	234.15	30.68	221.78	33.51	303	3.176**
103	Birmingham	186.71	27.68	199.85	36.01	379	-3.527***
105	Chase	180.18	29.58	174.27	30.10	297	1.672
106	Cherry	181.42	28.04	175.22	28.84	491	2.068
107	Crossgates	211.36	32.29	212.86	38.38	348	-0.223
109	ES Central	183.81	28.36	191.84	29.78	524	-3.116**
114	Franklin	198.56	30.92	192.74	29.24	350	1.617
115	Fulton	171.97	29.06	172.28	29.38	457	-0.044
116	Garfield	190.89	32.42	191.60	32.39	404	-0.226
119	Glenwood	168.91	27.83	170.55	27.54	568	-0.755
121	Hale	168.74	27.98	172.93	29.54	770	-1.930
123	Harvard	221.87	31.11	227.64	35.43	295	-1.372
124	Hawkins	215.84	30.45	206.61	33.08	522	3.052**
127	Keyser	181.91	29.94	203.60	33.82	520	-7.383***
129	Lagrange	181.93	33.17	171.60	31.14	360	2.968**
135	Mt Vernon	184.99	28.16	192.46	32.27	388	-2.363*
136	Marshall	191.70	30.99	186.00	29.80	429	1.864
138	Navarre	185.69	33.22	190.00	31.31	429	-1.404
139	Newbury	187.94	27.82	197.39	38.42	416	-2.599*
140	Oakdale	190.34	29.66	191.51	35.89	537	-0.388
141	Old Orchard	199.79	38.54	200.98	32.98	464	-0.382
142	Ottawa River	210.89	28.93	210.05	34.35	223	0.027
145	Pickett	166.56	26.51	162.72	27.56	620	1.698
148	Raymer	195.32	33.98	193.96	35.31	610	0.530
152	King	169.75	26.43	165.91	28.10	541	1.467
154	Sherman	166.47	28.81	170.27	29.80	683	-1.487
157	Stewart	165.96	28.13	171.90	27.42	438	-2.176*

*$p < 0.05$. **$p < 0.01$. ***$p < 0.001$.

Sample

Based on the availability of both fourth- and sixth-grade proficiency scores in Toledo Public Schools (TPS) from 1998–2003, the sample consisted of 20,834 fourth-grade students and 19,282 sixth-grade students. These students' proficiency scores were linked to their teachers in TPS. The TPS data were used because the sample sizes were sufficient to conduct our study, whereas the Springfield Local Schools (a small district in our partnership) did not have sufficient numbers of teachers and students to add to the analysis. Therefore, this sample data set was used for all statistical analyses.

Statistical Analyses

Statistical analyses were conducted using 10.0 version of SPSS and included independent t-tests, correlations, and one-way ANOVA. The following findings were obtained:

Science proficiency scores: These improved after the implementation of the TAPESTRIES program in Toledo Public Schools. Independent t-tests were performed to examine difference in achievement before and during the TAPESTRIES implementation. For fourth grade scores, nine schools significantly increased their average test scores during TAPESTRIES inquiry science implementation. Twenty-one schools experienced no significant changes in proficiency scores, but 15 of these 21 schools had trends toward higher scores after the TAPESTRIES implementation. See Table 1 and Figure 2.

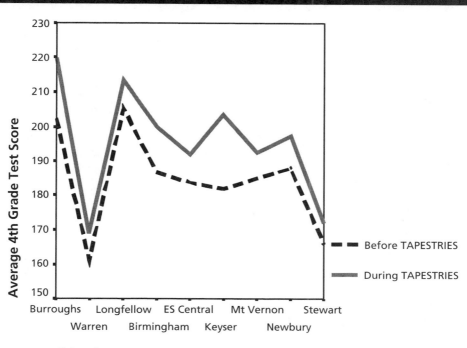

Figure 2. Significant Changes in Test Scores in the Fourth Grade (1998–2003)

Independent t-tests were performed to examine differences in achievement before and during TAPESTRIES. For sixth-grade scores, 19 schools (almost 50%) significantly increased their average test scores during the TAPESTRIES implementation. Twenty-two schools experienced no significant changes in proficiency scores, but 14 of these 22 schools had trends toward higher scores after the TAPESTRIES implementation. See Table 2 and Figure 3.

Table 2. Sixth-Grade Proficiency Scores Before and After Implementation of TAPESTRIES Program (1996–2003)

Code	School	Before TAPESTRIES, 1996–1998			During TAPESTRIES, 1999–2003			
		M	SD		M	SD	df	t
100	Arlington	193.05	21.79		196.22	28.86	553	-1.366
111	Elmhurst	211.60	20.00		205.92	25.89	351	1.363
110	Edgewater	187.88	18.80		203.22	25.98	201	-4.541***
130	Larchmont	193.86	25.37		194.39	23.64	303	-0.171
150	Riverside	174.41	20.34		178.84	22.30	568	-2.253*
156	Spring	170.97	28.56		172.73	36.12	707	-0.676
112	Fall Meyer	189.31	20.40		197.86	19.90	263	-3.384**
104	Burroughs	189.50	22.36		194.46	22.46	490	-2.685**
159	Walbridge	186.43	21.88		192.35	28.99	478	-3.187**
162	Westfield	185.33	20.61		179.12	31.60	357	1.988
160	Warren	167.06	16.08		180.88	21.16	187	-4.696***
131	Lincoln	164.48	51.14		172.66	27.82	261	-1.580
134	McKinley	180.41	24.97		181.10	27.63	673	-1.025
132	Longfellow	196.40	20.85		204.85	26.36	886	-4.924***
149	Reynolds	183.68	28.67		185.55	25.42	458	-.717
163	Whittier	187.40	22.45		189.35	25.79	927	-1.447
102	Beverly	211.63	23.39		204.59	23.67	314	2.490*
103	Birmingham	172.13	44.86		180.31	20.89	322	-2.241*
105	Chase	176.65	20.90		177.26	24.12	255	-0.757
106	Cherry	174.36	18.66		175.07	30.03	378	-0.605
107	Crossgates	199.76	23.40		191.28	35.88	324	2.209*
109	ES Central	182.25	21.26		183.42	27.11	467	-0.483
114	Franklin	187.73	19.87		189.63	21.59	348	-0.817
115	Fulton	168.09	19.92		175.72	30.76	383	-2.849**
116	Garfield	179.81	21.49		184.96	20.45	389	-2.685**
119	Glenwood	172.46	20.53		175.01	28.31	523	-2.328*
121	Hale	169.94	21.35		169.62	35.28	712	0.136
123	Harvard	196.85	25.48		206.27	29.47	287	-2.683**
124	Hawkins	194.16	23.55		193.17	24.92	556	0.054
127	Keyser	176.69	21.61		187.60	24.45	469	-4.730***
129	Lagrange	174.43	38.29		185.53	39.02	294	-2.304*
135	Mt Vernon	185.61	18.71		182.54	26.40	451	1.288
136	Marshall	176.61	21.70		180.71	27.85	405	-1.890
138	Navarre	185.17	19.31		177.96	32.69	417	0.861
139	Newbury	178.22	21.70		183.22	22.12	350	-2.019*
140	Oakdale	188.10	22.60		196.61	29.48	477	-3.240**
141	Old Orchard	193.10	25.92		196.04	24.92	476	-1.249
142	Ottawa River	204.40	20.73		196.77	26.82	182	1.941
145	Pickett	162.20	19.36		170.17	29.47	576	-4.540***
148	Raymer	189.03	23.38		183.63	29.32	567	1.310
152	King	167.97	20.59		175.96	34.72	464	-2.913**
154	Sherman	169.72	23.29		171.47	30.60	597	-0.690
157	Stewart	165.63	18.90		173.81	28.01	375	-3.276**

*p < 0.05. **p < 0.01. ***p < 0.001.

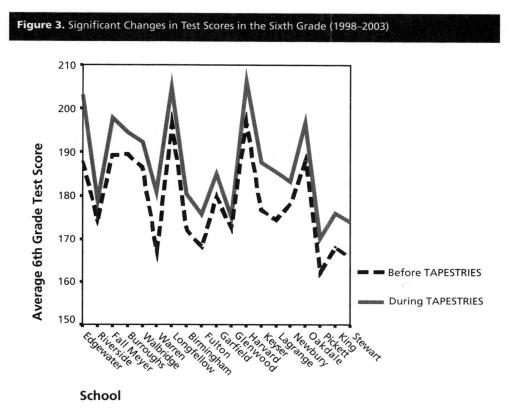

Figure 3. Significant Changes in Test Scores in the Sixth Grade (1998–2003)

School

Student achievement: In the fourth and sixth grades, the results differed significantly between the schools with the highest percentage of teachers' professional development (PD) hours and lowest percent of professional development (PD) hours. The 1998–1999 student proficiency scores were matched with the 1998–1999 PD hours. The 1999–2000 student proficiency scores were matched with the total of PD hours of the teachers these students had in 1998–1999 and 1999–2000. The 2000–2001 student proficiency scores were matched with the total of PD hours of the teachers these students had in 1998–1999, 1999–2000, and 2000–2001. The 2001–2002 student proficiency scores were matched with the total of PD hours of the teachers these students had in 1998–1999, 1999–2000, 2000–2001, and 2001–2002. Finally, 2002–2003 student proficiency scores were matched with the total of PD hours of the teachers these students had in 1998–1999, 1999–2000, 2000–2001, 2001–2002, and 2002–2003. Computing total PD hours across years allowed for accounting for the effect of the accumulated long-term PD. Correlating student performance on the proficiency test in science and PD hours of the teachers these students had the year they took the test yielded a significant positive relationship at both fourth-grade and sixth-grade levels. See Tables 3 and 4.

Table 3. Fourth-Grade Correlation of Student Performance and PD Hours of the Teachers

Measure	SSS_Fourth grade	PD
SSS_Fourth grade	--	0.039***

*** Correlation is significant at $p < 0.001$.

Table 4. Sixth-Grade Correlation of Student Performance and PD Hours of the Teachers

Measure	SSS_Sixth grade	PD
SSS_Sixth grade	--	0.110***

*** Correlation is significant at $p < 0.001$.

Cumulative effect: TAPESTRIES-trained teachers are associated with increased student achievement. Student achievement scores in science were considered in terms of the TAPESTRIES training of the teachers the students had when they took the fourth- or sixth-grade test. A new variable was created with 0 = years before TAPESTRIES, 1 = a single TAPESTRIES year but no TAPESTRIES-trained teacher in either fourth or sixth grade, and 2 = both a TAPESTRIES year and a TAPESTRIES-trained teacher.

For fourth and sixth grades, a one-way ANOVA revealed an overall significant difference in achievement across all the levels of the independent variable (see Table 5 and Table 6). The post hoc test revealed that a highly significant difference exists in achievement during TAPESTRIES years when students had one or more TAPESTRIES-trained teacher, compared to student achievement before TAPESTRIES—the average test score was significantly higher when students had one or more TAPESTRIES years, compared to the average achievement before TAPESTRIES. A highly significant difference was also observed in student achievement during TAPESTRIES between students who had one or more TAPESTRIES-trained teachers and students who had no TAPESTRIES-trained teacher: the average test score was significantly higher for students who had one or more TAPESTRIES-trained teachers.

Table 5. One-Way Analysis of Variance Summary for Fourth-Grade Achievement

Source	SS	df	MS	F
Between Groups	13739.72	3	4579.91	3.64*
Within Groups	26189892.06	20830	1257.32	
Total	26203631.79	20833		

*$p < 0.05$

Table 6. One-Way Analysis of Variance Summary for Sixth-Grade Achievement

Source	SS	df	MS	F
Between Groups	176414.40	2	88207.20	100.71***
Within Groups	16809810.75	19193	875.83	
Total	16986225.15	19195		

***$p< 0.001$

Supportive evidence of this finding was further obtained when the percentage pass rate in fourth- and sixth-grade proficiency tests by students whose teachers participated in the TAPES-TRIES program was compared to that of students in other school districts; TPS schools outranked all other large urban school districts in Ohio (Toledo is the fourth largest city) on the 2002 science proficiency tests (see Table 7 and Figure 4).

Table 7. Percent Pass Rate for Five Largest Urban School Districts in Ohio

School District	Percent Pass
Grade 4	
Toledo Public (Students of TAPESTRIES-trained teachers)	38%
Toledo Public (Students of non-TAPESTRIES-trained teachers)	23%
Cleveland City	26%
Columbus City	35%
Cincinnati City	36%
Dayton City	21%
Grade 6	
Toledo Public (Students of TAPESTRIES-trained teachers)	34.5%
Toledo Public (Students of non-TAPESTRIES-trained teachers)	28%
Cleveland City	25%
Columbus City	29%
Cincinnati City	32%
Dayton City	19%

Conclusions

The following conclusions can be drawn from this study:

1. Fourth- and sixth-grade science proficiency scores improved after implementation of a NSF funded Local Systemic Change (LSC) program.
2. Student achievement (fourth and sixth grade) was higher in schools where teachers had a greater number of professional development hours.
3. There is a positive cumulative effect of TAPESTRIES-trained teachers on student achievement as measured by a state science proficiency test.

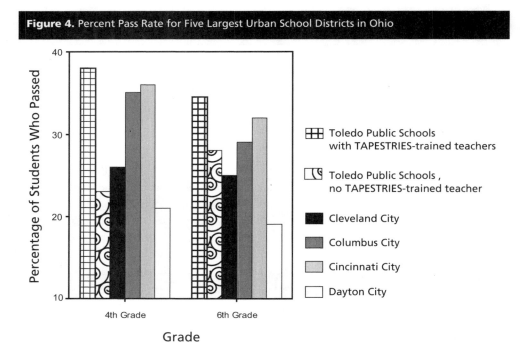

Figure 4. Percent Pass Rate for Five Largest Urban School Districts in Ohio

Legend:
- Toledo Public Schools with TAPESTRIES-trained teachers
- Toledo Public Schools, no TAPESTRIES-trained teacher
- Cleveland City
- Columbus City
- Cincinnati City
- Dayton City

Discussion and Implications

The findings from this study support the growing body of research that suggests that teachers are fundamental change agents (e.g., Fullan and Miles 1992), that classroom teachers impact student achievement (e.g., Sanders and Horn 1998), and, more specifically, that quality professional development has a positive effect on student achievement (e.g., Darling-Hammond 1999). The TAPESTRIES project is a direct application of the effective professional development principles outlined by Haney and Lumpe (1995). By focusing on standards-based goals, by preparing teachers in both content and pedagogy related to these goals, and by providing numerous support structures, the students of TAPESTRIES-trained teachers demonstrated higher academic performance as measured by Ohio's fourth- and sixth-grade science proficiency tests.

Although we cannot conclude that the use of this model directly resulted in higher achievement scores, it is fair to say that this model was used as a framework for a project that was successful in improving student achievement. Moreover, since the data show that the number of hours a teacher participated in this project was significantly correlated to higher student achievement and that there is a cumulative effect of teacher's professional development on student achievement, it is worthwhile to look more deeply at this model as a likely contributing factor that fostered positive change. Each component of this model was carefully examined and infused into the TAPESTRIES plan.

The Haney-Lumpe Professional Development Model and TAPESTRIES

For the following discussion, each component of the model, as numbered in Figure 1 (page 15), will be highlighted and discussed in relationship to the professional development program's planned activities.

1. *Concrete and teacher-specific experiences* were created based on preliminary needs-assessment data calling for in-depth and specific opportunities for teachers to focus on grade-level-appropriate science content and inquiry skills (Czerniak and Lumpe 1996). For example, teachers were grouped by grade level in the Summer Institute and all sessions focused on the science kits they taught in their schools.

2. The TAPESTRIES *schedule included regular project meetings that focused on practical issues* such as restocking the science kits. After the two-week Summer Institute, the academic year activities required teachers to attend monthly meetings. These meetings were sometimes "grade-level" meetings where teachers across the district could network and share ideas; other times were "building level" meetings where teachers could focus on and build upon their school science programs. Meetings allocated time for teachers to hash out current issues and were often led by the Support Teachers, versus project staff. For example, teachers discussed the tension felt between getting students to pass proficiency tests on the one hand, and the desire to teach inquiry-based science and to use alternative assessments on the other.

3. TAPESTRIES Support Teachers *served as lead teachers* and their contributions were so valued that the school district found additional funds to keep the services of half of these individuals, who served in this capacity beyond the original NSF funding. The role of the Support Teachers included (a) serving as liaisons between the project faculty and staff, the district, and the classroom teachers; (b) modeling and assisting in teaching and assessing in the classroom; (c) assisting with the district plan for building material distribution and replacement; and (d) acting as a peer "sounding board," "advisor," and "counsel" for classroom teachers. For TPS, one teacher was identified as the leader of the Support Teachers and served as a liaison between the project staff and the district's administration.

4. The primary focus of LSC projects is to build school capacity by providing professional development to *a critical mass of teachers;* thus, the TAPESTRIES program set out to directly educate at least 80% of the 1,400+ teachers within this district. By the end of the NSF funding period, nearly 1,000 teachers participated in TAPESTRIES (72%). A worthwhile note is that teachers who did not teach science in their building (e.g., art teachers, music teachers, and physical education teachers) often applied to participate in the program. Initially, the project staff had a difficult time determining whether these teachers should be allowed to attend the program. We decided that as long as teachers could connect their discipline or specialty to the science program in the school and could fully participate in all project activities, we would welcome their involvement. We believe this allowance was highly successful in helping us build a school culture for science teaching. Several of these teachers (art, physical education, music, intervention, etc.) found very creative ways to incorporate the science into their curricula, and in many cases were more dedicated and enthused about their contributions. For example, an art

teacher is able to teach about balance and motion by having students create sculptures that illustrate these concepts. A physical education teacher applied the principle of levers to body movements made in gym class.

5. The *building principals and other district administrators were included* in the TAPESTRIES experience as they attended yearly administrator meetings and retreats. The role of the principal was not extended to include evaluation of the project, as Toledo Public Schools use a nationally recognized peer evaluation model. However, the administrator meetings included activities focusing on "effective science teaching… what does it look like?" A few administrators participated in the entire TAPESTRIES program, including the Summer Institute and academic year monthly meetings. The administrators were encouraged to develop their own special projects that would meet their needs. One principal designed and implemented a plan to help further science reform efforts in her building.

6. With a large-scale grant, it is sometimes difficult to *allow teachers to make project decisions,* as an element of structure is also needed. However, Support Teachers served as the "ears" and "mouth" of the district and, as such, constantly helped the project evolve to better meet the district's needs. The grade-level meetings (as opposed to the originally planned building/school meetings) are an example of a change made by listening to the teachers. The Support Teachers participated in graduate courses every semester during their involvement with the project. One of these courses focused on the role of teacher leaders as school and district problem solvers and decision makers. Many project decisions were both spawned and actualized by these teacher leaders through this course. For example, the original project plans required more structured monthly meetings presented by project staff; however, the Support Teachers raised the issue that the teachers needed time to just "talk things out." Thus, the monthly meeting agendas were revamped to include guided discussions to get at issues of concern to the classroom teachers. Participating teachers and administrators were also allowed some project decision making by proposing "alternative" assignments to better meet their individual needs/roles within the district. Although difficult to manage, these assignments turned out to be of high quality and provided a more meaningful learning experience for the teacher or principal. Some principals did complete our assignments by teaching the science kits and so receiving first-hand experiences with students engaged in inquiry-based learning.

7. As developers of this project, much of our research focused on the role of teachers' beliefs in relationship to classroom practices. Therefore, we set out to *identify teacher beliefs about reform goals* at various points during the project activities. Other research related to this project directly examines belief-action relationships.

8. Although often viewed by our participating teachers as "boring" or not "meaningful," we stuck to our plan to include sessions focusing on *helping teachers become aware of reform goals*.

9. We also *helped the teachers develop a theoretical understanding of the national and state science reform goals*, and infused these principles as we planned for each professional development experience, hoping to model the theory as we practiced. For example, to set the stage for assessment, teachers first examined the National Science Education

Standards. Discussion on the Standards expanded to "what does this looks like in a classroom?" Next, teachers viewed a video noting how the teacher was assessing student learning according to the NSES. Teachers now had a visual image to work from as they tried out different types of assessments in their classrooms.

10. *Teachers were given frequent opportunities to pilot sample materials both during the training sessions and in the classroom.* The Summer Institute goals included allowing teachers to experience, as learners, the investigations in their science kits they would teach the following year. Teachers reported a high level of confidence in both their content knowledge and their ability to implement the investigations after this training. During the academic year, the teachers were given a small pilot task to complete during the month and were responsible for bringing back samples of student work to share at the monthly local meetings. These pilot tasks included having teachers try a project idea such as using graphic organizers with their science lessons, collecting student samples of work, and then bringing the samples to the next scheduled meeting.

11. At the meetings, teachers collaboratively reflected on these experiences and reexamined their belief structures about effective teaching and learning. *Reflective exercises* were also a formal part of the Summer Institute experience, as the final paper required teachers to both think back about their past practices and set goals for the future school year. Throughout the project, teachers participated in research lessons, providing them opportunities to observe selected taped science lessons and to critique both themselves and their peers in respect to these lessons, using a standardized protocol. Teachers then completed a written reflective analysis summarizing their thoughts about the effectiveness of the lesson itself and their beliefs about effective science teaching.

12. The Support Teachers were able to attend national meetings to meet with lead teachers from other funded grant projects and *compare and contrast district successes and challenges.* Although only the Support Teachers had the flexibility and resources to formally collaborate with teachers from similar projects, classroom teachers were able to "peer teach" with both the Support Teachers and project scientists (and in some cases with other teachers within their building) and were able to network with other teachers from their grade level at several monthly meetings as well as from another district at the annual symposium. The Support Teachers participated in the "virtual conferences" offered by Horizon, Inc. They were interested in learning from other Local Systemic Change projects. They were surprised to see that other projects were experiencing the same challenges that they were.

13. Teachers did not develop their own curricula, as research-based NSF-funded materials were already in place in the districts. However, *the project required teachers to take ownership of the curricula* by framing each lesson as a learning cycle episode and by developing and/or selecting assessments aligned with the Ohio Proficiency Outcomes. Specifically, the 5E model (Bybee 1997) was used to organize both the professional development sessions, where scientist and educator teaching teams developed 5E lesson plans to guide their instruction, and classroom practices, where teachers developed 5E lessons as they implemented the units in their classrooms. Both the teachers and

project scientists rated this aspect of the TAPESTRIES experience as extremely useful. They reported that the model was "what they had been looking for all these years" to help make hands-on experiences and "minds-on" opportunities.

14. As teachers implemented the curricula in their classrooms, *Support Teachers and project scientists assisted in the process*. At first, many of the participating teachers asked the Support Teachers and scientists to teach for them. We established a system to help the teachers help themselves by stepping back from the role of model to that of mentor to peer. For example, some teachers were very wary of using the kits for the first time so they asked the Support Teachers or scientists to teach for them. We were worried this support would only become a crutch, so the Support Teachers began to encourage the classroom teachers to co-present with them. The classroom teachers were later encouraged to go it alone, but many still used the Support Teachers to help plan the lesson, organize materials, or help with related assessment issues.

15. Each TAPESTRIES activity included some type of *formal or informal evaluation* that was shared with project staff. Follow-up activities included regular feedback and evaluation from district administrators, participating teachers, project faculty and staff.

16. Planning retreats were scheduled each semester to help us reflect on strengths and weaknesses of the program, set goals, and make needed modifications. Participating teachers attended *regular monthly follow-up meetings*. The annual symposium (our local professional conference) was an additional follow-up activity where the teachers could attend and/or lead sessions focusing on local needs-based issues.

Looking Beyond the Model

The Loucks-Horsley, Hewson, Love, and Stiles professional development model (see Figure 5) was released after the onset of TAPESTRIES and includes some valuable components missing from the Haney and Lumpe model. Through the TAPESTRIES project evaluation, we've gleaned new insights into effective professional development for science teachers which contributed to a reworking of our original model to include some of the Loucks-Horsley contributions, as well as new additions emerging from the TAPESTRIES experience.

Specifically, a critical component of quality professional development would not only identify teachers' beliefs about reform goals, but would also provide formal and frequent opportunities for teachers to examine and reflect on their belief structures. Program activities such as regular journaling, generating and peer-sharing of teaching metaphors, justification of personal beliefs through belief essays (that examine personal beliefs in light of the growing body of research on science teaching and learning), and sharing and discussing the belief profiles of teachers as identified by the belief research instruments—these are just a few strategies that could be used to help classroom and lead teachers examine the relationship between their own beliefs and classroom practices.

Another addition to our model would be in the adoption of high-quality, research-based curriculum materials and their use in professional development. Toledo Public Schools adopted a combination of the Full Option Science System (FOSS) (Lawrence Hall of Science 1993) and Science and Technology for Children (STC) (National Science Resources Center 1994) curriculum

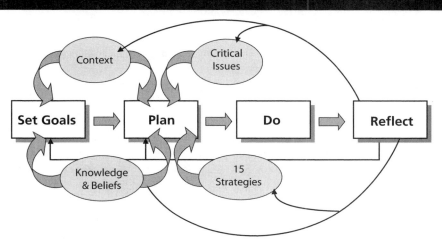

Figure 5. Loucks-Horsley, Hewson, Love, and Stiles Professional Development Model

programs. Both of these programs were funded by the National Science Foundation and are highly reputable programs. Using quality materials gives the school district a head start in paving the way to reform. Past research recommendations called upon the teachers to be thinkers and creators of curriculum, rather than passive recipients of existing curriculum. However, teachers constantly identify lack of time as a factor that impedes reform. Consequently, elementary teachers often don't have the time to develop quality lessons for each subject they teach. Curriculum developers at NSF spend years researching, developing, conducting field trials, and revising these materials (not to mention millions of dollars). It only makes sense that these materials offer higher quality and a more cohesive learning experience.

However, we believe teachers can still take on the role of empowered decision makers, even if they use preexisting curriculum materials as they are called upon to orchestrate the use of these quality materials so that they are developmentally and contextually appropriate for their students. Novice teachers (those both new to the profession and new to the teaching of inquiry-based science) rely more heavily on existing models of effective instruction. The NSF materials serve this population extremely well. As teachers develop skills and deeper understandings of the science content and processes, they are able to enrich a curriculum by modifying and contextualizing the learning experiences. Veteran science teachers (those experienced teachers possessing deep understandings of both the nature of science and the underlying body of knowledge) are able to mastermind a curriculum by weaving multiple resources and learning opportunities.

Finally, the answer to the often asked question as to whether or not the billions of federal and state dollars are well spent on science teacher professional development opportunities seems to be…"yes." However, this affirmation appears to be based on the quality of the professional development experience itself and also on the prioritization of the reform goals. In analyzing the TAPESTRIES data, we compared the Toledo Public School students achievement scores to the four other largest urban districts. When looking at the student scores of teachers who did not participate in the TAPESTRIES program, Toledo ranked either fourth or third (out of five) on the fourth- and sixth-grade tests, respectively. Yet, the Toledo student scores of the TAPESTRIES teachers were ranked first for both grade levels. This finding offers promise that Local Systemic Change initiatives, although expensive, may improve student achievement.

Further support for this finding is seen in the data of the three largest districts (Cincinnati, Columbus, Cleveland). These districts, despite demographic factors typically associated with lower student achievement, outscored both Toledo (non-TAPESTRIES teachers) and Dayton. These three large districts have all received large-scale funding and support under the NSF urban initiatives program and other federal programs.

Critics may comment that although large-scale reform projects are associated with positive impacts on student achievement, targeted districts of these projects (urban districts in this case) still lag far behind the state averages. This seems to be a reality that cannot be overcome (in the short run anyway) by these massive urban reform efforts, and the solutions likely include factors outside the scope of the reform projects. Professional development sustained over time is needed to help these projects reach their intended goals, yet unfortunately, most federal programs have a maximum of five years of external support, so funding often ends just as visible change is beginning.

In light of this and similar studies on the impact of quality professional development on student achievement, it appears that change does indeed take time, that teachers are critical to the change process, and that reaching our educational reform goals requires a substantial commitment of resources (fiscal and otherwise). So if *quality* professional development is provided in a systemic way (long-term and to a critical mass of teachers in the district/building), and if reaching our science education reform goals is truly a national priority (versus political rhetoric), then it seems that the ends do justify the means.

References

American Council on Education. 1999. *To touch the future: Transforming the way teachers are taught*. Author.

Brown, C. A., M. S. Smith, and M. K. Stein. 1995. Linking teacher support to enhanced classroom instruction. Paper presented at the annual meeting of the American Educational Research Association, New York, NY.

Bybee, R. 1997. *Achieving scientific literacy*. Portsmouth, NH: Heinemann Publications.

Carr, E., L. Aldinger, and J. Patberg. 2000. *Thinking works for early and middle childhood teachers*. Toledo, Ohio: The University of Toledo.

Cohen, D. K., and H. Hill. 1997. Instructional policy and classroom performance: The mathematics reform in California. Paper presented at the annual meeting of the American Educational Research Association, Chicago, IL.

Czerniak, C. M., and A. T. Lumpe. 1996. Relationship between teacher beliefs and science education reform. *Journal of Science Teacher Education* 7 (4): 247–266.

Darling-Hammond, L. 1999. *Teacher quality and student achievement: A review of state policy evidence*. Seattle, WA: Center for the Study of Teaching and Policy, University of Washington.

Fullan, M. G., and M. B. Miles. 1992. Getting reform right: What works and what doesn't. *Phi Delta Kappan* 73: 745–752.

Haney, J. J., and A. T. Lumpe. 1995. A teacher professional development framework guided by science education reform policies, teachers' needs, and research. *Journal of Science Teacher Education* 6 (4): 187–196.

Hussar, W.J. 1999. *Predicting the need for newly hired teachers in the United States to 2008–09*. Washington, DC: U.S. Department of Education.

Jones, R. 1998. What works: Researchers tell what schools must do to improve student achievement. *The American School Board Journal* 185 (4): 28–33.

Langer, J. A. 2000. Excellence in English in middle and high school: How teachers' professional lives support student achievement. *American Educational Research Journal* 37 (2): 397–439.

Lawrence Hall of Science 1993. *Full option science system (FOSS)*. Chicago, IL: Encyclopedia Britannica Educational Corporation.

Loucks-Horsley, S., P. Hewson, N. Love, and K. Stiles. 1998. *Designing professional development for teachers of science and mathematics*. Thousand Oaks, CA: Corwin Press.

Luft, J. A. 1999. Teachers' salient beliefs about a problem-solving demonstration classroom inservice program. *Journal of Research in Science Teaching* 36: 141–158.

Lumpe, A. T., J. J. Haney, and C. M. Czerniak. 2000. Assessing teachers' beliefs about their science teaching context. *Journal of Research in Science Teaching* 37 (3): 275–292.

Meyer, R. H. 2000. *Value-added indicators: A powerful tool for evaluating science and mathematics programs and policies*. Madison, WI: National Institute for Science Education.

National Board for Professional Teaching Standards. 2000. *Annual report*. Arlington, VA: Author.

National Commission on Mathematics and Science Teaching for the 21st Century. 2000. *Before it's too late*. Washington, DC: U.S. Department of Education.

National Commission on Teaching and America's Future. 1996. *What matters most: Teaching for America's future*. New York, NY: Author.

National Research Council (NRC). 1996. *National science education standards*. Washington, DC: National Academy Press.

National Science Resources Center. 1994. *STC: Science and technology for children*. Washington, DC: National Academy of Sciences.

Penick, J. E., and R. E. Yager. 1983. The search for excellence in science education. *Phi Delta Kappan* 64 (8): 621–623.

Riggs, I. M., and L. G. Enochs. 1990. Toward the development of an elementary teacher's science teaching efficacy belief instrument. *Science Education* 74 (6): 625–637.

Sanders, W. L. 1998. Value-added assessment. *The School Administrator* 11 (55): 24–27.

Sanders, W. L., and S. P. Horn. 1994. The Tennessee value-added assessment system (TVAAS): Mixed-model methodology in educational assessment. *Journal of Personnel Evaluation in Education* 8: 299–311.

Sanders, W. L., and S. P. Horn. 1998. Research findings from the Tennessee value-added assessment system (TVAAS) database: Implications for educational evaluation and research. *Journal of Personnel Evaluation in Education* 12 (3): 247–256.

Shroyer, M. G. 1990. Effective staff development for effective organization development. *Journal of Staff Development* 11: 2–6.

Valencia, S. W., and J. P. Killion. 1988. Overcoming obstacles to teacher change: Direction from school-based efforts. *Journal of Staff Development* 9: 2–8.

Wiley, A. E., and B. Yoon. 1995. Teacher reports of opportunity to learn: Analyses of the 1993 California learning assessment system. *Educational Evaluation and Policy Analysis* 17 (3): 355–370.

Wright, S. P., S. P. Horn, and W. L. Sanders. 1997. Teacher and classroom context effects on student achievement: Implications for teacher evaluation. *Journal of Personnel Evaluation in Education* 11: 57–67.

NOTE: This research is supported in part by funding from the National Science Foundation (NSF), project no. 9731306. The views expressed here are not necessarily those of NSF.

Appendix

Comparison of the Program to the National Science Education Standards

The National Science Education Standards envision change throughout the system.
The teaching standards encompass the following changes in emphases:

LESS EMPHASIS ON	MORE EMPHASIS ON	TAPESTRIES
Treating all students alike and responding to the group as a whole	Understanding and responding to individual student's interests, strengths, experiences, and needs	• Educators, STs, and the teachers themselves provided a variety of individualized lesson adaptations in the Summer Institute and academic year activities. • The suggestions provided by the CTs in the Summer Institute are listed under "Tips from Teachers" and "Sequence & Suggestions" on our website (*www.tapestries.ut-bgsu.utoledo.edu/*). • STs modeled this standard in the classrooms for their peers and helped CTs implement it into their classrooms.
Rigidly following curriculum	Selecting and adapting curriculum	• General session, "What Is Inquiry & Why Do It?" presented in Summer Institute addressed this standard. • TAPESTRIES PS helped STs implement more inquiry-based activities. • STs presented additional inquiry-based kits to CTs during the academic year. • STs aligned the district's curriculum to Ohio's Proficiency Outcomes. The STs identified the gaps in the curriculum and then developed inquiry lessons for each gap. • The STs were successful in convincing the school administration to replace one unit with the FOSS Landforms kit.
Focusing on student acquisition of information	Focusing on student understanding and use of scientific knowledge, ideas, and inquiry processes	• Scientists and educators modeled this in the Summer Institute with the teacher being the student. • STs modeled this in the classrooms and in the academic year's sessions. • Videos that illustrate this were used as case analyses to show teachers what this looks like in the classroom. • In the course assignments, CTs answered questions that focused on student understanding. They provided student samples and explained the level of student understanding. • CTs wrote assessment rubrics and provided a student sample for each level. • The BSCS 5E learning model evolved into a lesson plan template that focuses on student understanding.

Presenting scientific knowledge through lecture, text, and demonstration	Guiding students in active and extended scientific inquiry
	• Scientists and educators modeled this in the Summer Institute with the teacher being the student. • STs modeled how to meet this standard in the classrooms and in the academic year's sessions. • General session, "Higher Order Thinking," presented this topic in the Summer Institute, and STs built upon during the academic year sessions. • Videos that illustrate this were used as case studies to have teachers reflect on this in their classroom. • The 5E lesson plan template helped CTs implement this in their classrooms.
Asking for recitation of acquired knowledge	Providing opportunities for scientific discussion and debate among students
	• Scientists and educators modeled this in the Summer Institute with the teacher being the student. • STs modeled how to do this in the classrooms and in the academic year's sessions. • CTs learned cooperative learning strategies that would help facilitate student discussion. • Videos that illustrate this were used as case studies to have teachers reflect on this in their classroom.
Testing students for factual information at the end of the unit or chapter	Continuously assessing student understanding
	• General sessions on graphic organizers, Thinking Works (a curriculum connecting reading strategies to science—see Carr, Aldinger, & Patberg, 2000), and writing in science illustrated their use as an assessment. • Two general sessions focusing on assessment were presented in the Summer Institute. • Scientists and educators used graphic organizers, Thinking Works, and writing strategies in the Summer Institute with the teacher being the student. • STs modeled this in the classrooms and in the academic year's sessions. In the course assignments, classroom teachers answered questions that focused on assessment. They provided student samples and explained the level of student understanding in their own classroom examples. • CTs wrote assessment rubrics and provided a student sample for each level of understanding. • Assessment products are listed under "Assessment Ideas" and "Thinking Works" on our website (www.tapestries.ut-bgsu.utoledo.edu/).
Maintaining responsibility and authority	Sharing responsibility for learning with students
	• Scientists and educators modeled this in the Summer Institute with the teacher being the student. • STs modeled this in the classrooms and in the academic year's sessions. • Videos that illustrate this were used as case studies to have teachers reflect on this in their classroom.

LESS EMPHASIS ON	MORE EMPHASIS ON	TAPESTRIES
Supporting competition	Supporting a classroom community with cooperation, shared responsibility, and respect	• Two general sessions focusing on cooperative learning were presented in the Summer Institute. • Scientists and educators modeled this in the Summer Institute with the teacher being the student. • STs modeled this in the classrooms and in the academic year's sessions. • Videos that illustrate this were used as case studies to have teachers reflect on this in their classroom. • CTs suggestions were used to modify monthly meetings we held and to modify each year's summer institute.
Working alone	Working with other teachers to enhance the science program	• STs worked closely with CTs to implement inquiry-based science. • CTs participated in meetings during the academic year held in their school and grade level meetings for the district. • STs and CTs presented at the annual symposia. • Teachers used e-mail and the web to share ideas with others. • STs attended NSTA and other conferences to network with peers and gain ideas for improving the program.

The National Science Education Standards envision change throughout the system.
The **professional development standards** encompass the following changes in emphases:

LESS EMPHASIS ON	MORE EMPHASIS ON	TAPESTRIES
Transmission of teaching knowledge and skills by lectures	Inquiry into teaching and learning	• At the end of each kit session, CTs analyzed the method used by the scientists and educators. This debriefing provided an example that was used throughout their professional development. • CTs watched videos of other teachers teaching science and analyzed the teaching/learning process. • CTs completed "research" lessons—Japanese style lesson studies where they planned, taught, and reflected on their teaching and students' learning.
Learning science by lecture and reading	Learning science through investigation and inquiry	• CTs experienced the 5E learning model in action as they learned about their science kits in the Summer Institute. • STs modeled how to do this standard in the classrooms and in the academic year's sessions. • Videos that illustrate this were used as case studies to have CTs reflect on this.

Separation of science and teaching knowledge	Integration of science and teaching knowledge	• Scientists and educators team-taught the Summer Institutes thus integrating science content with pedagogy. • General session, "Constructivism & the 5E Model," presented in Summer Institute introduced this standard. • Using feedback from STs and CTs, the BSCS 5E learning model was expanded into a complex lesson plan for the teachers to follow. CTs developed their lessons using this plan. • STs and CTs read and discussed research-based articles on this topic.
Separation of theory and practice	Integration of theory and practice in school settings	• CTs implemented the lessons they developed. They wrote reflective essays critically analyzing the effectiveness of the lessons. • STs worked closely with teachers in their classrooms to implement the knowledge and skills learned in the Summer Institute and monthly meetings. • CTs saw this in action when scientists visited their classrooms.
Individual learning	Collegial and collaborative learning	• All TAPESTRIES PS modeled collaboration in the Summer Institute and throughout academic year events. • STs implemented this standard daily by working with CTs in their classrooms. • STs provided individualized professional development during the school year. • CTs worked in collaborative groups during class sessions. • STs and CTs were encouraged to attend and present at the annual TAPESTRIES symposia, SECO (Science Education Council of Ohio), NSTA, and other conferences.
Fragmented, one-shot sessions	Long-term coherent plans	• The TAPESTRIES program was a long-term program—starting with a 2-week Summer Institute, monthly after-school meetings, and an annual symposium. • Coherence was developed among the stakeholders: o STs developed and delivered presentations to the school board meetings. o STs conducted a needs assessment for science by interviewing every elementary principal or assistant principals in the district. o TAPESTRIES PS provided a yearly Principal Retreat. o TAPESTRIES co-PI's met with district leaders to develop long-range plans for sustainability.

Courses and workshops	A variety of professional development activities	• STs and CTs participated in Summer Institute, and in school-based or grade-level meetings during the academic year. • CTs participated in meetings during the academic year held in their school and grade-level meetings for the district. • CTs experienced one-on-one professional development with their STs. • STs were enrolled in graduate courses at BGSU and UT. • STs and CTs attended and presented at the annual TAPESTRIES symposia. • STs attended and presented at SECO, NSTA, and other conferences.
Reliance on external expertise	Mix of internal and external expertise	• TAPESTRIES staff included science education professors and scientists from two universities. • Educators who taught in the Summer Institute were area teachers, TAPESTRIES STs and CTs. • TAPESTRIES staff included a mixture of PIs, scientists, educators, graduate assistants, district leaders, and office staff.
Staff developers as educators	Staff developers as facilitators, consultants, and planners	• TAPESTRIES staff (PIs, scientists, educators, graduate assistants, district leaders, office staff) facilitated the Support Teacher's development and classroom teacher's implementation of knowledge and skills. • Scientists were assigned to STs to provide assistance in science content.
Teacher as technician	Teacher as intellectual, reflective practitioner	• Each ST and CT conducted more than one "research lesson" (a Japanese-style lesson study that involves the teacher writing a lesson in the inquiry style 5E learning cycle model. The teacher's assigned Support Teacher viewed the lesson, critiqued its effectiveness utilizing the NSF-Horizon Research Institute "Classroom Observation Protocol," provided written feedback to the teacher, and co-planned effective changes. • CTs wrote reflective essays focusing on students' learning and understanding science as part of required assignments.
Teacher as consumer of knowledge about teaching	Teacher as producer of knowledge about teaching	• STs discussed issues in the graduate courses. • STs were encouraged to publish articles. • CTs modified lessons, and created assessments. • CTs shared ideas with peers at monthly meetings and at the annual symposium.
Teacher as follower	Teacher as leader	• STs provided professional development for CTs during the academic year. • STs and CTs presented at the annual TAPESTRIES symposia. • STs wrote grants to funding agencies. • CTs shared ideas with peers at the annual symposium and at monthly meetings.

	Teacher as an individual based in a classroom	Teacher as a member of collegial professional community	• STs and CTs presented at the annual TAPESTRIES symposium. • STs attended and presented at SECO, NSTA, and other conferences. • STs participated in the annual Virtual Conference for LSC (Local Systemic Change) grants offered by Horizon, Inc. • CTs shared ideas with peers at the annual symposium and at monthly meetings.
	Teacher as target of change	Teacher as source and facilitator of change	• STs attended NSTA and other conferences to network with peers and gain ideas for improving the program. • STs presented additional inquiry-based kits to CTs during the academic year. • STs aligned the district's curriculum to Ohio's Proficiency Outcomes. The STs identified the gaps in the curriculum and developed lessons for each gap. • The STs were successful in convincing the school administration to replace one unit with the FOSS Landforms kit. • CTs shared ideas with peers at the annual symposium and at monthly meetings.

The **National Science Education Standards** envision change throughout the system.
The **assessment standards** encompass the following changes in emphases:

LESS EMPHASIS ON	MORE EMPHASIS ON	TAPESTRIES
Assessing what is easily measured	Assessing what is most highly valued	• Scientists and educators modeled this in the Summer Institute with the teacher being the student. • STs modeled this in the classrooms and in the academic year's sessions. • Student samples from other projects and videos that illustrate this were used as case analysis to show teachers what this looks like in the classroom. • CTs used the 5E model to focus on prior learning and assessment.
Assessing discrete knowledge	Assessing rich, well-structured knowledge	• Scientists and educators modeled this in the Summer Institute with the teacher being the student. • CTs saw this in action as Support Teachers modeled this in the classrooms. • STs modeled this in the academic year's sessions. • Videos that illustrate this were used as case analysis to show teachers what this looks like in the classroom. • CTs used the 5 E model to focus on prior learning and assessment. • CTs used graphic organizers to assess higher-level skills. • CTs implemented Bloom's Taxonomy focusing on higher order thinking.

Assessing scientific knowledge	Assessing scientific understanding and reasoning	• CTs attended a general session, "Higher Order Thinking," in the Summer Institute, and STs built upon during the academic year sessions. • Videos that illustrate this were used as case analysis to have teachers reflect on what this looks like in the classroom. • CTs used graphic organizers to assess scientific reasoning and understanding. • CTs implemented questions developed from using Bloom's Taxonomy and provided student evidence of scientific reasoning and understanding as part of required assignments.
Assessing to learn what students do not know	Assessing to learn what students do understand	• Scientists and educators used graphic organizers, Thinking Works, and writing strategies in the Summer Institute with the teacher being the student. • Two general sessions focusing on assessment in general were presented in Summer Institute and were further developed throughout the academic year. • General sessions on graphic organizers, Thinking Works, and writing in science illustrated their use as an assessment in the Summer Institute. These topics were expanded upon during the academic year. • STs modeled this in the classrooms and in the academic year's sessions. • Videos that illustrate this were used as case analysis to have teachers reflect on what this looks like in the classroom. • In the course assignments, CTs answered questions that focused on student understanding. They provided student samples and explained the level of student understanding. • CTs wrote assessment rubrics and provided a student sample for each level of understanding. • Assessment products are listed under "Assessment Ideas" and "Thinking Works" on our website (www.tapestries.ut-bgsu.utoledo.edu).
Assessing only achievement	Assessing achievement and opportunity to learn	• STs analyzed the school's curriculum (in comparison to state proficiency tests) to determine gaps in opportunity to learn concepts and skills. • STs analyzed low-proficiency test areas and used this to revise the TAPESTRIES program offerings.
End of term assessments by teachers	Student engaged in ongoing assessment of their work and that of others	• In assessment professional development sessions, CTs explored this standard and were given examples of students assessing themselves and their peers.

| Development of external assessments by measurement experts alone | Teachers involved in the development of external assessments | • STs and CTs developed and field-tested assessment items that mirror Ohio's proficiency tests.
• Assessment products developed by CTs are listed under "Assessment Ideas" and "Thinking Works" on our website (*www.tapestries.ut-bgsu.utoledo.edu*). |

The National Science Education Standards envision change throughout the system.
The science content and inquiry standards encompass the following changes in emphases:

LESS EMPHASIS ON	MORE EMPHASES ON	TAPESTRIES
Knowing scientific facts and information	Understanding scientific concepts and developing abilities of inquiry	• CTs developed concept maps of the science content for each kit being studied. These maps are under "Concept Maps" on our website (*www.tapestries. ut-bgsu.utoledo.edu*). • CTs experienced this in the Summer Institute and reflected on their use of it with children during the academic year. • CTs utilized the scientists via e-mail through our website to further their understanding of scientific concepts being taught during the school year.
Studying subject matter disciplines (physical, life, earth sciences) for their own sake	Learning subject matter disciplines in the context of inquiry, technology, science in personal and social perspectives, and history and nature of science	• Scientists and educators modeled this in the Summer Institute so that CTs could experience how inquiry facilitates the learning of the science content. • CTs attended a general session, "The Nature of Science," presented in Summer Institute. • STs modeled this in the classrooms and in the academic year's sessions.
Separating science knowledge and science process	Integrating all aspects of science content	• CTs experienced this in the Summer Institute and reflected on their use of it with children during the academic year. • Scientists were assigned to STs to provide assistance in science content. • Scientists visited elementary classrooms to facilitate children's understanding of science content. • CTs implemented integration by following the TAPESTRIES Lesson Plan (expanded version of the BSCS 5E model). • CTs integrated science across the sciences and with other subject areas as part of required assignments, since this was a focal point of the program. • CTs provided strategies for this integration that are located on our website.

Covering many science topics	Studying a few fundamental science concepts	• The school districts adopted only four science kits per grade level. • Exemplary lesson plans written by CTs are featured on our website.
Implementing inquiry as a set of processes	Implementing inquiry as instructional strategies, abilities, and ideas to be learned	• CTs experienced this in the Summer Institute as a student. • CTs attended a general session, "What Is Inquiry & Why Do It?" at the beginning of the Summer Institute. This session provided a springboard to engage CTs in inquiry activities. • TAPESTRIES PS helped STs implement more inquiry-based activities throughout the school year. • STs helped CTs implement inquiry-based kits during the academic year. • During the school year, CTs were required to provide evidence of this happening in their classrooms as part of the assignments. • Each ST and CT conducted more than one "research lesson." The category "Content" in the "Classroom Observation Protocol" developed by Horizon Research provided a focus on this for the teachers. Afterwards, the teachers wrote reflective essays about the strategies in the lesson.
Activities that demonstrate and verify science content	Activities that investigate and analyze science questions	• CTs attended a general session, "Higher Order Thinking." • CTs experienced this in the Summer Institute and reflected on their use of it during the academic year. • CTs experienced this in the Summer Institute as a student. • CTs viewed videos illustrating this and discussed how to have students communicate in their own classrooms. • STs helped CTs facilitate this in science classes. • CTs were provided a variety of graphic organizers that could be used to assess student explanations. • During the school year, CTs were required to provide evidence of levels of questions that they were asking in their classrooms and that their students were asking as part of the assignments.
Investigations confined to one class period	Investigations over extended periods of time	• STs helped CTs facilitate this throughout the school year. • CTs implemented this in their classrooms during the academic year.

Less Emphasis	More Emphasis	Activities
Process skills out of context	Process skills in context	• CTs experienced this in the Summer Institute as a student. • CTs viewed videos illustrating this and discussed how this could happen in their own classrooms. • STs helped CTs facilitate this in science classes. • CTs were provided a variety of graphic organizers that could be used to assess student explanations.
Emphasis on individual process skills such as observation or inference	Using multiple process skills—manipulation, cognitive, procedural	• CTs experienced this in the Summer Institute as a student. • CTs viewed videos illustrating this and discussed how implement this in their own classrooms. • STs helped CTs facilitate this in science classes.
Getting an answer	Using evidence and strategies for developing or revising an explanation	• CTs experienced this in the Summer Institute and reflected on their use of it during the academic year.
Science as exploration and experiment	Science as argument and explanation	• CTs experienced this in the Summer Institute and reflected on their use of it during the academic year.
Providing answers to questions about science content	Communicating science explanations	• CTs experienced this in the Summer Institute as a student. • CTs viewed videos illustrating this and discussed how to have students communicate in their own classrooms. • STs helped CTs facilitate this in science classes. • CTs were provided a variety of graphic organizers that could be used to assess student explanations.
Individuals and groups of students analyzing and synthesizing data without defending a conclusion	Group of students often analyzing and synthesizing data after defending conclusions	• CTs experienced this in the Summer Institute as a student. • CTs viewed videos illustrating this and discussed how to do this in their own classrooms. • STs helped CTs facilitate this in science classes.
Doing few investigations in order to leave time to cover large amounts of content	Doing more investigations in order to develop understanding, ability, values of inquiry and knowledge of science content	• CTs experienced this in the Summer Institute. • CTs worked with their STs to provide more investigations for their students during the academic year.

Concluding inquiries with the result of the experiment	Applying the results of experiments to scientific arguments and explanations	• Scientists and educators modeled this in the Summer Institute. • CTs experienced this in the Summer Institute by recording their results of experiments in their institute notebook. • During the school year, CTs were required, as part of an assignment, to provide evidence of this happening in their classrooms. • STs modeled this in the classrooms.
Management of materials and equipment	Management of ideas and information	• Scientists and educators modeled this in the Summer Institute. • CTs experienced this in the Summer Institute and reflected on their use of it during the academic year. • STs modeled this in the classrooms and in the academic year's sessions.
Private communication of student ideas and conclusions to teacher	Public communication of student ideas and work to classmates	• CTs experienced this as a student communicating their ideas to other teachers in the Summer Institute. • During the school year, CTs were required to provide, as part of an assignment, evidence of this happening in their classrooms. • STs modeled this in the classrooms and in the academic year's sessions.

Teaching Science With Pictures

Barbara Kay Foots
Houston Independent School District
Houston, Texas

Mary Reescano, Karl Spencer
VisualRealization.com

Setting

The state of Texas is divided into 20 Regional Education Service Centers (ESC). The largest, Region IV ESC, with offices in Houston, Texas, serves a seven-county area in southeast Texas. It consists of 54 school districts with 73,413 educators and 928,460 students located on 1,232 campuses. Schools located in three of the independent school districts in Region IV— Houston, North Forest, and Spring—were selected as pilot sites for a program designed to increase students' knowledge and understanding of science using scientific inquiry. The three districts are located in Harris County. See Table 1 for statistics on each district.

Since the National Science Education Standards (NSES) were released in 1996, requirements for science education for students and for the accountability of teachers and schools have changed. The most recent addition to the list of changes can be found in the No Child Left Behind Act. This federal law has increased the urgency to find effective ways to teach and learn science. Based on recent scores on state required criterion-referenced tests, and on the third international TIMSS results for science, little progress has been made in the achievement of students in the United States since the Standards were released.

Table 1. Statistics by District

District	Student Population	Number of School Buildings	Ethnic Breakdown	Economically Disadvantaged
Houston	208,090	306	African American: 30.5% Asian: 3.0% White: 9.3% Native American: 0.01%	80.2%
North Forest	11,699	15	African American: 79.1% Asian: 0.1% Hispanic: 20.1% White: 0.8% Native American: 0%	80.1%
Spring	23,034	24	African American: 28.9% Asian: 6.0% Hispanic: 27.4% White: 37.5% Native American: 0.2%	6.7%

Changing Emphases

The main purpose for designing the Visual Realization (VR) Program was to help students achieve the Changing Emphases for the Content Standards. Success in this task would in turn help students achieve the four goals of science education (NSES, p.13). The design of the VR Program allows for different emphases to be targeted. The program also addresses selected goals from the Teaching, Professional Development and Assessment Standards: *Content Standards:* (1) Learning subject matter disciplines in the context of inquiry, technology, science in personal and social perspectives, and history and nature of science; (2) Implementing inquiry as instructional strategies, abilities, and ideas to be learned; (3) Using multiple process skills—manipulative, cognitive, and procedural; (4) Using evidence and strategies for developing or revising an explanation; (5) Managing ideas and information; and (6) Applying the results of experiments to scientific arguments and explanations. *Teaching Standards:* (1) Guiding students in active and extended scientific inquiry; (2) Providing opportunities for scientific discussion and debate among students; and (3) Sharing responsibilities for learning with students. *Professional Development Standard:* (1) A variety of professional development activities. *Assessment Standards:* (1) Assessing to learn what students do understand; and (2) Students engaged in ongoing assessment of their work and that of others.

One of the changing emphases for teaching served as a constant reminder of our goals for this program, viz., "understanding and responding to individual students' interests, strengths, experiences, and needs," while addressing their weaknesses.

Teachers, Students, and Classroom

Teachers involved in the development of the Visual Realization Program shared the following characteristics:

1. They recognized the needs of their students.
2. They were open to change.
3. They were accustomed to working with students in different group settings and environments.
4. They were accustomed to adopting many different roles in the classroom.
5. They accepted the challenge of playing a major role in the development of an innovative science program.

The classes of each teacher contain a diverse student population (African American, Hispanic, white, Asian). The students like to "do" science. All students were included in the program activities, regardless of their academic achievement. All of the students are part of the net generation, and have grown up surrounded by technology and digital media. They have never known life before computers. They welcomed the opportunity for interactive learning using digital cameras and digital imagery because technology is not just technology to them—it is a part of their customary landscape. The teachers' classrooms encompass internet connectivity, with standard computers running in a Windows environment. The classrooms are equipped with lab tables, an overhead projector, TV, projection screen, and equipment to meet basic

Table 2. VR Program Development

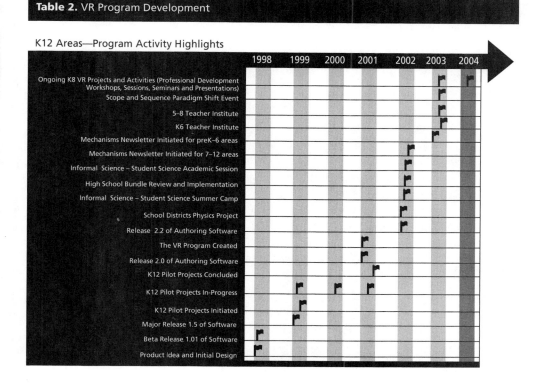

K12 Areas—Program Activity Highlights

	1998	1999	2000	2001	2002	2003	2004
Ongoing K8 VR Projects and Activities (Professional Development Workshops, Sessions, Seminars and Presentations)						⚑	⚑
Scope and Sequence Paradigm Shift Event						⚑	
5–8 Teacher Institute						⚑	
K6 Teacher Institute						⚑	
Mechanisms Newsletter Initiated for preK–6 areas					⚑		
Mechanisms Newsletter Initiated for 7–12 areas					⚑		
Informal Science – Student Science Academic Session					⚑		
High School Bundle Review and Implementation					⚑		
Informal Science – Student Science Summer Camp					⚑		
School Districts Physics Project					⚑		
Release 2.2 of Authoring Software					⚑		
The VR Program Created				⚑			
Release 2.0 of Authoring Software				⚑			
K12 Pilot Projects Concluded				⚑			
K12 Pilot Projects In-Progress		⚑	⚑	⚑			
K12 Pilot Projects Initiated		⚑					
Major Release 1.5 of Software		⚑					
Beta Release 1.01 of Software	⚑						
Product Idea and Initial Design	⚑						

laboratory requirements. In addition, digital imagery technology is available for the teachers to check out or have assigned to their classrooms.

Development of the Program

Many activities were conducted before the VR Program was developed.

Note that, unlike many programs, the software was developed first, with applications for education K–12 in mind, and was reviewed and tested by educators, business personnel, and technology specialists. (A description of the software is included in "The Program" section.) In 1998, we collected information from students, teachers, and administrators in K–12 on their interests and their perceptions of the needs in science teaching and learning, and in current practices. This was done through surveys, interviews, requests, and pilot projects. We also gathered information from the teachers on their educational backgrounds, years of teaching experience, comfort levels with teaching inquiry, perceived classroom needs, and descriptions of their students and teaching routines. Other questions elicited information on their knowledge and use of technology in teaching and assessing science. Below is a sample of other questions we asked the teachers.

1. Do you have industry experience? (e.g., research scientist) If so, describe.
2. Do you have access to the internet? __ home/off campus __ on campus __ none
3. How would you rate your overall technology skills (e.g., digital camera, laptop, projector, etc.) on a scale of 1 to 5 ((1) Expert …(5) Novice)? __
4. What percentage of classroom time is spent in laboratory or field excursion activities (e.g., laboratory experiments involving simple machines, dissection, or field excursion activities such as AstroWorld Physics Day, Nature Center studies)? __
5. What technology tools do you have in your classroom (e.g., digital camera, laptop, projection panel, overhead projector)?
6. What technology tools do you have access to check out and bring into your classroom (e.g., digital camera, laptop, projection panel, overhead projector)?
7. Which of these best describes your expertise with teaching the Texas Essential Knowledge and Skills (TEKS)? (Note: TEKS contains scientific processes (inquiry) and science concepts.) **Select One:** (1) Novice; (2) Less than adequate; (3) Adequate; (4) More than adequate; (5) Expert
8. Which one of these broad topics contains science concepts that you are MOST comfortable teaching? **Select One:** (1) Earth science systems; (2) Living systems; (3) Motion, forces, and energy; (4) Nature of science; (5) Structures and properties of matter.
9. Which one of these broad topics contains science concepts that you are LEAST comfortable teaching? **Select One:** (1) Earth science systems; (2) Living systems; (3) Motion, forces, and energy; (4) Nature of science; (5) Structures and properties of matter.

Extensive research was conducted on "best practices" for teaching and learning science and for professional development. Our research findings included the following:

- While constructivism is often viewed from either cognitive (within the individual) or sociocultural (within a community of learners) perspectives, the learning of science can be seen to entail both individual *and* social processes.

- In order to help students apply what they learn to real-world situations, learning should be situated in *authentic activity*.
- Technology is seen by many as a unique agent that can anchor students' learning or support/augment the construction of meaning.
- The goal of Project-Based Study (PBS) is to enhance science instruction by involving students in exploring solutions to real questions, learning science content, and understanding science concepts through extended inquiry, collaboration, and use of technology. While the notions behind it are not new, PBS in its current form has developed only recently and has yet to be explored or enjoyed to its fullest potential.
- Teacher quality is the factor that matters most for student learning.

Finally, we identified the participating teachers and began designing the Visual Realization (VR) Program.

The Program

The major challenge faced by the developers was in designing a program that would support the goals for school science that define a scientifically literate society (NSES, p. 13), encompass the eight categories of the content standards, and address our findings. We also wanted to design a program that could be used with any science discipline; therefore, we chose to concentrate on the *unifying concepts and processes* standard as stated in the NSES: "This standard describes some of the integrative schemes that can bring together students' many experiences in science education across grades K–12. The unifying concepts and processes standard can be the focus of instruction at any grade level but should always be closely linked to outcomes aligned with other content standards" (NRC 1996, p. 104). Meeting this challenge led to a program that is suitable for *all* students in grades K–12. The pilot studies were done with students ages 10–18 in both regular classes and advanced placement classes.

The VR Program Goals

1. Provide an interactive learning environment where all students are involved in experiencing science according to their interests and abilities;
2. Address the need for students to develop research and technological skills for science, which directly relates to local and national trends and science requirements;
3. Provide numerous learning opportunities for students in traditional and nontraditional settings to collect and analyze data, evaluate information, and offer possible solutions for science-related problems and issues; and
4. Provide teachers continual opportunities for growth through practice-based professional development experiences that will equip them with knowledge and skills needed to teach science on an inquiry basis.

The VR Program synergistically combines three components into a unique approach featuring a technology enhancement that students can use without having to know "programming stuff" to get results. Each component of the VR Program is designed to both complement and support the other two. Students work in collaborative teams, with each team member assigned to be responsible for specific tasks. The program can readily stand alone at any level, and can also be incorporated into established efforts, projects, programs and curricula. The program is also unique in that there is not a prescribed sequence of study. It promotes both the design of curricula (understanding by design) that engage students in exploring and deepening their understanding of important ideas as well as in the design of assessments to reveal the extent of their understandings.

Each element targets one or more changing emphases. A definition and explanation of each program component is followed by an explanation of how these emphases were addressed by that component.

Practice-Based Professional Development

Most teachers write lesson plans based upon their district and state requirements, and on available resources. It's important to offer professional development activities that will help them develop effective teaching plans that include the interests of their students while also increasing students' knowledge of and achievement in science. Effective professional development is a continuum of professional learning experiences. It is ongoing and collaborative, stresses content learning and inquiry-based teaching strategies, uses instructional technology, and requires active participation. The professional development component of the VR Program combines online practice sets, one-on-one mentoring, and a continuum of different experiences (workshops, on-site assistance, communication networks, resources, etc.).

Participating teachers learn how to (1) incorporate project-based studies and digital imagery into the teaching of conceptual science; (2) teach students to use digital cameras for collecting, analyzing, and reporting data through digital imagery authoring; (3) design project-based study lessons that are aligned to the required curriculum; and (4) complete a study model to demonstrate knowledge and understanding of project-based studies and digital imagery integration. The *More Emphasis* conditions addressed by practice-based professional development are (1) implementing inquiry as instructional strategies, abilities, and ideas to be learned; (2) guiding students in active and extended scientific inquiry; (3) providing opportunities for scientific discussion and debate among students; and (4) a variety of professional development activities.

Prior to a one-day orientation and training session held for the program teachers, one-on-one sessions were held with them at their schools. Gathering information prior to the one-day session allowed the planners to tailor the session to the teacher attendees. Each teacher was asked to bring to the session a list of the objectives, concepts, and other materials that they planned to teach during the next six weeks. They were also asked to prepare to present their plans to the session attendees. The agenda for the day is provided below.

Topics
1. Survey, Pre-Test, Visual Realization Program and Project-Based Study Models
2. NSES Goals, Eight Categories of Content Standards and Changing Emphases
3. Teaching Strategies and Scientific Inquiry Techniques
4. Visual Realization: Discovering a New Way to Teach and Learn
5. Planning and Designing a Project-Based Study

6. Teacher Presentations
7. Digital Imagery Hardware Technology Usage: Digital Cameras, Microscope Cameras, Flex Cams, etc.
8. Creating Digital Imagery Files: Software Techniques for Authoring and Managing Digital Imagery
9. Action Plans/Timeline (Collaborative Groups)

From the teachers' presentations, science topics to be developed were identified. Based on their plans, the teachers were assigned to collaborative groups; each group selected a topic to develop, and made task assignments. Before the next one-day session, team members made initial plans and completed their task assignments. The teachers were instructed to use teaching strategies and activities that would teach students the skills and knowledge identified by the team as important to know for the topic at hand. The teaching plans had to involve at least two weeks of instruction time. Between sessions, a member of the planning team visited each teacher to check up on his or her progress and to assist him or her if needed. The planning team members were also available to the teachers upon request. Presentations were made at the next one-day session.

Digital Imagery Technology

Digital imagery technology is the union of images, multimedia files, audio and video files, and other electronic graphic elements that are produced or maintained using imaging technology (digital camera or microscope camera). The technology allows dynamic digital imagery content to be captured and added to a digital content repository for authoring. *Authoring* consists in writing or constructing descriptive notes as an overlay or attachment to the file. The technology allows learners to easily author unlimited "regions" on any digital imagery. *Region authoring* is the ability to manipulate, add to, type over, and enhance any region on a digital imagery file without compromising the original file size in any way. This is done by layering, and allows content to be saved in a database for searches/sorts on any region with ease of use.

Region authoring is distinct from editing, because the copyright of the original digital imagery file is not compromised but associated text merely sits as an overlay on top of the visual. Region authoring is like writing on an erasable white board with erasable markers, while editing uses a permanent marker to write on the same board. The technology also allows a general description of the entire digital imagery file to be stored in a separate viewable area while performing region authoring. The dynamics of adding a general description, and of unlimited region authoring for visuals, allows more authentic and reliable content in any science discipline.

Changing Emphases Addressed by Digital Imagery Technology

This was the component that the teachers needed the most instruction in and assistance with incorporating into their teaching plans; it comprises the *More Emphasis* goals of learning subject matter disciplines in the context of inquiry, technology and science in personal and social perspectives, and history and nature of science, as well as management of ideas and information.

Taking the digital pictures was easy; *why* take the picture and *what* to do with them afterwards—these questions presented a major challenge for both teachers and students. The VR

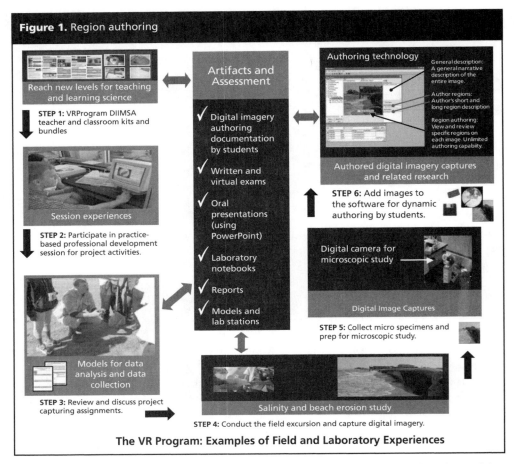

Figure 1. Region authoring

Reach new levels for teaching and learning science

STEP 1: VRProgram DIIMSA teacher and classroom kits and bundles

Session experiences

STEP 2: Participate in practice-based professional development session for project activities.

Models for data analysis and data collection

STEP 3: Review and discuss project capturing assignments.

Artifacts and Assessment

✓ Digital imagery authoring documentation by students

✓ Written and virtual exams

✓ Oral presentations (using PowerPoint)

✓ Laboratory notebooks

✓ Reports

✓ Models and lab stations

Authoring technology

General description: A general narrative description of the entire image.

Author regions: Author's short and long region description

Region authoring: View and review specific regions on each image. Unlimited authoring capability.

Authored digital imagery captures and related research

STEP 6: Add images to the software for dynamic authoring by students.

Digital camera for microscopic study

Digital Image Captures

STEP 5: Collect micro specimens and prep for microscopic study.

Salinity and beach erosion study

STEP 4: Conduct the field excursion and capture digital imagery.

The VR Program: Examples of Field and Laboratory Experiences

technology is used to author captured digital imagery files. By authoring, the students learned that they were able to provide detailed descriptions and annotations to accompany their individualized work, demonstrating understanding of the content. A student taking part in an environmental study stated that, "Authoring pictures with the software taught me a lot about the parts of an animal and what they were used for. Once I gathered my information, I was able to easily put it together and learn from it by clicking and creating regions on various parts of the picture." Using the features of the technology allowed the students to easily manage their information and record their ideas and research findings.

Project-Based Study (PBS)

PBS enhances science instruction by involving students in exploring solutions to real questions, learning science content, and understanding science through extended inquiry, collaboration, and use of technology.

PBS is characterized by:

1. a *driving question* that is meaningful to the learners and that is anchored in a real-world context;
2. student-conducted *investigations* that result in the development of *artifacts* or products; and
3. *collaboration* among students, teachers, and the community; and the use of cognitive tools, and particularly *technology,* to help students represent and share ideas (Krajcik et al., 1994).

While particular projects can and do differ, these are the common elements.

Four study models have been defined for this program. These models can be used alone or in different combinations to achieve stated goals: (1) Laboratory; (2) Field Excursion; (3) Campus-Based; and (4) Case. In each model, students must collect data that include digital pictures. Teachers use one or more of these models in developing their teaching plans, which were submitted and approved by the planning team.

Laboratory

This is an empirical project or series of projects, conducted within a laboratory setting. This model involves students' exploration of the use of laboratories in science in different ways. Traditionally, laboratories have been used to collect data and report results on experiments provided by the teacher. Now, students are expected to design these experiments themselves so that they can test hypotheses and collect, analyze, and interpret data, and then report results firsthand in a variety of formats. The laboratories conducted must be linked to other instructional activities (convergent learning). The historically typical practice of an entire class conducting the same pre-outlined experimentation at the same time has shifted to students' conducting a variety of unique and original laboratories, or different procedures of the same lab simultaneously. This model also provides the vehicle for students to conduct the sorts of skills laboratories that are needed for field excursions.

Field Excursion

This model requires students to work in collaborative teams in order to determine the methods they will use to answer the identified driving question. In addition to exploring these driving questions, students identify and explore new notions, concepts, or issues that arise. Excursion leaders provide on-site instruction and assist the students as they gather and document characteristics of (and/or samples collected from) explored areas. After each excursion, the teams analyze the data collected, formulate conclusions based on the data collected, and communicate findings with a report or presentation.

Campus-Based

This is similar to a field excursion study, but all research, digital imagery, and specimen collection are conducted locally—on campus and in surrounding locations. This model is effective for conducting project-based studies when it is not feasible to conduct a full field excursion and is frequently combined with the laboratory model.

Case

This is a non-empirical historical project, involving research in primary and secondary references, as well as digital imagery from all available non-empirical sources. Case studies develop students' skills in group planning and interactions, oral and written communication, critical thinking, and research skills. This model allows for the study of contemporary science problems that students encounter in the news.

Changing Emphases Addressed by PBS

Content Standards
- Using evidence and strategies for developing or revising an explanation
- Applying the results of experiments to scientific arguments and explanations

Teaching Standards
- Guiding students in active and extended scientific inquiry
- Providing opportunities for scientific discussion and debate among students
- Sharing responsibility for learning with students

Assessment Standards
- Assessing to learn what students do understand
- Students engaged in ongoing assessment of their work and that of others

Each model has a suggested a set of instructions and procedures. From this basic information, the teacher groups develop a full plan. Though each model has its own unique features, all of them require students to conduct research and create a product. After an overall topic is assigned, the students research the topic independently and in class. This preliminary groundwork helps to guide the students as they begin to identify a driving question. As students conducted background research, they were asked to keep a number of issues in mind: *What area of the topic strikes my interest? What research has been conducted in this area already? What types of methods, materials, and procedures are regularly used in this area? Which of these methods, materials, and procedures are available to me? Why are the topic and my area of it, of particular importance? What questions do I have about my topic that I have not yet asked?*

Research sources included internet, school library, city and community libraries, textbooks journals, teacher handouts, and other reference materials. Research is continued throughout the project. Each collaborative team identified a question. This question fueled further research project efforts and guided students as they defined the parameters of the project.

Conducting a Field (Excursion) Research Study

The following example outlines a field excursion to Herman Brown Park in Houston, Texas. To complete this study, students will be involved in collecting field, library, and laboratory data. The collection of field data will occur during an excursion to Herman Brown Park. The role of the teacher and the tasks that the student teams must complete are listed below.

Pre-Excursion Activities

The teacher should

1. Provide instruction on scientific inquiry and team dynamics;
2. Select a topic focus;
3. Develop a teaching plan for the study;
4. Organize collaborative teams;
5. Describe the study to the students;
6. Develop presentation criteria;
7. Select appropriate activities, including labs, related to the topic for the students to conduct, complete, and discuss prior to the field excursion;
8. Provide adequate class time for the teams to meet and plan the excursion;
9. Approve research problems and plans;
10. Make necessary arrangements for the excursion; and
11. Assemble necessary materials/supplies for the excursion;

Post-Excursion Activities

The teacher should

1. Provide adequate class time for the teams to analyze collected data and complete necessary reporting documents;
2. Provide class time for the collaborative teams to present results to the class; and
3. Conduct a virtual exam.

The collaborative teams should complete the following tasks:

Pre-Excursion Tasks

- Task 1: Conduct all pre-excursion activities and complete required documentation/reports;
- Task 2: Conduct library research related to the excursion topic; and
- Task 3: Brainstorm possible questions to investigate during field experience (excursion);
- Task 4: Select one question to investigate. The question should be stated in the form of a problem. The team members should develop an explanation of why this problem was selected;
- Task 5: Present their problem and explanation to the class for questions and feedback;
- Task 6: Design a plan of action that includes the procedure for collecting data, prepare a list of materials and supplies needed, construct tables to record collected data, and assign tasks for each team member to complete during the excursion. Conduct additional research, if needed;
- Task 7: Submit Task 6 results to another team for feedback. Then, submit revised plan of action to the teacher for approval;

Excursion Task

- Task 8: Collect necessary data for their problem during the excursion. The data should include pictures, drawing, charts, diagrams, measurements, written descriptions as well as samples (soil, water, etc.). Data and samples collected will be analyzed during class;

Post-Excursion Tasks

- Task 9: Analyze collected data, design and conduct experiments if necessary, write a narrative summary, and complete reporting documents (graphs, charts, tables, pictures). Include research information to support your data; and
- Task 10: Prepare a presentation based on the criteria provided by your teacher. Present excursion results to the class.

In contrast, a campus-based or laboratory model may require the collaborative teams to design one or more experiments. The design of the experiment included a hypothesis, variables, a list of materials and procedures, tables, charts, graphs, and an explanation of how digital imagery would be used in the experiment(s), including documentation and a presentation plan. A case study frequently involves the other three models.

Evaluation

Assessment was interactive and continual (i.e., researched and authored digital imagery content, virtual exams using their captured digital imagery without authored content, PowerPoint presentations using their captured digital imagery files, and associated research). Students were tested over materials that they helped produce through the design of, and active participation in, activities and research. In addition to digital imagery and other documentation, students presented their findings using digital imagery technology and PowerPoint presentations. Evaluation measurement instruments used include surveys, questionnaires, student achievement on standardized tests, virtual exam results and student portfolios. Teachers profiled and targeted key areas for improvement using data from the measurement instruments completed by the students. One such survey follows.

Sample Student Post-Analysis

The following statements are excerpts from the evaluation instruments.
Statements A-1 and A-2 were identified using this scale: (1) Strongly Agree; (2) Agree; (3) Somewhat Agree; (4) Somewhat Disagree; (5) Disagree; and (6) Strongly Disagree.

A-1. The Virtual Exam was effective because of my:

Involvement in capturing and authoring images:	1 2 3 4 5 6
Experience in researching the information for the images:	1 2 3 4 5 6
Creating or having ownership of the authored images:	1 2 3 4 5 6
Understanding of what I was authoring on the images:	1 2 3 4 5 6
Overall, I thought the Virtual Exam using the software was effective:	1 2 3 4 5 6

A-2. I was able to retain more Science content because of my:

Involvement in capturing and authoring images: 1 2 3 4 5 6

Experience in researching the information for the images: 1 2 3 4 5 6

Creating or having ownership of the authored images: 1 2 3 4 5 6

Understanding of what I was authoring on the images: 1 2 3 4 5 6

Statements C-1, C-2, D-1, D-2 show the typical BEFORE/AFTER questions.

C-1. How would you rate your experience with computers BEFORE this project?

1 – Expert … 6 – Novice

Word-processing skills	1	2	3	4	5	6
Searching, file copying, and deleting	1	2	3	4	5	6
Internet Explorer	1	2	3	4	5	6
Netscape Navigator	1	2	3	4	5	6
MS-PowerPoint	1	2	3	4	5	6
Image authoring technology	1	2	3	4	5	6

C-2. How would you rate your experience with computers AFTER this project?

1 – Expert … 6 – Novice

Word-processing skills	1	2	3	4	5	6
Searching, file copying, and deleting	1	2	3	4	5	6
Internet Explorer	1	2	3	4	5	6
Netscape Navigator	1	2	3	4	5	6
MS-PowerPoint	1	2	3	4	5	6
Image authoring technology	1	2	3	4	5	6

D-1. How would you rate your technology skills using a digital camera and the computer to manipulate images BEFORE participating in this project?

1 – Expert … 6 – Novice					
1	2	3	4	5	6

D-2. How would you rate your technology skills using a digital camera and the computer to manipulate images AFTER participating in this project?

1 – Expert … 6 – Novice					
1	2	3	4	5	6

Summary

The VR Program is not static. Its structure and components provide active learning experiences that enhance student understanding and address the need for students to develop inquiry research skills in science. The collaborative learning environment that is created puts the potential for achievement at a relatively high level, thus leading to increased student motivation, improved academic achievement, and the acquisition of real-world skills, which lead to a better understanding of science. Problem finding and solving, critical thinking, and communications skills were also increased as students collaborated with peers, leaders, professionals, facilitators, and mentors by e-mail, voice, and other collaborative methods.

The VR Program allows

1. teachers to activate, motivate, and stimulate students in science;
2. technology integration in science education to be successful;
3. students to explore a subject, evaluate information, capture digital imagery, think critically, and work toward a rewarding resolution;
4. students to use digital imagery equipment to capture, author content, and document studies; and
5. easy implementation of inquiry-based curriculum to enhance and assist in the learning process.

The end result is *Involvement + Experience = Understanding, Ownership, and Long-Term Retention.*

References

Blumenfeld, P. C., E. Soloway, R. W. Marx, J. S. Krajcik, M. Guzdial, and A. Palincsar. 1991. Motivating project based learning: Sustaining the doing, supporting the learning. *Educational Psychologist* 25: 369–398

Collis, B. and G. Knezek. 1997. *Teaching and learning in the digital age—research into practice with telecommunications in educational settings.* Eugene, OR: International Society for Technology in Education.

Converse, R. E. 1996. Technology and the science program: Placing them in proper perspective. In *Issues in Science Education,* eds. J. Rhoton and P. Bowers, 49–56. Arlington, VA: National Science Teachers Association.

Darling-Hammond, L. 2000. *Solving the dilemmas of teacher supply, demand, and quality.* New York: National Commission on Teaching and America's Future.

Driver, R., H. Asoko, J. Leach, E. Mortimer, and P. Scott. 1994. Constructing scientific knowledge in the classroom. *Educational Researcher* 23 (7): 5–12.

Kozma, R. B. 1991. Learning with media. *Review of Educational Research* 6 (2): 179–211.

Krajcik, J. S., P. C. Blumenfeld, R. W. Marx, and E. Soloway. 1994. A collaborative model for helping teachers learn project-based instruction. *Elementary School Journal* 94: 483–497.

Loucks-Horsley, S., P. Hewson, N. Love, and K. Stiles. 1998. *Designing professional development for teachers of science and mathematics.* Thousand Oaks, CA: Corwin Press.

National Research Council (NRC). 1996. *National science education standards.* Washington, DC: National Academy Press.

National Research Council (NRC). 2000. *Educating teachers of science, mathematics and technology: New practices for the new millennium.* Washington, DC: National Academy Press.

Finding Out What...and How They Know

Margaret Foss
Hawkins Middle School
Hawkins, Wisconsin

Setting

Hawkins Middle School is located in a small rural city, the county seat of one of the poorest counties in Wisconsin, ranking fifth lowest in per capita income. Approximately 50% of the students receive assistance in the form of free and reduced lunch. Primary employers in the school district include the government (county hospital, school, city and county government) and two window manufacturers. A large number of residents are engaged in the business of logging.

The district is fairly small (1,100 students pre-K–12). Students are organized into four buildings, three of which are in the county seat, pre-K–5 in one building, 6–8 in a middle school and 9–12 in a high school. The fourth district building serves students grades pre-K–8 in a small town 20 miles east. The district has been suffering from declining enrollments since a copper mine closed five years ago.

More Emphasis Conditions

Two National Science Education Standards (NRC 1996) have been the focus of this project: to experience the richness and excitement of the natural world, and to engage in intelligent discourse about science and technology.

Students are always the focus in education, but in this project that emphasis becomes even stronger and richer as students take on a shared responsibility for their own learning. Students select their topics of study, work in cooperative groups and share responsibility for the classroom. Primary emphases in the teaching include a desire to respond to individual needs, conceptual understanding as a learning goal, and the development of inquiry skills. Assessment to support these efforts is natural and ongoing.

We allow students the freedom to develop and test personal explanations for phenomena, analyze ideas, and defend conclusions; this approach fosters their regular engagement in intelligent discourse about science. This rich dialogue among learners lends itself to nontraditional forms of assessment such as performance-based assessment and teacher observation, allowing the teacher a window into what and how the students know. These assessments were designed to measure students' understanding and routinely involve the students in self-assessment.

Classroom Participants

Our classroom focuses on project-based learning (Chard 1998). Work in all subject areas was intentionally integrated. Students in this self-contained fifth-grade classroom requested the experience through an application process. Of 20 students, 3 needed emotional/behavioral assistance, 2 qualified for Title I, and 3 were gifted; they were led by a second teacher. She earned a BA in microbiology, became licensed to teach in a graduate program, and has 13 years experience teaching, with the prior 2 years spent teaching fifth grade in the same district.

Program Description

The general expectation for this project was that students would learn the same general content and skills as other fifth graders, but would engage in learning through activities and personal experiences rather than through reading and answering questions. They would be invited to select the specific facets to study within larger, teacher-selected topics. In order to assess student progress fully, some care needed to be taken to allow for sufficient flexibility, since no two students would be focusing on the same subtopics. At the same time, a unified description of the targeted skill was needed, since all students were expected to develop similar skills but at levels appropriate to each learner.

Student work was project based and individually paced, to allow them to accelerate to the fullest extent possible, while working toward international standards. Student work in science, social studies, health, and language arts was integrated and designed to use a real-world setting as much as possible. A strong connection to Wisconsin State Academic Standards anchored the curricular goals and projects addressed.

The long-term plan for the classroom (Jacobs 1997) included several unifying themes. The first was integration of subjects to provide a contextually accurate sense of the natural world and our history of interactions with it. The second was developing strong skills through engagement in intelligent discourse and through encouraging student inquiry. The most important was the focus on the learner—responding to individual needs, concentrating on understanding, and encouraging intrinsic motivation through student choice.

A timeline was used to frame the studies and to facilitate the integration of social studies into the science and health topics. Quarters were divided into centuries of American history, with first quarter addressing prehistory through the 1600s, second quarter the 1700s, and third the 1800s; we ended the year in the 1900s. Students were placed in four permanent groups to study specific states (one per region): South: FL, East: PA, Midwest: MN, and West: CA. Other groupings were also used flexibly throughout the year, but the state groups provided constant support for students and also encouraged cooperation.

A variety of skills were addressed during the year, including traditional science skills and communication skills. Each quarter a particular set of skills was emphasized: first quarter targeted questioning, basic research skills, and curiosity; second quarter focused on data collection and analysis; third quarter explored the use of primary sources and public presentation skills; fourth quarter expanded on the public presentation of findings. In addition, students wrote constantly about what was going on in the classroom. They recorded their progress on projects daily in journals and produced a weekly newsletter to explain to parents and other interested persons what was going on in the classroom. This writing allowed them to play with ideas as well as objects in their project-based studies.

When presented with new experiences, students were encouraged to select a particular facet to study in depth. This routine of choosing fostered their interest, hence increasing both motivation and a shared responsibility for learning. This made students' work necessarily personal, which increased their depth of understanding. Self-assessment contributed to this focus on the student as well.

Format for Projects

The general format for project work involved six steps: (1) determine prior knowledge, (2) experience the topic as a group, (3) generate questions, (4) select focus topics, (5) complete planned work, and (6) present project (Chard 1998; Kilpatrick 1918). The steps are flexible in the manner in which they are used. For example, many methods of determining prior knowledge were used throughout the year, including class brainstorming, writing individual concept maps, drawing pictures, and writing prose. Each phase involved class decision making. Although broad topics were teacher selected, students always selected their own subtopics. Project guidelines were developed by the teacher, but timelines and some details were negotiated with the class. Project work itself could be individual or group, as chosen by students. Rubrics for assessing student work were teacher developed and provided to students prior to beginning project work, but always included a student self-assessment prior to teacher assessment. Projects were often group efforts, as seen in the prairie mural in Figure 1. The student explaining her mesic prairie plant had created only one of the plants in the mural.

Figure 1. Presentation of Mesic Prairie Mural

Students created a mural of plants they had researched and shared information about their plants with the class.

Assessment

Two major goals guided all the assessment attempted during the year. First, students were to develop increasing awareness of their own learning. Fifth graders are capable of metacognition and self-assessment when introduced to these skills. Secondly, progress would be measured against criteria, rather than through comparison with other students. This allowed students, parents, and teacher to see progress over time in an individual (Stiggins 1997; Wiggins 1998).

The assessment and self-assessment were integrated fully in the learning environment, rather than existing as a necessary evil accomplished in private by a teacher. Students assessed their own work, including work habits, every day. This was accomplished through daily journal writing about project work that had been accomplished during the day. Students described their progress in detail; they rated their use of time, effort, and clean-up using a teacher-developed rubric (see Table

Table 1. Student rubric for self-assessment of work habits. Students marked the level of their daily work in each row.

	Wow	**OK**	**Oops**	**Unacceptable**
Time use	I used my time well today, getting a lot accomplished on this	I wanted to waste time today, but I decided not to	I started to waste time, but after a reminder I got busy	I wasted more time than I should have today
Effort	The work I did was my best work. I'm proud of it	I started out badly, but reminded myself to work better	I needed a reminder to work carefully	The work I did today was a little careless
Clean-up	I cleaned up all my materials right away	I almost forgot to clean up, but remembered later	I needed to be reminded to clean up	I left things for others to clean up

1).   Student journal entries were read and discussed at a weekly student-teacher conference held during independent math work time. To prepare for the conference, students would set a personal goal for the week and describe their progress toward its achievement. At the conference, the teacher read and assessed journal entries for content and grammar (including spelling), and discussed both project progress and the self-rating of work skills. Goals were discussed, modified if necessary, and made specific enough for progress to be noted the following week. This allowed students to discuss their learning in depth with regard for both *what* and *how* they were learning.

All project work was assessed using a rubric developed by the teacher in advance of the project. These rubrics were carefully discussed in class so that students would have a clear understanding of expectations before they began their work. The rubrics and project directions were designed to be general enough to allow for differences in subtopics, but specific in skill descriptions and expectations, including work habits. When a project was completed, students would spend a short time assessing their work with the aid of the project rubric before they presented their project or submitted their work in any way. Rubric sheets were then returned to the teacher for teacher evaluation of the project and work (see Table 2, page 65).

Every quarter, students were encouraged to reflect on their progress and establish quarterly goals. The reflection included reviewing all the quarter's weekly goals, then tallying the number of goals achieved. New goals were selected and students described them in detail. They also specified the assistance they would need from parents and teacher in order to attain these goals. This was a major topic of discussion in the student-led parent conference (Stiggins 1997).

To prepare for the conference, students went through their paperwork collected throughout the quarter and selected three papers they were proud of. They explained on a sticky note their reason for selecting each item. Students reviewed the report card format and prepared themselves for explaining their achievement with their parents. Students had never done anything like this before, so they spent a lot of time in class practicing before the big day. The teacher modeled examples of a conference, then students were given some time to practice their conferences in small groups. Once the big day arrived, the students did a great job. They were able to articulate what they had learned and how they learned it with a richness of detail that nobody else could provide. In addition to their personal preparation for conferences, students worked in their state groups to share various facets of classroom life with their parents. Student groups each created a presentation board and all the boards were displayed at conferences and were also used at a requested school board presentation.

The report card was modified to reflect more accurately the emphasis on criterion-referenced assessment and individually paced learning in the classroom (see Figure 2). Student progress in

Figure 2. Modifications to the report card. Reporting categories were changed to reflect the change in classroom learning environment to emphasize learning in context through projects and assessment based on individual progress.

Project: Learning!

Quarterly Progress Report

Basic Skills

Mathematics Skills mastered (See attached Math checklist)

Skill area	Qtr 1	Qtr 2	Qtr 3	Qtr 4
% accuracy				
Chapter/Objective completed				

Reading

Skill area	Qtr 1	Qtr 2	Qtr 3	Qtr 4
AR point total				
Journal score				
Literature read by the group				

Writing

Skill area	Qtr 1	Qtr 2	Qtr 3	Qtr 4
Mechanics (Spelling, grammar)				
Fluency (word choice, quantity, creativity)			1	
Final product (editing, revising)				

Writing Rating Scale

Outstanding	Acceptable	Emerging	Struggling –
consistently quality work, advanced skills	appropriate to age level	skills are progressing, good effort	skills need work

Other skills

Skill area	Qtr 1	Qtr 2	Qtr 3	Qtr 4
Typing (lesson completed)				
Health Journal				
Foreign Language (5th grade) Skills mastered				
Art				
Music				
PE				

Project work

	Qtr 1	Qtr 2	Qtr 3	Qtr 4
Time use (Avg. rating)				
Effort (Avg. rating)				
Cleanup (Avg. rating)				
Project Score (Avg. rating)				
Subjects addressed (See grade level check-off sheet for details)				

Project Evaluation Rubric

4 points	3 points	2 points	1 points
I used my time well today, getting a lot accomplished	I wanted to waste time today, but I decided not to.	I started to waste time, but after a reminder I got busy	I wasted more time than I should have today.
The work I did was my best work. I'm proud of it.	I started out badly, reminded myself to work better	I needed a reminder to work carefully.	The work I did today was a little careless
I cleaned up all my materials right away	I almost forgot to clean up, but remembered later	I needed to be reminded to clean up	I left things for others to clean up

4/25/05

math was assessed by percentage accuracy on chapter tests, along with number of chapters completed. Reading progress was measured through the accumulation of points from comprehension tests taken after reading children's literature. Writing was rated in three strands, cumulatively on all written work throughout the quarter, using the rating scale in Figure 2. This rubric was also used for the foreign language grade.

Project work was rated on the average score in each of the targeted skill areas—time use, effort, and clean-up—and overall project quality for all projects undertaken in a quarter. Typically, students completed four to six projects during the quarter. The skill areas were chosen as perceived areas of need in fifth graders in this school.

Students were presented with the "new" report card and discussed the changes at the beginning of the year so that all learners would have a sense of the expectations. After that, the assessment became extremely nonintrusive. Gone were the pages marked in red, screaming failure, along with the quantities of incomplete lessons needing to be turned in. In their place were opportunities to answer real questions and make models, explore real situations and discuss ideas. Using these almost incidental assessments allowed students to focus more on their learning than on their comparison with neighbors, a much more natural way to assess progress.

The Pond Project

Students were challenged in the beginning of the year to create a pond biome in the classroom. This project allowed students to grow in their personal research skills and to use measurement and simple ratios while they were learning about pond life and its complex interactions. Students were introduced to the pond biome with a canoe trip on the schoolyard pond. At the pond, students used skills they had learned in the classroom to identify macro-invertebrates and test water (Figure 3).

Figure 3. Water Testing at a Pond

Once familiar with the pond, students selected a biotic factor (viz., plants and animals) to research. Their task was to create a model of their organism—four times larger than real life. The expectations of the project were discussed prior to beginning the work and students were provided with the rubric shown in Table 2.

| | | | | chapter 4 |

Table 2. Sample Rubric: Pond Project (save this sheet for grading when you are done)

Category	Wow – 5 pts	Ok – 4pts	Oops – 3 pts	Self rating	Teacher rating
Scale	Size of creature is accurately to scale	There is a minor error in scale	There is major error in scale		
Information	Enough information is provided to get a clear sense of the organism	A few questions remain unanswered about the organism	Lots of holes exist in the information provided		
Accuracy	Organism is a color and shape that closely resembles reality	Organism is unrealistic in some way	Organism is a caricature or quite unrealistic		
Connections	Many connections made between organism and others	One or two connections made, but not any more	Others provide connections to your organism in class		
Time use	Used my time well, working steadily on this project each day	Started to waste time, but when reminded got busy	Wasted time or waited until the last minute to start		
Work quality	Work to be proud of	Needed reminders to work carefully	Careless or sloppy work		
Clean-up	Cleaned up all materials right away	Needed to be reminded to clean up	Left things for others to clean up		

The pond models were hung in the classroom after students presented their findings. The class lived "in the pond," discussing animal and plant interactions for several weeks after the presentations.

Evidence of *More Emphasis* Conditions

The sense of learning community was strong. Students shared learning tasks, challenges, and victories effectively through the permanent student groups. These heterogeneous groups provided continuity and support for all learners. In fact, groups were encouraged to support one another's weekly goals and were rewarded with chances at a weekly prize, when all students in their state group achieved their goal. Three of the groups attained this goal fairly consistently (70% of the time). One of the groups struggled with it, but did manage to achieve all their group's goals at least once each quarter. This group support allowed several of these students to change patterns of low achievement that had plagued them in prior years.

The focus on responding to the individual was the most critical component of the project. Meeting the learners where they were was at times challenging, but was rewarded by high levels of student interest and understanding of the content. When asked "How do you feel about your learning this year?" Students wrote these responses:

1. I feel better when we do stuff than reading it, because I learn stuff easier and I have to research and draw.
2. I think I am learning a lot more than other years because when I do projects and hands-on things I remember things a lot better.
3. I am glad I am in this class because I can work at my own speed. So instead of being behind I will be in the right spot.
4. I feel that I am doing very well and learning a lot.
5. It's fun without using textbooks and doing projects.
6. I like it. You have no books and worksheets. I remember more of it now.
7. I think that this is the best year that I have had out of all the school years. And it is because of this class, so this is the best school year ever. I feel OK about my learning this year because of the help in this class does most of it.
8. I think that project based learning is a great way of learning and I am learning a lot more this year.
9. I feel good because I'm learning a lot more and in a different way.
10. It's a little harder than I thought.
11. I think I learned more than last year. I think I remember things better with projects.
12. I like it. It is much more fun and interesting. It is also easy but challenging enough.

These responses indicate high student involvement in the learning community and in their own learning. As you can see, students were feeling challenged, but not pressured by the format of the classroom. Their enthusiasm was wonderful.

Inquiry was an emphasis in the classroom in at least two ways. Students were involved in developing skills that support real scientific inquiry (questioning, researching, data analysis, presentation of findings) and they were routinely exploring real-world issues (water quality, rural life, a variety of environmental issues). Students were provided actual experiences in the sciences, encouraged to engage in activities typical to real scientists (as often as safety permitted) and discuss their findings with their peers. Their understanding of the big ideas of science was greater than other classes I have taught. These students were able to engage in a discussion of ideas in which they supported their position with data. Often they disagreed, but this just provided an opportunity to reexamine the data.

This level of discourse about science and about their learning was evidenced in the quality of the student-led conferences and the students' own articulation of their learning. Student-led conferences were very favorably received by parents. Many expressed their pride at their child's achievements. Nearly all parents (95%) made a regular effort to attend conferences. Parent comments on the learning experience were invited mid-year. The following comments demonstrate their pleasure:

1. She is learning how to do research and find answers to her questions. She has become a very independent learner.

2. I know she really enjoys the different things and projects that are offered.
3. Because the learning is more hands-on, he can advance at the rate appropriate for him, he is given the opportunity to be reflective about his learning, and he is exposed to so many different topics.
4. Each child is in a way responsible for themselves and how much they learn, but the teacher provides excellent guidance to these students.
5. She has shown more interest than previous years.
6. He feels good about what he learns and how he learns it. He's become more eager to share what he learns each day. Many social skills have developed this year.

When asked to rate their child's learning this year compared with the previous year, 92% of the parents felt their children were learning more than they had before. All the students experienced growth in their communication skills (increased fluency and mechanics), through the regular journal and newsletter writing. They were all able to describe the benefits they individually received through the *More Emphasis* (NRC 1996) changes employed.

Although no standardized tests were administered during the school year, achievement was measured regularly through project work and pop quizzes. Student performance on science quizzes was comparable to previous years (average scores: this year 82% to last year 79%). In related subject areas, students completed nearly twice as much math as their grade-level peers. Student reading scores increased over the previous year (30% average increase). Student surveys showed a strong perception of learning (76% felt they were learning more than last year, with 18% undecided).

The focus on natural, contextual assessment contributed much to the understanding of what and how students learn. Opportunities to assess and evaluate progress occurred more frequently this year than in previous years and were enhanced by the use of performance assessment, the observation of student skills, and a modified reporting system focused on growth and individual achievement.

Performance-based assessment of students proved to be an effective way to ensure that students achieve the desired learner outcomes. By discussing expectations of skills and depth of understanding *before* students begin a project, a lot of the guesswork was eliminated from the school experience. Students understood what was expected and monitored their project based on the level of accomplishment they had targeted. By making the expectations clear, students were able to consistently achieve high levels of performance (92% of points received on projects averaged over the year). It was clear what they had learned and what they could do.

Observation of student skills is an integral component of learning how students learn. In this modified classroom setting, observations of student work were ongoing. Students were engaged daily in individual and small-group projects. The teacher watched and occasionally used probing questions to aid in focus and understanding. The weekly conference provided regular opportunities to discuss their learning with the students. This informal discussion provided a wonderful opportunity to develop metacognitive skills. Conversations about students' perception of progress and their needs gave the teacher a window on how they were learning.

Modifications to the report card provided an important escape from traditional norm referenced evaluations. In a setting where student growth and individual achievement were prized, it helped immensely to be able to report progress to parents and students as measurements against a standard. By focusing on the growth of the students, rather than a comparison with their peers, students were better able to experience success as learners. For example, one student, who in particular was meticulous about all her work, tended to work more slowly than the others, but always maintained a high level of accuracy (98% average in math and projects). By assessing student work against a standard, it was possible to celebrate this student's proficiency as careful diligence, a much more meaningful interpretation of what and how she learned.

Summary

In this project emphasizing student involvement in experiencing the richness of the natural world, assessment proved to be a critical tool in the understanding of what and how students learn. Students were engaged in a learning experience that was integrated across subject areas and focused on student choice. They were learning concepts, not facts. By making clear expectations of skills, students were able to develop strong inquiry, researching, and communication skills. They were doing, not watching. The assessment that measured progress throughout the year was student centered, involving students in intelligent discourse about their learning, providing the teacher with multiple perspectives on what and how the students learned. The benefit to the students was clear in their high performance and the methods proved not to be cumbersome for the teacher. The focus was criterion referenced, not norm referenced. Using these modifications in a fifth-grade classroom provided a wealth of insight into what… and how students learn.

References

Chard, S. C. 1998. *The project approach: Making curriculum come alive.* New York: Scholastic.

Jacobs, H. H. 1997. *Mapping the big picture: Integrating curriculum and assessment K–12.* Alexandria, VA: Association for Supervision and Curriculum Development.

Kilpatrick, W. 1918. The project method. *Teachers College Record* 19 (4): 319–335.

National Research Council (NRC). 1996. *National science education standards.* Washington, DC: National Academy Press.

Stiggins, R. J. 1997. *Student-centered classroom assessment.* Second edition. Upper Saddle River, NJ: Merrill.

Wiggins, G. 1998. *Educative assessment: Designing assessments to inform and improve student performance.* San Francisco, CA: Jossey-Bass Publishers.

Teach Them to Fish

Hector Ibarra
West Branch Middle School
West Branch, Iowa

Setting

The reader may question how the "Teach them to fish" proverb relates to science education. Yet, a shift in emphasis from presenting knowledge through lecture and demonstration to encouraging active learning, in which students learn with understanding, exemplifies this proverb in the classroom. Lifelong learning is what we, as teachers, seek to develop in our students.

I teach sixth- and seventh-grade science in the West Branch Middle School. West Branch is a community of 2,188 people in eastern Iowa. Agriculture, manufacturing, and service industries provide the major employment opportunities in this community. The school district has 825 students, with 385 in elementary school, 195 in middle school, and 245 in high school. There is a separate building for each of these levels. In middle school, there is an average of 22–23 students per class. The schools are an important part of the community, with parents and other community members attending school events. This community is also home to the Herbert Hoover Presidential Library.

National Science Education Standards

Four goals for school science underlie the National Science Education Standards (NSES). These goals and the *More Emphasis* conditions I have addressed in my program are as follows:

    1. Goal: Students experience the richness and excitement of knowing about and under-

standing the natural world.
More Emphasis conditions included in program:

Teaching Standards
• Understanding and responding to individual student's interests, strengths, experiences, and needs;
• selecting and adapting curriculum; and
• continually assessing student understanding.

Assessment Standard
• Assessing to learn what students do understand.

Content and Inquiry Standards
• Integrating all aspects of science content; and
• studying a few fundamental science concepts.

2. Goal: Students use appropriate scientific processes and principles in making personal decisions.
More Emphasis conditions included in program:

Teaching Standards
• Guiding students in active and extended scientific inquiry.

Assessment Standard
• Assessing scientific understanding and reasoning.

Content and Inquiry Standards
• Understanding scientific concepts and developing abilities of inquiry;
• implementing inquiry as instructional strategies, abilities, and ideas to be learned;
• performing activities that investigate and analyze science questions; and
• using evidence and strategies for developing or revising an explanation.

3. Goal: Students engage intelligently in public discourse and debate about matters of scientific and technological concern.
More Emphasis conditions included in program:

Teaching Standards
• Supporting a classroom community with cooperation, shared responsibility, and respect; and
• providing opportunities for scientific discussion and debate among students.

Assessment Standard
• Students engaged in ongoing assessment of their work and that of others.

Content and Inquiry Standards
- Communicating science explanations;
- applying the results of experiments to scientific arguments and explanations; and
- public communication of student ideas and work to classmates.

4. Goal: Students increase their economic productivity through the use of the knowledge, understanding, and skills of the scientifically literate person in their careers. *More Emphasis* conditions included in program:

Teaching Standard
- Focusing on student understanding and use of scientific knowledge, ideas, and inquiry processes.

Assessment Standard
- Assessing achievement and opportunity to learn.

Content and Inquiry Standards
- Learning subject matter disciplines in the context of inquiry, technology, science in personal and social perspectives, and history and nature of science;
- investigations over extended periods of time; and
- doing more investigations in order to develop understanding, ability, values of inquiry and knowledge of science content.

Teacher, Students, and Classroom

I have been a teacher at the sixth- through eighth-grade level for 28 years. Currently I teach sixth-grade general science and seventh-grade Earth science. I maintain ongoing professional development through graduate courses, structured inservice programs, professional associations like NSTA, both regional and national conventions and workshops, networking, professional journals such as *Science Scope*, summer institutes that are one to five weeks in length, and the development of cross-curricula activities with other colleagues in my school. Of the student body, 2.5% are minority students, and 5.2% participate in the reduced lunch fee program. My science classroom is a combined classroom/laboratory. The classroom tables are organized in the middle of the room, with laboratory tables to one side and storage along two sides. Equipment for extended projects also can be found along two sides of the room. Science classes meet every day for 45 minutes.

A Typical Day

I use a *guided inquiry* teaching approach in my classroom. This provides the students with a problem or question to investigate, a list of materials to be used, science definitions associated with the investigation, and a data table to record the information (Figure 1). I have developed these activities after scrutinizing a number of activities in books and journals. My students do hands-on inquiry activities in 85% of our science class periods. A typical class is organized in the following manner:

1. I provide 5 to 10 minutes of overview on the concept by me to lay the groundwork for the day.
2. I present the students with a question.
3. Students write answers to "I think" questions related to the question I have given them (assessing preconceptions and building upon past experience).
4. About 60–70% of the time I ask the students to share their "I think" responses, giving students an opportunity to learn what someone else thinks.
5. In paired groups, students work collaboratively to design an investigation in order to answer the question in the activity.
6. The paired groups of students carry out the investigation as I circulate through the room, observing the student activity, answering questions with questions of my own, rather than answers (as the students conduct the investigation, I can hear the questions they ask each other… "Did you notice what happened when I did…?").
7. Students collect data, recording information in their portfolios.
8. Students develop answers to the question; if something doesn't quite turn out the way they expected, they reconstruct their thinking and continue to explore.
9. Students write conclusions and reflect back to their answers to the "I think" question(s).
10. Students share their findings with the class; data from each group may be recorded on a white board; students see how their answers compare to their classmates.
11. I provide final closure: I may ask, "Why were the data observed and collected different between groups of students?" "Did the class do the same investigation?" "What was different or what was done differently in the investigation that caused the differences in the answers reported by the various groups?" "What did we learn…(about the question of the day)?"

With each investigation the students (a) design ways to gather information about what is known, (b) identify variables, (c) gather information and organize observations, (d) interpret their data, (e) use the evidence to develop explanations, and (f) often consider alternate explanations. A 45-minute class period is not very long, so I have developed activities that can be completed in that time, or have a natural break where we continue with the activity the next day.

More Emphasis on Teaching Standards
Selecting and Adapting Curriculum

I have developed curriculum maps for both sixth- and seventh-grade classes that organize my thinking about the units and concepts to be taught (Figure 2). The curriculum maps identify essential questions for each concept, content, and skill the students need to demonstrate (and are consistent across all units), as well as assessments, activities, and resources. The sixth-grade general science units include (a) lenses/mirrors, (b) electricity and magnets, (c) simple machines, (d) simple

Figure 1. Excerpt From an Activity on Anemometers

Investigating anemometers: Devices such as anemometers, Beaufort scales, and wind vanes are used to make short-term weather forecasts. Admiral Sir Francis Beaufort created the Beaufort scale in 1806 to indicate the strength of the wind. The British admiralty accepted the scale for the open sea in 1838 and it was adopted in 1874 by the International Meteorological Committee for international use in weather telegraphy.

I think

    A. Why was the Beaufort scale developed?

    B. Why is the Beaufort scale of little use in this century?

    C. Winds from the south bring what type of weather conditions?

    D. Winds from the north bring what type of weather conditions?

Words to know: anemometer, Beaufort scale, wind vane

Materials: anemometer, Beaufort scale, and wind vane

machines and planetary exploration, (e) planets and constellations, (f) alternative energy/solar cars, (g) life cycles, (h) timber stand improvement, and (i) chemistry.

The seventh-grade Earth science units include (a) nature of science, (b) meteorology, (c) properties of air, (d) rocks and minerals, (e) the universe, (f) groundwater/pollution, (g) plate tectonics and continental drift, (h) geologic time, (i) the Moon, and (j) atomic structure.

The curriculum has been adapted using activities I have developed. I write a handful of new activities each year and revise all activities after each unit. When I first moved to inquiry, the idea of a major overhaul of my activities was overwhelming. I decided to do a handful each year until I had moved all of them to an inquiry approach. I revise all activities after each unit because I have learned from my observations of students doing activities that there is always something that I can fine-tune. If students are asking me to clarify what I have asked on an activity, I realize I need to improve the question(s). A recent addition to the activities has been the "I think" questions that offer information on student preconceptions and experiences. Most of these activities can be done with a limited budget.

The textbook is used solely as a resource, rather than a way to disseminate science knowledge. The activities include references to pages of the textbook for students to easily look up information. I go to journals, the internet, and colleagues for ideas. Students also have the internet as a resource available to them. I believe the teacher is the most important resource to the students as they develop the skills of learning.

Focusing on Student Understanding, Use of Scientific Knowledge, Ideas, and Inquiry Processes

The daily overview of concepts and the investigations the students carry out are the first step in developing student understanding. Students complete portfolios that contain an overview

Figure 2. Excerpt From Curriculum Maps

	Sixth-Grade General Science Simple Machines
Essential Questions	What are examples of simple machines? Why can't a simple machine be 100% efficient? What are 2 things that must occur for work to be done? How does a machine make work easier?
Concept	Six simple machines – lever, pulley…. Properties of simple machines. Forces (friction, gravity, drag, and motion). Work. Newton's first law. Application of concepts – Balloon cars.
Skills	Works in a cooperative atmosphere. Generates questions and makes predictions. Executes procedures based on inquiry. Makes observations, collects, interprets, organizes, and explains data from graphs & tables, draws conclusions, and communicates results. Uses appropriate instruments to obtain data. Analyzes data & recognizes patterns. Applies what is learned to real world situations. Applies knowledge of safety and use of equipment.

Assessments	Identifies simple machines.
	Identifies the properties of a simple machine.
	Identifies the affect of forces on the ability to do work.
	Designs, constructs, and evaluates performance of a balloon car
	    (rubric).
	Develops a written plan to construct a balloon car.
	Makes scale drawing of balloon car, complete with measurements
	    (rubric).
	Practical lab exams.
	Portfolios.

Activities	Investigate friction. Investigate wedges, screws, and incline planes. Investigate wheel and axle. Investigate 1st, 2nd, and 3rd class levers. Investigate fixed, belt, and moveable pulleys. Worksheets. Design, construct, test, and race a balloon car. Balloon car problem and solution worksheet. Balloon car journal.
Resources	Textbook as a resource. Structured inquiry activities developed by teacher. Balloon car rubric.

Figure 2. Continued

	Seventh-Grade Earth Science **Earthquakes**
Essential Questions	What causes earthquakes and volcanoes? Why wasn't the theory of plate tectonics accepted until the 1960's? How can an earthquake be felt in Iowa?
Concept	Earthquakes, volcanoes, and tsunamis. Richter scale and seismology. Continental drift and plate tectonics. Pangaea and Eurasia. Sea floor spreading, trenches, and subduction. Earth's crust, mantle, and core. Faults.
Skills	Works in a cooperative atmosphere. Generates questions and makes predictions. Executes procedures based on inquiry. Makes observations, collects, interprets, organizes, and explains data from graphs & tables, draws conclusions, and communicates results. Uses appropriate instruments to obtain data. Analyzes data & recognizes patterns. Applies what is learned to real world situations. Applies knowledge of safety and use of equipment.
Assessments	Recognizes areas of earth that have earthquakes & volcanoes. Explains causes of earthquakes and volcanoes. Describes the theory of continental drift and plate tectonics. Explains how fossils and rock support the theory of continental drift. Describes different forms of faults. Locates major plates on earth and ring of fire. Plots earthquakes and volcanoes. Practical lab exams. Portfolios.
Activities	Investigate earthquakes and volcanoes. Investigate continental drift. Investigate mountain ranges. Investigate interior parts of earth. Investigate faults. Investigate density.
Resources	Textbook as a resource. Mt. St. Helens video. Plate Tectonics video. Earthquakes video. Structured inquiry activities developed by teacher.

drawing of the unit they complete. Following that is a prediction each student makes about the question I have given them. Data tables are included in the portfolio, followed by the conclusion. The portfolios are one way I am able to determine their level of understanding. Additionally, the questions I ask as I walk around the room while they do the investigations give me a clear idea of their understanding. Finally, the class sharing and discussion at the end of the investigation give me a clearer picture of their understanding of the concepts for the day, as well as their ideas and understanding and use of the inquiry process.

Guiding Students in Active and Extended Inquiry

The manner in which I have developed the activity sheets is the first way in which I guide the students in inquiry. My practice of answering their questions with questions of my own is a means of guiding students and making me a facilitator of learning. This is often frustrating to the sixth-graders when they first come to my class. I have often heard "Don't ask him a question, because he just asks you one right back." I have learned there are four types of questions that are successful in guiding students as they carry out investigations. These questions serve to

1. Clarify: Can you be more specific?
2. Focus: Can you give me an example?
3. Probe: What do you think will happen?
4. Prompt: What can you do…?

It took me a while to develop this questioning skill, but it is necessary for an inquiry approach to teaching. I needed to immerse myself in inquiry to be able to teach as an inquirer. Being a facilitator means helping students to learn to think critically and logically, and to develop the relationships between evidence and explanations.

The summary discussions where I ask why differences in results may have occurred are a further step in guiding the students. Extended inquiry occurs with select units; for example, a weather unit has students collecting data over a 30-day period. Special projects have students carrying out activities and doing data collection and analysis over a two- to six-week period. Some activities, such as a solar car activity, build on their previous study of magnets, electricity, simple machines, and alternative energy. The solar car activity truly applies all they have learned in the previous units. Imagine how exciting it is to hear this student dialogue: "My car goes in reverse. I have to rebuild it." "No, you don't. Remember…"

Providing Opportunities for Scientific Discussion and Debate Among Students

At the end of the activity, the sharing of findings by each student with the entire class provides opportunities for discussion and debate. As students carry out the investigations, they often check with other groups to see what they are doing and why. Collaborative learning is occurring.

Continually Assessing Student Understanding

Assessing understanding is key to the educational process in my classroom. Through observations made as I walk around the classroom during investigations, answers to my questions, and class discussion I am able to determine what I may need to provide in my classroom summary at the end of the activity. For some projects, I have developed a rubric that students complete. A *balloon car* rubric is an example (Figure 3): each student evaluates the car they have developed, providing information on what common problems may be and how to correct the problems.

Figure 3. Excerpt From Balloon Car Rubric

Grade A:
All of the following conditions are met:
1. Balloon powered car travels at least 10 feet.
2. Car has extensions that make the car longer or car has an extension to support the balloon. Wider axles do not qualify as extensions.
3. One set of wheels turns together with the axle (dependent) and the other set of wheels turns on the axle separately and independently.

Grade B:
Condition 2 or 3 from Grade A is met and the car travels 6–9 feet.

Grade C:
1. Car travels between 2 and 5.9 feet.
2. One set of wheels turns on the axle and the other set turns with the axle.
3. No extensions for wheels or balloons are present.

Grade D:
1. Car travels 1.9 feet or less.
2. Grade C conditions are not met.

Grade F:
1. No car is made or brought to the race.

All cars must have at least three wheels. If the car has only three wheels, the pair of wheels must turn separately.

Supporting a Classroom Community With Cooperation, Shared Responsibility, and Respect

On average, 60–70% of the time I ask students to share aloud their answers to the "I think" questions. Students understand there is no wrong answer. No one says, "That's dumb," or makes any negative comment. Indeed, students often find there are common threads in their answers to the "I think" questions. This is a time when the group shares an expectation for respect so that we can learn from each other.

Collaborative learning is another example of cooperation in the classroom. I have developed a system whereby students work in pairs for each investigation. The pairings change every week, eliminating the self-grouping with friends that often occurs in school. This also eliminates the feeling of being left out that the students chosen last often feel. At the beginning of the year, I develop a table with each student's name. Each name has a number. The weeks of the school year are across the top of the table. Students can easily see the number of the student they are working with for the week (Figure 4).

Figure 4. Example of Assigned Lab Partner Sheet for up to 24 Students

Week	1/1	1/8	1/15	1/22	1/29	2/5	2/12	2/19	2/26	3/4	3/11	3/18
Name	1	2	3	4	5	6	7	8	9	10	11	12
1.	23	24	2	3	4	5	6	7	8	9	10	11
2.	22	23	1	24	3	4	5	6	7	8	9	10
3.	21	22	23	1	2	24	4	5	6	7	8	9
4.	20	21	22	23	1	2	3	4	5	6	7	8
5.	19	20	21	22	23	1	2	3	4	5	6	7
24.	12	1	13	2	14	2	15	4	16	5	17	6

Understanding and Responding to Individual Students

Answers to the "I think" questions draw upon student experiences and interests. The group sharing helps me understand the baseline they are coming from. This helps me focus my questions when I go around during the investigation.

More Emphasis on Assessment Standards

Assessing Scientific Understanding and Reasoning

Through the investigations, the portfolio summaries, and classroom discussions I am able to develop a clear picture of student understanding of scientific understanding and reasoning. Twelve years ago, I developed the idea of the students completing portfolios (a summary of each investigation). In the portfolios, the students record their Plan of Attack (POA). The POA includes (a) answers to "I think" questions; (b) "Questions I have" developed by the student; (c) their procedure (what they are going to do); (d) a data table; (e) a conclusion; and (f) where appropriate, an application section. I have learned the importance of reflective writing, and am able to see growth in their investigative skills as they practice inquiry and write activity summaries in their portfolios.

Assessing to Learn What Students Do Understand

I use a variety of assessments and have them specified on the curriculum maps for each unit. Examples include: (a) identify translucent objects, (b) change the direction of a fan's blade, (c) draw and label simple schematic circuits, (d) construct an electromagnet, (e) write a report, (f) scale planets to size and distance from the sun, (g) design a solar car, (h) use a model to understand moon phases, and (i) complete practical lab exams. Unit tests and standardized tests such as the Iowa Test of Basic Skills also give me a picture of student understanding.

Students Engaged in Ongoing Assessment of Their Work and That of Others

Students assess their work as they listen to the group discussion at the end of an investigation where results are shared, reasons for differences are discussed, and possible alternative activities are identified. Additionally, for select projects they complete a rubric that assists them in evaluating their projects. For a solar car project, each student critiques one other student's solar car according to a rubric. In the process, students learn about concepts applied by a peer in the design of the car.

I have developed a self-report knowledge inventory for students who are challenged in learning (resource students, at-risk students, and self-contained and integrated [SCI] students). Students complete the self-reports (Figure 5) at the end of a unit as they think about their understanding of the unit's concepts. These students also take a revised version of the unit test.

Figure 5. Excerpt From Student Self-Report Knowledge Inventory

1. I have never heard of this.
2. I have heard of this but cannot do it.
3. I think I somewhat understand how to do this.
4. I can do this.
5. I can do this and can explain this to another student.

Add up to 5 words per statement to show you can do this if you score any a 4 or 5.
Add up to 2 words per statement to show you can do this if you score any a 3.

____Use a spectroscope
____Use an illustration to show the main sequence of stars
____Do investigations to show Newton's first law
____Do investigations to show Newton's third law
____Do investigations to separate visible light

More Emphasis on Content and Inquiry Standards
Understanding Scientific Concepts and Developing Abilities of Inquiry

The activities I have developed for the typical day include students discussing concepts, investigating the concepts, and learning vocabulary that helps them speak knowledgeably about those concepts. The reason I use *guided* inquiry as a teaching approach rather than *open* inquiry is that I believe some structured knowledge is necessary in order for students to be able to communicate scientific concepts. Including vocabulary in the investigations helps students begin to build and understand explanations for their observations. The names and "words to know" associated with the investigations become useful and meaningful. "Words to know," based on direct experience, results in understanding rather than memorization. One sees students' increasing comfort with inquiry in their portfolios as they go through the year. (I occasionally use worksheets to reinforce concepts.)

Learning Subject Matter Disciplines in the Context of Inquiry, Technology, Science in Personal and Social Perspectives, and History and Nature of Science

As students learn subject matter, we often discuss how what we are discussing in the classroom relates to the real world. Application is essential to helping them understand that science is a part of their everyday lives. Several units have an *environmental education* component, where we discuss the impact of inefficiency, pollution, and waste in light of what they mean to the students and to the world as a whole. Specific projects—on oil filters, lighting and water efficiency, and alternative energy—help them gain knowledge to make decisions for the future.

A science club offers students out-of-class time to explore a variety of interests. Since 1993, state and national awards have acknowledged students' numerous projects for their scientific process. Students also have the opportunity to carry out extended projects.

Technology is a part of the classroom as students (a) design solar cars and Lego rovers, (b) use digital cameras and digital microscopes, and (c) discuss how technology can help or hinder the concept under investigation for the day. We often use a "what if?" approach in discussing technology, including the benefits and other possible consequences.

History and nature of science are a part of the investigations. I have a growing number of activities where historical information is included and is part of the "I think" question(s) at the beginning of the activity.

Integrating All Aspects of Science Content

Through extensive use of investigations and a guided-inquiry teaching approach, students integrate science knowledge and the science process. When I hear students say "Sweet!" as they observe, or change how they are doing something with amazing results, I know they are tying knowledge and process together.

Studying a Few Fundamental Science Concepts

I have developed the curriculum for each grade to have 11–12 units. Essential questions/concepts are identified for each unit. Typically, there are four or five concepts we focus on for each unit. So, by the end of each year the students will have studied 48–55 concepts.

Implementing Inquiry as Instructional Strategies, Abilities, and Ideas to be Learned

The curriculum maps show the relationships between the essential questions/concepts, content, skills, assessments, activities, and resources for each unit. These really identify the strategies to used, the abilities or skills the students demonstrated, and the ideas (concepts) learned.

Activities that Investigate and Analyze Science Questions

Each investigation begins with a question the students will be answering. As they develop the investigation, they work toward understanding and the ability to answer the question. Group discussions enable the students to understand why differences in results may occur. My questions to them, such as "Why do you think…?" also help them analyze what they are seeing.

Investigations Over Extended Time

Not every investigation can be completed within one 45-minute class period. Some units lend themselves well to investigations over an extended period. The mineral unit is an example. The physical properties of minerals are studied over two weeks. Activities associated with a weather unit and simple machine unit occur over several weeks. Separate units build on each other, culminating in a project that incorporates learning from each in a final design.

Using Evidence and Strategies for Developing or Revising Explanation

Students use evidence (their observations and data) to develop conclusions, which are recorded in their portfolios. In the closure at the end of the class period, I ask students to share their findings and conclusions. There is class discussion, with a wide variety of explanations provided for some units. The class discusses why there are differences, and what variables or measurements in the investigation may have yielded the results. This is an opportunity for students to go back and do the investigation again, paying close attention to those variables or measurements.

Doing More Investigations

Eighty-five percent of the class periods are spent doing investigations; follow-ups help develop understanding, ability, values of inquiry, and knowledge of science content. The frequency with which students do investigations helps them develop the ability to work through the scientific process with ease. It becomes second nature to them for two reasons. First, repetition strengthens learning. Second, investigations are an exciting way to learn and provide a needed break from the textbook and worksheet learning that commonly occurs in other classes.

Public Communication of Student Ideas and Work to Classmates

The students share answers to their "I think" questions aloud with the group 60–70% of the time. This helps students see where they have common thinking and how an idea may be put to the group that someone else has not thought of. Public sharing also occurs at the end of the investigation, when students share with the class what they have learned in the investigation. Additionally, these students have shared projects with the School Board, City Council, and at state, regional, national, and international conferences.

Communicating Science Explanations

Students communicate findings in the closure at the end of the class period. As they do so, they share findings and thoughts as to why the results occurred. In addition, students have done presentations to parents at Open Houses for parents. Students take their parents through the same investigations they have done in the classroom during the day, explaining what they have learned.

Applying the Results of Experiments to Scientific Arguments and Explorations

In the closure time as students discuss their findings, they discuss their findings in relationship to the concept(s) I introduced at the beginning of the class period. Additionally, in my summary I share with the group what the students observed and how this supports (or does not support) the concept(s) being covered in this unit.

Evidence Learning Is Occurring

Assessments within my curriculum help to determine student understanding and abilities, monitor student progress, and collect information to grade student achievement. The traditional assessments I use include practical lab exams, unit tests, and the Iowa Test of Basic Skills (ITBS). The latter is a standardized test students take in the fall of each year. Science is one component of the

ITBS. Over the past 16 years, I have seen the results vary from year to year and class by class. The data yielded from implementation of the *More Emphasis* conditions of NSES show the same unsystematic variability, but continue to show that learning is occurring (Figure 6). Creativity and problem solving are difficult to measure using these standardized tests.

Figure 6. Iowa Test of Basic Skills Results Over Time for Students in My Classroom

Activity Related to NSES *More Emphasis* Conditions	Year and National Percentile Rank of sixth graders—test taken in the fall before these incoming students have had much introduction to my teaching approach and assessments		Year and National Percentile Rank of seventh graders (previous year's sixth graders)—these students have now had a full year exposure to my teaching approach and assessments		Year and National Percentile Rank of eighth graders (previous year's seventh graders) – these students have now had two full years' exposure to my teaching approach and assessments	
	Year	Rank	Year	Rank	Year	Rank
1991: Six units per grade use an inquiry approach	1991	91	1992	92	1993	85
1993: Three-fourths of the units per grade use an inquiry approach	1993	89	1994	74	1995	78
1995: All units use an inquiry approach	1995 1998	73 60	1996 1999	69 43	1998* 2000	67 90
1999: Implemented the Plan of Attack portfolios, group discussion of results of investigations	1999	67	2000	94	2001	65
2000: Developed curriculum maps for each grade, focusing on activities, assessments, skills, and essential concepts/ questions for each unit	2000	81	2001	79	2002	90
2001: Added historical information to investigations along with "I think" and "questions I have" to investigations. Continued to refine the *More Emphasis* teaching, assessment, content conditions used in the classroom	2001 2002 2003	77 81 91	2002 2003	94 83	2003	87

*Test not taken in fall 1997.

Other evidence of learning is found in the portfolios, which show (a) student understanding of the question of the day, (b) procedures to answer the question and (c) conclusions. I see increased use of the scientific process, creativity in how students develop the Plan of Attack, and comfort with the "I think" portion of the portfolios. The observations I make as the students carry out their investigations, along with the responses they make to my questions, also show student understanding.

Students completed an entry survey as they entered sixth grade in 2003 and did so again at the end of the school year (spring 2004). The survey explored general attitudes toward science and science classrooms, with students using a Likert scale to indicate level of agreement or disagreement. For the 2003–04 school year these surveys showed no change between pre- and post-responses to the statement "I enjoy designing and conducting experiments." The post-survey showed a 17% increase in the number of students marking *strongly agree* or *agree* to the statement "I often test my own hypothesis." The post-survey showed a 9% increase in the number of students marking *strongly agree* or *agree* to the statement "I like classes that encourage me to discover some ideas for myself." Finally, the post-survey showed a 10% increase in the number of students marking strongly agree or agree to the statement "I learn well by problem solving with a lab partner." One may ask whether a survey of student attitudes is evidence of learning, yet the results clearly show attitudes changing for the three measures. Student attitudes are an important piece of the foundation required for learning; I believe the number of students in Science Club shows a growing interest in science and use of the scientific process in exploratory activities. Over the past few years, teams of students have submitted a number of projects for award consideration. In 2003–04, 25% of my students worked on special projects. Students have received a number of awards. Judges at the state, regional, or national level evaluate these projects or award applications. The success of the students is evidence that learning is occurring, albeit in the Science Club as compared to the classroom. Yet, skills they learn in the classroom transfer to these projects.

Awards Won by West Branch Middle School Science Students

2004: Region VII EPA National Award

2004: President's Environmental Youth Award

2004: eCYBERMISSION finalist environmental awards

2003: Second place, National eCYBERMISSION environmental awards

2003: Semi-finalists in Bayer NSF Community Issues Award for Region 3

2002: Semi-finalists in Bayer NSF Community Issues Award for Region 3

2002: Governor's Environmental Excellence Award: Waste Management

1999: Semi-finalists in Bayer NSF Community Issues Award for Region 3

1999: Student selected as Youth Conservationist of the Year in Iowa

1997: Region VII EPA National Award

1997: President's Environmental Youth Award

1997: Two sixth graders represented Iowa at the first National Solar Car Races in Dallas, Texas. (This team finished tied for third in the national races.)

1996: Student selected as Youth Conservationist of the Year in Iowa

In addition to these examples of learning, the student quotes at the end of the solar car unit point out the benefits of the inquiry approach and use of the *More Emphasis* approach:

"Never before have I ever learned about building a car, conserving energy, using different forms of energy, working as a team, experimenting, and problem solving all at the same time!"

"Many kids don't remember stuff they are forced to learn out of a book. But we will remember building solar racers and how they worked."

"The project allowed us to see the real thing happening. We weren't just reading about how solar panels make electricity. We were actually applying the ideas and making it happen."

"When you read it out of a book it is harder to understand than when you do it yourself. You have questions that you actually can see have a purpose."

"If you build a car and it runs, you end up getting sucked into learning why it works. You end up looking things up because you want to learn."

"You get to see why it is good instead of someone telling you this is how it works."

"We had to be creative, use our ideas, and work together."

"I learned how to make designs and overcome problems."

"Working as a team played an important role in the success of our car."

Learning is occurring.

Summary

Students are active learners in my sixth- and seventh-grade science classes. Guided inquiry enables them to learn content as they carry out investigations—an almost daily activity. Student achievement is higher when both the concrete content and the inquiry investigations are a part of the science classroom. The inquiry approach increases student creativity, problem solving, independence, curiosity, and favorable attitudes toward science, school, and learning. The program is successful, as demonstrated by discussions following investigations, by student involvement in Science Club and award-winning projects, and by traditional testing methodology.

Science is an important component of everyday life. I believe that students learn best through process. If one stresses content, one forces students to memorize for that lesson. By teaching the process of learning (including problem solving skills, creativity, and critical thinking skills), students will learn for a lifetime. To be able to question, explore, and problem solve leads to lifelong learning.

References

Ibarra, H. 1998a. Add inquiry-based learning to your science curriculum. *Middle Ground* 2: 31–33.

Ibarra, H. 1998b. Balloon-powered cars. *Science Scope* 22 (3): 21–23.

Ibarra, H. 2001. *Learning without limit—Solar powered racers: Racing with the sun.* Tampa, FL: Showboard.

Llewellyn, D. 2002. *Inquire within: Implementing inquiry-based science standards.* Thousand Oaks, CA: Corwin Press.

National Research Council (NRC). 1996. *National science education standards.* Washington DC: National Academy Press.

National Research Council (NRC). 2000. *Inquiry and the national science education standards: A guide for teaching and learning.* Washington DC: National Academy Press.

Rakow, S. ed. 1998. *Pathways to the science standards—middle school edition.* Arlington, VA: National Science Teachers Association.

Creating a Classroom Culture of Scientific Practices

Joseph S. Krajcik
University of Michigan

Ann M. Novak, Chris Gleason, Jay Mahoney
Greenhills School
Ann Arbor, Michigan

Setting

Three of us teach at Greenhills School, an independent grade 6–12 school in Ann Arbor, Michigan, where we enjoy a partnership with professors in the School of Education at the University of Michigan. We teach a total of five seventh-grade science classes and four eighth-grade classes. We have between 11 and 30 years of teaching experience. Greenhills School is a college preparatory program with an average of 75 students per grade. Students of color comprise 21% of our student body of nearly 500 students. Our admission process seeks to attract and accept students from the upper half of nationally standardized test norms. Our school is tuition based with 15% of students receiving financial aid.

Overview

We illustrate how seventh-grade students take part in scientific practices by engaging in projects where they experience, firsthand, the richness and excitement of developing a deep understanding of the natural world. Two major projects make up the curriculum, which focuses on helping students learn content standards and on applying their understandings to important, everyday components of their lives. Through extended investigations and collaboration, supported by the use of learning technologies and teacher scaffolds, students investigate important and meaningful science questions to develop understanding of fundamental science concepts while developing abilities of inquiry.

All along, students discuss and debate ideas and apply results of their investigations to scientific arguments and explanations. As teachers, the learning outcomes that we strive for are to help our students develop deep understandings of science concepts through scientific practices.

More Emphasis Conditions and the Goals of Science Education

Seventh-grade students engage in investigating the natural world through two extended projects. In the first project, students investigate the driving question, "How clean is the water behind our school?" Students investigate the water quality of a small neighborhood stream and look at land-use practices in the watershed that can potentially impact the stream. In the second project students explore the question: "How can I make new stuff from old stuff?" (McNeill, Lizotte, Harris, Marx, and Krajcik 2003). This project focuses on explaining chemical reactions in terms of atoms rearranging to form new molecules and the Law of Conservation of Matter. In both projects students are carefully supported through a series of scaffolds to transition from a teacher-structured classroom in which scientific practices are introduced, modeled, and coached, to one where students use scientific practices on a routine, daily basis to discover, explore, and explain scientific phenomena. Scaffolds allow students to take part in more cognitively challenging activities than they would otherwise. Scaffolds are slowly and methodically withdrawn as students gain more experience and expertise with various aspects of scientific practice, as they take over the various cognitive tasks. All work is done in collaboration with other students and the teacher, where students present ideas, obtain feedback, and revise their thinking based on these discussions. In this dynamic process, students engage in a variety of these practices throughout an investigation. Although the learning outcomes of our curriculum and instruction incorporate many of the *More Emphasis* conditions from the National Science Education Standards (NSES), we will mainly focus our discussion on inquiry standards that reflect scientific practice and which foster students in developing in-depth understanding of fundamental science concepts. Our goal is to create a learning environment that reflects a classroom culture in which students use scientific practices to explain phenomena as they find solutions to authentic questions that are important to their daily lives.

How Do We Help Students Develop Scientific Practices?

Scientific practices are the activities that scientists engage in as they investigate the natural world. These daily practices include asking questions, designing investigations, finding, incorporating and using information, collecting and organizing data, creating protocols and graphs for data interpretation, and applying the results to create scientific arguments and explanations (Wu and Krajcik 2003). The NSES (NRC 1996) provide the vision and the direction for science teachers to create and implement curricula that promote classroom cultures where scientific practice is the means of exploring phenomena. Through such a process students develop deep understanding of fundamental science concepts because they actively construct understanding through experience.

Through various lessons that we refer to as *benchmark lessons*, we model, coach, and guide students so that they become more proficient in asking meaningful questions, conceptualizing and designing ways of gathering information they need to conduct an investigation, developing protocols for data collection, creating their own tables to organize data, using graphical organizers to make sense of ideas, and analyzing schemes to look for patterns that will facilitate interpretation of data. Using these practices, students create data tables, graphs, models, pictures, and other forms of representations to clearly articulate their results and findings in both written and oral explanations.

All of our projects are inquiry, project based, and include the following major components: contextualizing science, investigation with collaboration, and the development of artifacts.

Contextualizing Science: The Driving Question

Science is one of the most relevant subjects in students' lives. Yet many students don't see the connection between science class and their everyday experiences. Teachers can use driving questions (Krajcik, Czerniak, and Berger 2002) that are anchored in real world situations and hold meaning for students to help them see these connections. These driving questions, and associated subquestions, should be rich in science content and allow students to perform investigations to explore them.

Scientists ask questions that drive and contextualize their work. Teachers need to model this for students and facilitate students in developing such questions as a regular habit of good scientific practice. Introducing a driving question and involving students in a process to generate related subquestions both contextualizes learning and models what scientists do.

In our water project we use the driving question, "How clean is the stream behind our school?" The stream meanders along our school property and eventually flows into a large river that is the major source of drinking water for our community. It is part of the watershed where most of our students live, including some who live in condominiums that directly adjoin the stream. For these reasons, this driving question is important and meaningful. It sets a stage, or context, for future investigations. The driving question, combined with a stream walk to introduce students to the waterway under investigation, creates a framework that focuses and directs instruction. Students observe the stream and surrounding area, making observations of potential influences that would impact the water quality. They develop a meaningful context for science learning. Important content is embedded in finding solutions to this authentic question, including concepts from chemistry, Earth science, environmental science, and biology (Novak and Gleason 2001).

As teachers we can now further draw students into the project by making connections with students' real-life experiences; we use these experiences to help students generate ideas and subquestions related to the driving question. Through a class discussion, some students may share that they check the pH of their fish tanks or hot tubs at home or see lifeguards conduct tests at the beach or pool. Other students may share that they have aerators in their fish tanks. Based on students' experiences we, as teachers, are now able to ask students, "So, what questions can we investigate about the stream, based on your experiences?" A student may suggest, "We can ask what's the pH of the stream?" The teacher can continue probing students to further think about pH by asking, "What else can we ask about pH?" Several good questions should arise, including, "What is pH? Why is pH important to study for water quality? What is the pH of various substances that can get into the stream? How do substances get into the stream in the first place?" A similar discussion can take place, based on the student comment about aeration. Questions that arise may include, "What is aeration? Why is oxygen important to a stream's quality? Is there enough oxygen to support life in the stream? Do changing conditions affect oxygen levels?" In the water project many subquestions can be generated early in the project and others added as students develop understanding of water quality concepts.

Our second project's driving question "How do you make new stuff from old stuff?" (McNeill, Lizotte, Harris, Marx, and Krajcik 2003) takes a slightly different approach. Like the water project, it has a driving question to focus and contextualize the unit. Unlike the water quality project, its sub-questions are not generated by students but rather presented as a series of experiments and activities that build on each other to promote students' developing rich understanding of chemistry concepts. The project's focus is on having students develop explanations. Students develop increased proficiency in asking more complex questions in approaching an experiment, in asking questions during the experiment that aid their observations and in asking questions that facilitate the analysis of the experiment.

These are a few examples of how teachers can model, facilitate and support students to begin to approach science with the practice of asking questions. Driving questions and sub-questions set the stage for all activities and investigations for a project. They help to create a meaningful context for science learning. It is through investigating these questions that students develop deep understanding of science content.

Investigation: Helping Kids Engage in Scientific Inquiry

"Investigations form the essence of doing science" (Krajcik, Czerniak, Berger 2002). Once a driving question is introduced with supporting questions to contextualize the project, students need to be guided in active scientific inquiry with investigations that take place over extended periods of time. These investigations should emphasize exploring a few science concepts thoroughly. The goal is to assist students to construct rich, in-depth understandings of a few fundamental concepts through inquiry. Components of investigations include the scientific practices of (a) asking and refining questions, (b) finding, incorporating, and using information, (c) designing experiments, (d) collecting and organizing data, (e) creating graphs and protocols for data interpretation, and (f) applying the results to create scientific arguments and explanations to defend conclusions.

Collaboration is also a vital part of scientific practice and a major component of our program. Scientists work together, engaging in intellectual discussions and joint projects to investigate and work toward finding solutions to important scientific issues. In our projects, students work together to find solutions to meaningful questions in which important science concepts are embedded. Students' collaborations parallel what scientists do. Our learning goal is to create a community of learners in a classroom culture of healthy sharing, discussing, and debating of ideas.

For our water quality project, seventh-grade students investigate the stream in a longitudinal study during the fall and the spring. With teamwork as a focus, each student group is responsible for a portion of the stream where they will determine the health of the water in supporting aquatic organisms. Students collaborate to identify three locations at their stream section where they will collect data. They jointly plan where and why data should be collected at these locations and develop a rationale. They discuss and debate predictions for each test based on visual observations of the stream, combined with the scientific understandings they have developed through background research and benchmark or key lessons completed earlier. Students jointly collect the data while discussing observations and recording information in field notes. Using portable, handheld technology connected to sensors as scientific instruments, students collect pH, temperature, dissolved oxygen and dissolved substances data along with other, qualitative data to make conclusions about the health of the stream (Novak and Gleason 2001; Novak, Gleason, Mahoney, and Krajcik 2002). The portable technology allows students to go out to where the science is happening, rather than doing science in the classroom only (Tinker and Krajcik 2001; Novak and Krajcik, forthcoming).

Our students are thus essentially involved in the same activities as scientists. However, getting them to work like scientists takes a great deal of support from us initially. So how do we support students in doing inquiry? We help our students learn the process of inquiry through teacher-designed investigations and activities that model the process. Our students can't initially just go out to the stream to collect data. They first need to develop an understanding of the concepts and gain experience in the process of inquiry, including the use of the portable technology tools. "How will we investigate the stream?" is a question we pose to students. "What tests and activities will we conduct? What procedure will we follow to collect the data? How will we organize the data once it is collected?" These, and other questions, lead to benchmark lessons that are teacher-directed activities that foster students in developing an understanding of the science concepts while using scientific practices to explore phenomena.

Benchmark lessons introduce students to key ideas, including science concepts such as pH, solutions, dissolved oxygen, turbidity, thermal pollution, watershed, point and non-point source pollution. The students also gain experience in using technology tools that will assist them in data collection and interpretation, in addition to gaining experience in the processes of inquiry and collaboration. Each benchmark lesson models scientific practices. For example, one question we investigate, "What is the pH of various substances that can get into the stream?" is used to introduce students to pH and the disastrous effects on aquatic organisms that result with pH changes in the stream. In addition, several other components of investigation are introduced. The first is in asking questions that serve to contextualize, focus, and drive the investigation. But other questions naturally follow: "What substances should we test? How much of each substance should we use? Does the substance have to be in solution? What tools will we use to test the substances? Should we test a substance more than once? How will we record our data? What safety precautions, if any, need to be taken? What will the pH numbers we obtain tell us about the stream if our stream has similar pH numbers?" Table 1 includes subquestions explored through benchmark lessons, concepts developed through investigating these questions, and the technology tools used to assist students in the process.

Questions investigated through benchmark lessons lead students to research background information, create procedures and data tables, and methodically conduct investigations. Students make bar graphs or charts to graphically represent their data. This helps students transform their data into other forms that may aid them in seeing patterns and so more fully understand their

Table 1: Benchmark Lessons From the Water Quality Project		
Subquestion explored as Benchmark lesson	Concept goals	Technology Goals
1. How much water is on earth and how much of that is usable?	Water distribution, water use, conservation, water pollution	None
2. Where does the water come from?	Water cycle, renewable vs non-renewable resource	None
3a. What substances can pollute the water? 3b. What effect do these substances have on water quality? 3c. How much is too much?	Water quality, water quality standards, water quality's effect on living organisms, water pollution • pH/acids/bases, neutralization • solutions: solute/solvent • thermal pollution • turbidity: density, suspended particles, erosion	Introduction to hand-helds • pH probe • conductivity probe • temperature probe
4. Is there enough oxygen to support life in the stream?	Dissolved oxygen	Dissolved oxygen probe
5. How do substances get into the water in the first place?	Water cycle, watershed, topography, point and non-point source pollution	None

results; this in turn will help them develop thorough and sound explanations. The teacher acts as facilitator, coach, and guide, initially providing a great deal of support with each aspect of an investigation. As more and more activities and experiments are conducted, such as for temperature or dissolved oxygen, students gain more experience and expertise in designing investigations and are able to take on more responsibility, both cognitively and technically, in the process. A classroom culture is thus created where students routinely engage in scientific practices to explore phenomena. Students are learning science by doing science (Krajcik 1993).

Following benchmark lessons, student are ready to go out to the stream to collect data. Once teams have collected water quality data, they need to analyze their data. We carefully provide students with structure in the form of scaffolds initially; this assists them in thoughtfully and methodically examining their data and in making connections between the data and the science concepts, and so in developing sound explanations. These scaffolds come in the form of questions such as, "What should we do with the data now that we've collected it?" These questions are followed by group discussions, together with formal guideline sheets that we provide students. These guidelines provide students with both a procedural and a conceptual structure for data analysis. Chapter appendixes 1 and 2 are examples of student guideline sheets; these facilitate student collaboration in data analysis because they provide students with specific guiding questions to discuss, requiring them to make claims about their results, provide evidence to support their claims, and discuss reasons for the results by tying scientific principles with direct observations of the stream. This moves them toward developing sound scientific explanations about the quality of the water, based on various tests. As students gain more experience in data analysis, they have more insight to develop explanations supported by claims, evidence, and reasoning. This allows us to slowly remove the scaffolds because students take on the responsibility themselves. After students have analyzed data, the entire class has a formal meeting to share results, and to defend and debate findings. In this culminating experience, students attempt to reach consensus about the overall health of the stream and the causes associated with their overall findings.

Just as with the water project, students collaborate throughout our chemistry project. Asking questions, intellectually debating ideas, discussing potential outcomes of experiments, sharing findings, making explanations, and jointly working to try to understand the meanings of experimental outcomes is a constant cycle in which our students engage.

The focus with the chemistry project is on getting students to write thorough scientific explanations. While students engage in some experimental design, they more often focus on developing deep understanding of chemical reactions through a series of experiments and activities. The teacher works to help students thoughtfully and methodically conduct experiments and make connections between the experiments and the science concepts they are investigating. Using the format of claim, evidence, and reasoning, students create oral and written explanations of various phenomena.

The curriculum's design includes three major learning sets; each learning set is a collection of related lessons organized to answer a subquestion and is comprised of experiments and activities that build on the previous one. The first learning set focuses on *Properties and Substances: How is stuff the same and different?* This learning set is heavily dependent on scaffolds, with guiding questions that provide students with careful structure to support them in writing scientific explanations that include claims and evidence from the experiments, supported with scientific reasoning. Various supports are slowly withdrawn as the curriculum progresses and students become more proficient in thoughtfully and completely developing scientific explanations. The second learning set's focus is on *Chemical Reactions: When do I make new stuff?* And the third learning set investigates *Conversion of Mass: What happens to mass when I make new stuff?*

With each successive experiment or activity, students gain more experience in thinking, discussing and analyzing their results more scientifically. Students think critically and logically to see connections and make relationships between evidence and explanations. Students come to see that minor adjustments to experiments, intentional or unintentional, may have major consequences. Vibrant discussion of concepts and experimental design, in both small and large group settings, become routine as students wrestle with ideas together.

The teacher facilitates the dialogue with probing questions that encourage the students to think, to listen to each other's ideas and to make connections between science concepts. Investigation and collaboration are essential components of helping students develop scientific practices. Figure 1 represents one way to visualize the process of investigation.

This *investigation web* illustrates the nonlinear fashion in which students engage in an investigation. Our learning goal is to create a community of learners in a classroom culture that reflects these practices. Our water project and the chemistry project have been developed with these learning outcomes as the guide. If we have been successful the result should be students who have developed a rich understanding of the science. How can we assess the degree to which students have developed understanding? Student work provides us with insight into the level of each student's learning.

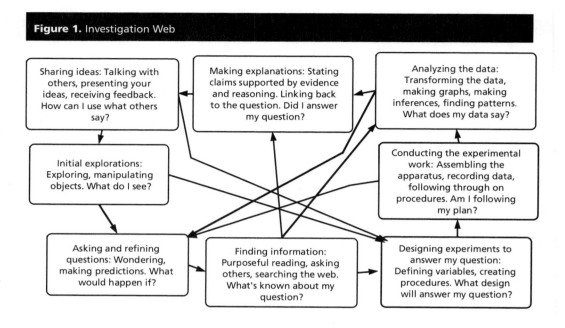

Figure 1. Investigation Web

Artifacts: Tools to Develop and Assess Student Understanding

Artifacts are student-created products that reflect what they have learned. As teachers, we need to provide students with a variety of ways to create artifacts that assist them in constructing knowledge, while at the same time assist us with assessing their understandings. We use a variety of assessment tools, including water quality booklets, concepts maps, pre- and posttest scientific explanations. Some are embedded within instruction while others precede or follow instruction.

Students create *Water Quality Booklets* that represent their understanding of water quality concepts and processes. Each student creates a booklet of his or her stream section that includes all aspects of the investigation, including the question, general background information about water, test location rationale, stream section drawing, data collection, an analysis—including graphs with explanations of quantitative and qualitative data—and a conclusion. Students write down background information, make predictions, and collect and analyze data for five different water quality tests. As part of the first two tests, students are provided with feedback, either from the teacher or through a peer editing process where they revise their background, predictions, and analyses. Chapter appendix 3 is one example of a peer edit sheet students use to provide each other with feedback on their background information about the impact of biological, geological, and social worlds on water quality. Classroom discussions (along with these criteria sheets) support students through this process of thinking, writing, obtaining feedback, and revising. Students take great ownership of their booklets; they are produced over a period of several weeks in the fall and then again in the spring. The assessment is embedded throughout the instruction; each portion of the booklet assists students in developing understanding and also provides the teachers with evidence of their emerging understanding. Each portion represents a mini-artifact, and the composite booklet is a complex and complete product that reflects the level of deep understanding students possess about water quality.

Concept mapping is used in both the water and chemistry projects. It is used both at the beginning and end of each unit for pre- and post-assessment. Students also develop concept maps during instruction as a tool for developing understanding. They serve as a means to assist students in constructing understanding because they facilitate students to find connections between ideas (Novak and Gowin 1984). All of these maps provide the student and teacher with constant feedback about learning prior to, during, and after instruction. In addition, they provide us, as teachers, with valuable information that informs our teaching, directing us to areas where students need further study to develop a more complete understanding of the science or to highlight areas where students have developed ideas that are inconsistent with those of scientists.

Pre and post written tests are another means to assess student understanding. Comparison of student answers from pre and post questions that address similar concepts provide teachers with measures of how students' ideas have evolved over the course of the study. When returned to students in a timely manner, tests can also serve as learning tools. Students are able to gauge their own growth, both with written tests and with concept maps. Nothing is more powerful and delightful to students than to compare a pre-assessment, whether a test or concept map, with a posttest or concept map to "see" the enormous amount of growth they have undergone toward developing a deep understanding of the science.

Another artifact that reflects learning is students' scientific explanations of experimental results. Students' analyses of their qualitative and quantitative water quality measures, as well as their explanations in successive chemistry experiments, progress toward more thoughtful and complete written explanations as students gain more experience in an inquiry, project-based approach where they are supported in thinking deeply about ideas, sharing their understanding, revising their thinking, and reporting their understandings—both orally and in text.

The development of meaningful artifacts is a crucial component in assisting students to learn and in providing teachers with evidence of student understanding. Using a variety of artifacts ensures a more complete picture of what the student knows. They also aid teachers in improving instruction because they give them insights into areas where students need additional support to develop understanding.

Evidence to Support the Program's Success

Throughout the years, a number of studies have been conducted in the classrooms that show both the benefits and the challenges of supporting students in doing various scientific practices to support inquiry. In 1999, we studied the benefits and challenges for both teachers and students to do inquiry in the classroom. The results of this work helped us realize the importance of supporting student more in designing investigations. In 2000–2001 an extensive study was undertaken of student learning in regard to the use of handhelds. We have pre- and post-tests that show substantial learning gains (Krajcik and Starr 2001). In addition, students made substantial gains on pre and post concept maps (Novak and Gleason 2001) and improved in their ability to analyze data; both become more complex over the course of the school year. These more complex analyses were evidenced in students' Water Quality Booklets.

In 2001–2002, an extensive study was carried out to see how teachers develop scientific practices in the classroom (Wu and Krajcik 2003). Wu and Krajcik showed that because the teachers provided thoughtful scaffolding of some important scientific practices—such as data recording/analysis and the design of investigation—students were able to carry out these practices on their own as the year progressed. During 2002–2003 we studied how students developed understanding of substantial ideas related to the nature of chemical reactions and their capabilities in writing scientific explanations. The findings show that students made significant and substantial progress on all major learning goals.

Summary

Teachers carefully support students through scaffolds in the use of scientific practices as *the* means of investigating the world in which they live. "*How clean is the water behind our school?*" and "*How do you make new stuff from old stuff?*" are two seventh-grade extended projects that reflect classroom cultures where students (a) routinely use scientific practices in order to (b) explain phenomena, as they (c) find solutions to authentic questions important to their daily lives.

References

Krajcik, J. S. 1993. Learning science by doing science. In *What research says to the science teacher: Science, society and technology,* ed. R. Yager. Arlington, VA: National Science Teachers Association.

Krajcik, J. S., C. Czerniak, and C. Berger. 2002. *Teaching science in elementary and middle school classrooms: A project-based approach,* Second Edition. Boston, MA: McGraw-Hill.

Lizotte, D. J., C. J. Harris, K. L. McNeill, R. W. Marx, and J. S. Krajcik. 2003. Usable assessments aligned with curriculum materials: Measuring explanation as a scientific way of knowing. Paper presented at the annual meeting of the American Educational Research Association, April, Chicago, IL.

McNeil, K. L., D. L. Lizotte, C. J. Harris, R. Marx, and J. S. Krajcik. 2003. Using backward design to create standards based middle school inquiry-oriented chemistry curriculum and assessment materials. Paper presented at the annual meeting of the National Association for Research in Science Teaching, March, Philadelphia, PA.

National Research Council (NRC). 1996. *National science education standards.* Washington DC: National Academy Press.

Novak, A. M. and C. I. Gleason. 2001. Incorporating portable technology to enhance an inquiry, project-based science classroom. In *Portable technologies: Science learning in context,* eds. R. Tinker and J. S. Krajcik. Netherlands: Kluwer Publishers.

Novak, A. M., C. Gleason, J. Mahoney, and J. S. Krajcik. 2002. Inquiry through portable technology. *Science Scope* 26(3): 18–21.

Novak, A. M. and J. S. Krajcik. Forthcoming. Using learning technologies to support inquiry in middle school science. In *Scientific inquiry and nature of science: Implications for teaching, learning, and teacher education,* eds. L. Flick and N. Lederman. Netherlands: Kluwer Publishers.

Novak, J. D. and D. B. Gowin. 1984. *Learning how to learn.* Cambridge, England: Cambridge University Press.

Tinker, R., and J. S. Krajcik, eds. 2001. *Portable technologies: Science learning in context.* Netherlands: Kluwer Publishers.

Wu, H.-K. and J. S. Krajcik. 2003. Inscriptional practices in inquiry-based classrooms: How do seventh graders construct and interpret data tables and graphs? Paper presented at the annual meeting of the National Association for Research in Science Teaching, March, Philadelphia, PA.

APPENDIX 1: Analysis Guideline Sheet

Name:_____

Fall Stream Analysis Guidelines
October/November, 2003

All five of the water quality test analyses will follow the format of this guideline sheet. You will essentially replace the term "pH" with each of the other four tests when analyzing each of the other tests.

Label this section, **Fall pH Analysis**

You have collected data for the pH of the stream. You have graphed this data with the standards. You now need to analyze this data.

1. Label this Section Header as "Fall pH Analysis"

2. Introduce the analysis in one or two sentences.

3. Analyze the data using the information below as a guide. Incorporate all into a complete discussion.

   - Make a **CLAIM** about your results. Decide if the results of your data reflect excellent, good, fair or poor water quality by *comparing* the results to the standards (ie. "Our pH results at all three locations suggest that the water quality is fair according to the standards.") If the results are different at each location be sure to address each location.

   - Provide **EVIDENCE** to support your claim. *Report* your *results* at each location using the averages (ie. At Location A our pH average is…., at Location B….) Refer to the graph that you've already created.

   - Discuss **REASONS** why you may have gotten the results. *Also discuss reasons that these results are positive or negative (excellent, good, fair or poor) for aquatic life in the stream.*

   - Tie in the scientific principles from your *background* information to help you explain. Look for cause and effect relationships (Is the pH acidic? Basic? Neutral? - What may have caused this? What will be the consequences?)

   - Look at your *physical data* and comment about how it may have affected your results. Look for cause and effect relationships (Do you see any physical evidence that could explain your results?).

   - Compare your results with your predictions.

4. Conclusion: Wrap up your pH analysis with a conclusion. Your conclusion should address the specific test (what we are looking for with the test), a summary of your results and what the results mean in terms of water quality including the standards as well as life in the stream.

APPENDIX 2: Water Quality Analysis—Student Worksheet

Water Quality Fall Analysis–Worksheet

Fill in each box with notes for the test using the Guideline sheet. Next, use these notes to write up a complete analysis for that test. Use this format for each test analysis.

Test Analysis Name: Section Header (ie. Fall pH Analysis)	
Introduction	
Make a **CLAIM** about your Results (Excellent? Good? Fair? Poor?)	
Provide **EVIDENCE** to support your claim (Your Data: averages of each location) Provide evidence from physical observation	
REASONS—explain results • Why did you get these results? Explain* • Are these results positive Or negative? Explain.* *Connect **scientific principles** from background information with your evidence (Test results and physical data) completely discuss/explain Use cause and effect	
Compare your results with your Predictions. Discuss.	
Conclusion. Wrap up the Section.	

APPENDIX 3: Peer Editing Worksheet—Water Background Information

Author's Name:_____

Three Worlds: Biological, Geological, and Social Worlds
Peer Editing

The purpose of peer editing is for you to provide feedback to one of your classmates that will allow that student to revise his/her paper resulting in a higher quality paper.

You will also see the quality of another person's paper and it may provide you with ideas to improve your own paper.

Please provide feedback to your peer by writing notes in the margins that can be suggestions to improve the paper as well as positive statements when you identify good ideas.

Sign your name at the bottom of the paper. Use the same color for both comments and your name. You include your name to:
- Let the person know who wrote the comments so that if he/she has questions he/she knows whom to ask.
- Let the teacher know so that you may receive peer-editing credit for your work.

If you are the second person to peer edit please choose a different color of ink than the first person.

We are going to peer edit this paper with the following three goals in mind:
1. **Content**: Is all of the science included and is it accurate?
2. **English**: Proper grammar? Complete sentences? Spell-checked?
3. **Format**: Header? Introduction? Main body? Conclusion?

Editor:_____	Requirements	Editor:_____
	Header: Has the writer included a header at the beginning of the section?	
	Introduction: Is there a sentence or two that presents the main idea of the section?	
	Main body: Is each world clearly and completely defined? Does the writer include two examples from each world?	
	Conclusion: Does the writer wrap up the section with a concluding thought that ties everything together?	
	English: Proper grammar, sentence structure and spell-checked?	

More Emphasis on Scientific Explanation:

Developing Conceptual Understanding and Science Literacy

Joseph S. Krajcik, Elizabeth Birr Moje, LeeAnn M. Sutherland
University of Michigan

Alycia Meriweather, Sheryl Rucker, Paula Sarratt,
Yulonda Hines-Hale
Detroit Public Schools

Setting

This chapter describes a process for engaging middle school students in writing scientific explanations in the context of project-based science. In four Detroit classrooms, teachers enacted strategies for explanation writing that aimed to help students develop deep understanding of science concepts, inquiry processes, and writing skills. Although this process is now being used in many classrooms and as part of other research projects, these four teachers and the university research team initially worked together to unpack the meaning of "explanation" as described in the National Science Education Standards (NSES) and to create a plan for helping seventh graders to understand that meaning. This chapter describes the resulting schema and the practices in which students engage in a chemistry unit on air quality and in a biology unit on communicable diseases. The chapter also describes the multiple ways in which we scaffold explanation writing across time so as to provide opportunities for all students to be successful using this form of scientific discourse.

This work has evolved out of a partnership between researchers at the University of Michigan and four teachers in the Detroit Public Schools (DPS). Each of the four teaches in a different school. Two of the middle schools are neighborhood schools, the third is a magnet school, and the fourth is a school of choice attended by students from across the city. Demographic data suggest that the range of student experiences and performance across these four schools reflects the range across the district. The student population of all four schools is predominantly African American (approximately 98%). Across the district, 70% of students qualify for free and reduced lunch.

Against this backdrop, the four female teachers who participate in this project teach multiple sections of seventh-grade science, averaging 32 students per class. The teachers have between four and nine years of teaching experience in varied educational settings. The science classrooms at these different schools vary greatly. At one school, the small and crowded classroom was clearly not built for teaching science. It has no lab tables or sinks; the teacher has access (by appointment only) to a school computer lab shared with teachers across the building. In contrast, the classroom in another school is spacious, with lab tables and working computers for each pair of students. In other classrooms, desks are pushed together to create student groupings and a larger communal surface on which to work. Off to one side of the classroom, a bank of working computers stands ready to accommodate groups of three to four students. Although their schools and classrooms look very different, all four teachers share a desire to (a) engage students in challenging tasks, (b) encourage students to like science and to learn science, and (c) guide students to develop skills and understandings they can use immediately and in their futures.

More Emphasis Conditions and the Goals of Science Education

This chapter focuses on those NSES *More Emphasis* conditions apropos of our view of scientific literacy, particularly writing. We believe that if students are to make meaning of school science and to take their understandings into their everyday worlds, then they must go beyond doing inquiry to understanding how and why scientists engage in particular practices, as well as how those practices compare with the practices of other discourse communities (e.g., the home) and other disciplines. This belief is congruent with NRC content standards for science as inquiry which state, in part, "As a result of activities in grades 5–8, all students should develop the abilities necessary to *do* scientific inquiry [and to] develop understandings *about* scientific inquiry" (p. 143, emphasis added).

Our work brings those principles to life in classrooms in which we attend closely to the NSES standards regarding students' ability (a) to develop … explanations … using evidence; (b) to think critically and logically to make the relationships between evidence and explanations; and (c) to communicate scientific … explanations (pp. 145 and 148).

The Content and Inquiry Standards call for the science education community to place *More Emphasis* on (a) using evidence and strategies for developing or revising an explanation; (b) science as argument and explanation; (c) communicating science explanations; (d) applying the results of experiments to scientific arguments and explanations; and (c) public communication of students' ideas and work to classmates.

We also address related aspects of the Teaching Standards: *More Emphasis* on (a) student understanding and use of scientific knowledge, ideas, and inquiry processes; (b) providing opportunities for scientific discussion and debate among students; and (c) continually assessing understanding. We particularly attend to student thoughtfulness, as exhibited in rich, well-reasoned explanations of phenomena. Each of these conditions simultaneously places more emphasis on understanding scientific concepts, as opposed to knowing scientific facts and information. Having students do, discuss, read about, and write about their understanding places more emphasis on studying a few fundamental science concepts in depth rather than covering many science topics at a more cursory level. Each of these *More Emphasis* conditions is interwoven in the project-based science units, in teacher enactment of those units, and in our focused attention on scientific explanation to support content understanding and literacy learning.

Teachers, Students, and Classroom

The majority of students in these four schools are African American and low socioeconomic status (SES), but they are diverse within those categories. Students have varying degrees of interest, engagement, and performance in science. Although 13.6% of students in the district met state science standards on the statewide achievement test in 1999, the range in these four schools is 0.8%–72% for those who met science standards. In reading, 19.1%–61.9% of students in the four focus schools met state standards in reading, and 28.4%–100% met state standards on the eight-grade writing assessment. Many of the students exhibit multiple difficulties with writing tasks (e.g., usage, spelling, sentence structure, and generating text), although students in some classes are able to compose substantive paragraphs that synthesize what they have learned. As the teachers work together to systematically address scientific explanations as a tool for content literacy, they are always cognizant of the very different starting points for the students in their classrooms.

Unique Features of the Program as Aligned With NSES Vision of *More Emphasis*

For this project, the team of science teachers and the district's instructional specialist partnered with a team of researchers from the University of Michigan's School of Education to develop and to enact strategies that help students think more deeply about science content (see Moje et al. 2004 for detailed discussion of this work). In the two project-based units discussed in this chapter, student learning is framed and motivated by questions of interest to real people in real places, such as: "What affects the quality of air in my community?" and "How can good friends make me sick?" (Krajcik, Blumenfeld, Marx, Bass, and Fredricks 1998). Both units contain multiple opportunities for students to engage with phenomena and to develop inquiry skills as they study the chemistry of air quality and the biology of communicable disease. Students turn their wonderings into research(able) questions, make hypotheses and predictions, write and carry out procedures, systematically gather data, analyze data, and come to a defensible conclusion. The Air Quality unit, taught early in the fall, serves as most students' introduction to inquiry. In this context, writing explanations is a vehicle for helping students think more deeply about complex (often abstract) chemistry concepts as they also develop science literacy.

Although the teacher/researcher team had discussed conclusions and explanations as important aspects of scientific literacy for some time, we focused on explanations in earnest when teachers voiced frustration with students' brief, simple answers when asked to *explain*, *give reasons*, or *tell why*. For example, in the Air Quality unit, teachers reported that their students could readily repeat the definition of matter as "anything that has both mass and volume." However, students could not provide a rich explanation of how scientists have determined that air is matter. Students learn scientific principles about matter as they conduct investigations in which they see that air has both mass and volume. Yet students typically did not connect the results of their own tests as evidence of the important scientific principles they illustrate. Peker and Wallace's (2003) review of research on students' scientific explanations indicates that, in general, students do not connect pieces of information they acquire into a coherent whole when asked to write an explanation. As applied in these classrooms, students tended to see investigations and experiments as discrete activities, separate from the synthesis in writing of what they had learned from those activities. Their ability to make sense requires students to analyze and synthesize, but doing so on a deep, rich level of understanding is not an intuitive response to the task. In fact, Blumenfeld (1992) concluded that when some students find a problem difficult, they may be unwilling to expend the effort or take the risks necessary to think it through. The four practicing teachers on this team, well aware of that phenomenon, have been particularly invested in determining how to scaffold explanation writing so that students feel successful and remain engaged with the task, while they learn the science content and important communication skills. They want to encourage students to expend the energy necessary to make sense of complex science concepts. Explanation writing is one way to do that. Nevertheless, to help students organize information into a cogent explanation—consistent with scientific practice—we first needed to consider what it is that makes an explanation "scientific." We then developed ways to scaffold the sense-making necessary for the 12-year-olds in their classes to make such explanations.

As a result of our early conversations, our analysis of student work, our reading of the national standards and benchmarks, and our reading of other work on explanations, we drafted guidelines for writing explanations that included five components. Two of those were later interwoven into the teaching of explanations (and are discussed elsewhere in this chapter). The resulting schema for scientific explanations includes three central components: (a) a claim about the problem, (b) evidence for the claim, and (c) reasoning that links the evidence to the claim using scientific principles (Harris, McNeill, Lizotte, Marx, and Krajcik, forthcoming; Moje et al. 2004; Sutherland et al. 2003). To help students learn a process for writing explanations that include each of those components, we developed scaffolds of three types:

1. explicit teaching of the *components* of a good scientific explanation;
2. explicit attention to the *differences* among explanations that serve different purposes; and
3. systematic *introduction and practice* of explanations so that students' skills develop as the inquiry demands of the curricula become increasingly complex across the year.

In the following sections, we first describe the components of a scientific explanation, and second, describe the process we have successfully used to scaffold students' thinking and writing.

Scientific Explanations: The Components

Years of literacy research on writing reveals that weaker writers often simply write what they know without a plan for writing (see Harris and Graham 1992). Because writers who have difficulty often do not plan, breaking explanations into their components—claim, evidence, and reasoning—aims to help writers gain control of the task of explanation writing (Collins and Godhino 1996). Teaching the components of an explanation mimics what good problem solvers do: They "solve major problems by breaking them into smaller, component problems" (p. 180). Breaking down explanations into smaller, manageable, and teachable components serves as an initial scaffolding of explanation writing.

Claim

Our curricula and teachers' enactment help students learn that in science, a *claim* is a statement of one's understanding about a phenomenon or about the results of an investigation (experiment). A claim may be made about data that students have been given or have gathered themselves. If an investigation has independent and dependent variables, then the claim must show the relationship between those variables. In practice, teachers have also found it important to stress that a claim must be a complete sentence that does not begin with "yes" or "no," and that is typically the first sentence in an explanation. Although it is not necessary that a claim be the first sentence, our experience with teaching students to write scientific explanations, consistent with literacy research, has shown that freedom to vary the guidelines is best managed *after* the guidelines and their purpose have been learned. At first, many students must systematically learn steps that can be revised as they gain control of the process.

Evidence

An explanation must also contain accurate and sufficient *evidence* in support of the claim. Data can come from investigations one conducts, from observations one makes, from reports of research others have done, or from other sources (e.g., a web-based search about levels of pollution in different cities or about rates of diseases by geographic location). Where possible, explanations incorporate more than one piece of data as evidence. Our analysis of historical pre- and posttest data in these classrooms revealed that students often respond to a call for evidence by simply rewriting in sentence form the data represented in a table or graph. They repeat rather than interpret data, often not accounting for trends or patterns. Students often identify a point or two on a line graph, for example, but do not make a statement that recognizes the trend: "As X increases, Y increases."

One of our goals is to help students understand that data must be marshaled as evidence in support of a *particular* claim. In more complex situations, more than one claim can be made about a single data set, and more data may be represented than are necessary to support a particular claim. Therefore, students must determine which data to use to support the claim they have made. The idea that multiple claims might be made about the same data develops across the school year as inquiry activities become more complex, and students' options for research questions (and resulting claims and evidence) become increasingly open-ended. Initially, the data they gather or analyze are far less complicated, including only simple bar and line graphs.

Reasoning

Finally, students learn that the accepted scientific understanding or principles that undergird the explanation must be made explicit in a process we have termed *reasoning*. Reasoning is the most difficult aspect of explanation writing, and is the most difficult aspect for teachers to teach.

Reasoning typically requires relating scientific principles—what we already know in science—to what one is currently doing or learning. Even when students can readily make a claim and provide evidence, we found that they seldom refer to the pertinent scientific principles they have been studying in class. Students in these early rounds of explanation writing, for example, would write, "air is matter," and would provide evidence from two investigations done with a volleyball and handheld pump to illustrate that the ball gains both mass and volume when inflated. Students did not understand, however, that an explanation needs to tell why evidence about volume and mass counts as evidence for this claim. Those results count as evidence because "scientists call anything that has mass and volume *matter*." If one claims "air is matter," then that person needs to provide evidence that air has both mass and volume because scientists have agreed that they will call *matter* anything that has mass and volume. The links and connections are difficult for students to make initially, thus explanations are best taught in the context of simple investigations with relatively straightforward possibilities for claim, evidence, and reasoning.

Although we agreed on what was intended by our joint use of the word *reasoning*, teachers found that *reasoning* was not a helpful word for students. Describing reasoning as a way to "link" or "connect" also did not resonate with students in their classrooms. As a group, the teachers developed the metaphor of reasoning as a "bridge" between claim and evidence, which they could readily represent graphically to further scaffold students' understanding. See Figure 1.

Teachers reported that the bridge analogy seemed far more helpful for many of their students than did the suggestion that reasoning makes a link or a connection. Teachers report that this visual organizer seems to be helpful for many students, but especially for those who struggle most with writing tasks.

Language

Teachers teach two additional components of our original schema as integral to explanation writing, but they no longer name them as separate components: precise and accurate scientific language, and clear writing that "anyone, anywhere" can understand. We chose to abandon these as components of a scientific explanation in order to stress that writing in any discourse community (e.g., a content area) should include the appropriate use of language of the field. All writing should also be sensitive to a particular audience and should provide whatever information might be necessary for that audience to make sense of written text. Teachers use the "anyone, anywhere" language to help students understand that they cannot use vague pronoun referents, and that they must provide enough detail so that someone unfamiliar with the investigation can understand what was done and what resulted. To help students develop audience awareness, teachers pose questions like, "If Mrs. Brown in the next classroom read your explanation, would she understand what happened and why, and why it is important in science?" Other potential audiences include a cousin or friend at another school, a younger sibling, or an older student. Naming the audience better situates the explanation and cues students to the nature of the information they must provide and the language they should use in communicating their ideas.

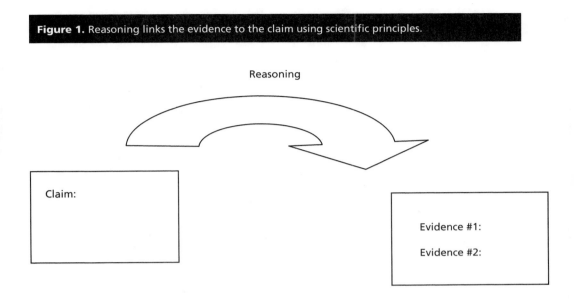

Figure 1. Reasoning links the evidence to the claim using scientific principles.

Reasoning

Claim:

Evidence #1:

Evidence #2:

Scaffolding the Introduction of Scientific Explanation

Introducing Explanation

Another layer to the scaffolding process involves teaching students *about* scientific explanations. As a team, we devised a systematic plan for teaching explanations across the seventh-grade school year. The first step in teaching students about scientific explanations is the same first step that we completed as a team: answering the question, "What does it mean to explain?" Students already have experience with the word "explain," so teachers begin by building on that prior knowledge.

Using whole-class instruction, teachers ask students to name instances in which they might have to explain something, and guide students to think about those examples. If prompting is needed, teachers ask students how they explain when they get home late, or when they don't have their homework done. They ask students how they explain why they think one athlete or sports team is superior to another. After students have begun to think about how they explain in their everyday parlance, teachers introduce *claim* and *evidence* as labels for parts of those explanations students offer. Beginning with this discussion of "everyday" explanations helps students to consider what counts as a claim and evidence in various discourse communities (e.g., home, school, and other content areas). Teachers use multiple analogies and real-world examples to help students see that not all explanations are equally valid in all discourse communities. In this phase, which involves only conversation about explanations, teachers also help students distinguish between opinion-based and evidence-based claims. Teachers have found that the amount of time they need to devote to this phase varies, but typically, they spend at least a week using discussion and bellwork time to consider claims and evidence in and outside of science.

Generating Criteria

Teachers next put examples of scientific explanations on the overhead and model a process of critiquing the strengths and weaknesses of each. Through that process, teacher and students co-construct possible criteria for evaluating scientific explanations. Although the teachers begin with the criteria we have generated in mind they guide students to develop criteria in their own language.

The collaboratively created rubric that results is an artifact to which teacher and students refer all year. Teacher-made charts and diagrams adorn the walls of each of these classrooms, providing visual reminders of what it means to write a claim, provide evidence, and use reasoning. Although the framework can be given to students without this step, students have a deeper understanding of why the components matter; and they have more buy-in to the process and framework when they have worked cooperatively to generate criteria themselves.

In addition, as teachers incorporate explanation writing into their instruction, they must continually help students move back and forth between the components and the overall function of an explanation. Otherwise, writing claim, evidence, and reasoning becomes formulaic, and students lose sight of the reasons that one would write an explanation. In this framework, an explanation has components, but its purpose is to function as a whole.

Constructing Explanations

Teachers create multiple opportunities to model explanation construction, both orally and in writing. A think-aloud process that makes the teacher's thinking visible to students helps those students to understand what an explanation writer does to construct an explanation. In the process, the teacher identifies the claim, evidence, and reasoning in the examples he or she creates, and relates the explanation as a whole back to the original question, problem, or phenomenon. The point of this step is to help students think about explanation construction by modeling what a good writer does.

Critiquing Explanations

Students often think that once something is written, it is finished. Whole-class, teacher-led critique of explanations helps students to see that written explanations can be revisited, rethought, and revised. Beginning to teach explanations through activities that require relatively simple explanations keeps students from having to learn difficult content at the same time that they are learning how to write in a new way and with new language. Teacher critique and think-aloud discussions are a good first step. A teacher can initially create sample explanations for critique purposes. Once students have written explanations, anonymous student responses can be used for whole-class critique. Teacher-guided critique, in which the teacher asks probing questions in a discussion, is a useful second step. Next, once students have had practice in teacher-led critique, they can exchange with a peer and critique one another's written explanations. In any critique, strengths and weaknesses should be highlighted, and concrete suggestions for improvement should be offered. Focus attention on the written product, not on the writer: "These data come from the table, but it's just a list of numbers; this explanation doesn't show how the numbers are related to each other," instead of "You didn't show how the numbers are related to one another."

The teacher models in a whole-class setting, then guides students to critique in either small-group or whole-group structures. It is the small-group or paired sharing, in which students compare similarities and differences, and justify their use of evidence, that we wish to emphasize is the goal of this work, for it is in those comparison activities and justification activities that deeper conceptual understanding takes place. Simultaneously, students develop a better sense of what it means to explain in science. Teachers guide students to think about scientific explanations as requiring particular kinds of claims, particular kinds of evidence, and particular ways of incorporating and discussing scientific principles. Students are strategically supported as they transition from teacher-modeled explanations, critiqued as a whole group, to writing explanations based on investigations they design and carry out themselves.

Providing Students With Feedback

The critique process is further augmented by teacher feedback to individual students. Teachers provide feedback on the quality of the explanation as a whole, as well as on the quality of the individual components. Comments such as "Be more specific" are very difficult for students to translate into meaningful revision. It is far more helpful to offer specific comments, guiding questions, or alternative examples of how students might word an idea. A feedback and revision cycle, which draws from research on process writing in the English language arts, encourages students to think more deeply, to communicate more effectively, and to understand that ideas—in science—may be revised when they are reconsidered from different perspectives or are fleshed out in more detail. Teacher feedback is key to students developing these complex understandings about science literacy.

Scaffolding Explanations Across Time

Practice is essential, and many students will need a great deal of practice to become proficient explanation writers. Although the framework applies to many types of scientific explanations, different content, different types of data, and different types of problems or questions posed will require somewhat different shaping of an explanation. Consider explanation writing a long-term process that may require more than one unit and, in fact, may require an entire school year for some students to develop proficiency.

As each unit (and the school year) progresses, students are given fewer prompts and scaffolds until, ultimately, they are expected to write a scientific explanation or to explain when asked—including claim, evidence, and reasoning—with no scaffolds. Teachers learned in the first year of enacting these explanation strategies that it is important not to fade scaffolds too quickly, however. As teachers used questions we had generated to help students in one complex investigation (about the composition of air), they saw students' struggles with content understanding exacerbated by their struggles to explain that understanding *in writing* and *in a scientific manner*. The experiences of teachers and students in these classrooms revealed that using explanations to help students develop deeper understanding of content must be addressed systematically throughout the school year and across units. Explanation writing is not a one-semester or one-unit task.

Whether scientific explanations are written individually or in collaboration with others, cycles of feedback and revision enable students to deepen their conceptual understanding; they are also able to write with greater clarity and precision for a specific audience. In the Communicable Diseases unit, students write scientific explanations of phenomena observed directly but also as gathered by others and reported by the Centers for Disease Control, for example, or in articles in the popular press about SARS, hepatitis B, or outbreaks of influenza. Everyday and scientific discourses are also bridged via a collection of reading material, written in conjunction with the curriculum, which provides students with opportunities to apply and extend understandings developed in class to situations that are part of their everyday lives. For example, the movement and arrangement of molecules in solids, liquids, and gases is a central concept in the Air Quality unit. Students undertake a classroom inquiry activity, see a teacher demonstration, and enact a "human model" to simulate molecules' movement and arrangement in each of the common phases of matter. In the reading materials, students are given a scenario in which they are asked to explain drying a pair of jeans—by hanging them on a clothesline or putting them in a clothes dryer—in terms of molecules, phase changes, and heat provided by the sun or dryer. As students explain, they develop a richer understanding of the meaning of the particulate nature of matter in an everyday situation. Throughout these units, teachers create a learning environment in which students use scientific explanations as a vehicle for making sense of phenomena, for engaging deeply with scientific ideas, for organizing those ideas, and for communicating understanding to a real audience in a meaningful context of inquiry.

As indicated, claims are initially generated in response to rather simple questions, but the content understandings and the explanations become more complex across the span of a unit and across the span of the school year. Components are initially prompted with explicit scaffolding: "What evidence from your investigation supports your claim?" and "What scientific principle is important to this investigation?" Students move from (a) questions that prompt each component of an explanation; to (b) the symbols C, E, and R for claim, evidence, and response; to (c) only the instruction to "write a scientific explanation." They move from writing in boxes connected by an arrow to writing a paragraph. Over time, they learn how to critique explanations and how to revise explanations, using sample explanations and then in considering their own writing.

Students in these classrooms write more detailed and more complete explanations across time. However, we have also learned that content and context matter. The explanations students must write in the Air Quality unit require them to determine relationships between dependent and independent variables. In the unit that follows, students write explanations about data presented in tables and for which there are no independent variables, dependent variables, or trends to determine. The content, however, is even more abstract. That unit is followed by the Communicable Diseases unit in which students are provided with complex trends, and they need to consider which data out of large data sets are appropriately marshaled as evidence for a particular claim. In many instances, more data are provided than what is needed for any claim a student would make. Assessing the quality of students' explanations across time, then, becomes a complex but important task for teachers.

Aligning Teaching, Assessment, and Content: The *More Emphasis* Conditions

Teachers typically generate rubrics with their students that are in checklist form and focus on inclusion of each component: (a) "I remembered to make a claim;" (b) "My claim does not begin with yes or no;" (c) "I used at least two pieces of evidence;" and (d) "I included the scientific principle that makes a bridge from my evidence to my claim." Teachers and researchers, however, assess students' conceptual development and their development of writing skills in a variety of other ways. Our first pass at analyzing students' work involves classifying their explanations holistically, using broad categories such as *developing*, *partially developed*, and *developed*, or simply level 1, 2, or 3. This type of system is quick and easy to use, and provides a global view of how students are making sense of the content and of explanation writing. Teachers can continually monitor student understanding using a holistic system. Teachers also use journal topics, quizzes, and other methods of formative assessment to gauge student understanding throughout the units.

Table 1. Assessing Student Work Using a Holistic System

	Level 1	Level 2	Level 3
Makes a claim about the problem.	Does not make a claim OR makes an inaccurate claim.	Makes a claim that reveals *partial* understanding. The claim may include *both* accurate and inaccurate details, or it may omit important details.	Makes an accurate claim.
Provides evidence for the claim.	Does not provide evidence OR provides inaccurate evidence for the claim.	Provides some accurate evidence for the claim, but it is not sufficient evidence OR may include *both* accurate and inaccurate evidence for the claim.	Provides accurate evidence and sufficient evidence for the claim.
Provides reasoning about "what we know in science" that links the evidence to the claim.	Does not provide reasoning OR provides inaccurate reasoning.	Provides *partial* reasoning that links the evidence to the claim, but the reasoning is not sufficient OR may include *both* appropriate reasoning and reasoning that does not link the evidence to the claim.	Provides explicit reasoning that links the evidence to the claim. The scientific principle or "what we know in science" is described and used appropriately.

For teachers and researchers to assess students' explanations more closely (primarily to shape instruction), we created a general rubric that defines three levels for each component. Low scores indicate inaccuracies or omissions. For example, an explanation might not include evidence, or the evidence in a table or graph might be misinterpreted. High scores indicate accuracy, appropriateness, and sufficiency.

We use the rubric, as previously described, as a guide from which we tailor criterion-based rubrics to each individual question posed in investigations or on pre/posttests. A tailored rubric provides examples of each category so that it is clear as we assess students' responses what "accurate but not sufficient evidence" might look like given a *particular* task. We might create, for example, a criterion-based rubric in which we have more than three levels for a given component because we need to know more specific information about what students are doing. For example, there is a substantive difference between the claims: (a) The age of a car has an effect on the amount of pollution, and (b) the older the car the more particulate matter it releases into the air. Once we were able to tease apart those differences, we were better able to help students understand that a good claim specifies the direction of the relationship; it does not simply state that there is a relationship.

Results of This Attention to Scientific Explanation Writing

Both quantitative and qualitative analysis of students' work revealed that once we started intensive work on explanation writing, students immediately began to write better claims, and we saw far fewer instances of "listing" data in favor of marshaling data as evidence for the particular claim. Reasoning stood out as the weakest element of students' explanations, as it was sometimes missing, and often implicit rather than explicit (see Moje, et al. 2004 for additional analyses). Therefore, for the next year, we spotlighted reasoning, with the teachers increasingly confident about teaching *claim* and *evidence,* and spurred by their students' writing improvement to continue to "dig in" to this work. It is in this round of discussion that teachers created the bridge analogy for use in the 2003–04 school year. Those data are not analyzed at the time of this writing; therefore, only teacher report is available. Across classrooms, teachers report that students' explanations are "getting better" more quickly. One teacher has said that her students *ask* if they can use the claim, evidence, reasoning bridge even when tasks do not specifically ask for an explanation. Students' requests suggest that they find the scaffolds helpful as they organize and present complex science ideas in writing.

One teacher noted that she needs to remind herself to provide opportunities for "practice, practice, practice." To help students access scientific discourse in other contexts, she has them read short newspaper and magazine articles. She asks students to find the claim the writer is making and to "look for the scientific resources within the article" that are "there to reinforce or support the claim of the article." She uses this language to help students learn that it is "scientific resources" of a particular type that are unique to *scientific* explanations and that shape a particular kind of argument. We have now built more of these kinds of activities into the curriculum, which we again expect to strengthen students' conceptual understanding and explanation writing.

The four teachers agree that repeated, sustained practice opportunities are essential, as explanation writing is a cognitively demanding task for which students need much support. The strategies we have devised for developing and revising explanations continually place more emphasis on student understanding; on the use of scientific knowledge, ideas, and inquiry processes; on the development of argument and explanation; and on communication, discussion, and debate as key to being good classroom scientists who can also apply their understandings outside the classroom.

Near the end of the 2002–03 school year, we administered a test, rather like a short final exam, to students in these classrooms and others—two classes each from 10 teachers in 10 different DPS seventh-grade classrooms. The test was purposefully designed around the school district's "core outcomes," which all teachers are expected to address during the school year. So, while students using our curricula were studying atoms, molecules, and phase changes, so were students across Detroit Public Schools, but using other materials. About a given content area (e.g., the particulate nature of matter), the test asked two multiple-choice questions and one constructed-response (open-ended) question that called for a scientific explanation.

Students in classrooms in which our curricula were used outperformed other students in the district by statistically significant margins (p<0.001) on all three measures: (a) multiple-choice questions, (b) open-ended questions, and (c) overall performance. Closer analysis of two open-ended questions—scored in accordance with our explanation rubric—revealed that students using our curricula outperformed their peers in control classrooms by statistically significant margins (p<.001) on both the evidence and reasoning components of their written explanations. Differences in *claim* scores were not statistically significant, suggesting that students across the district (in similar percentages) were able to read (interpret) a relatively simple table or graph and to make a conclusion (claim) about those data. This indicates that students across the district, as represented by these 10 classrooms, were learning this important skill. However, drawing a conclusion and making an explanation are decidedly different and differentially complex tasks.

Aside from the trends we see across the range of students in our work, we find the development of *individual* student's explanation writing a particularly exciting aspect of this endeavor. Both the data and teachers' reports reveal that students across a range of skill levels (low-, average-, and high-achieving students) make progress. Teachers are steadily developing facility with and confidence in their ability to teach explanations, reporting that their own improved understanding of explanations, and their intense attention to developing ways to teach explanations, is improving their students' work. We see improvement in students' thinking about the science concepts and in their writing skills across levels of performance and across measures.

A sample explanation from one student's Air Quality pre- and posttests illustrates the development evident in many students' work. In this test item, students are given a scenario in which a white sock placed over the tailpipe of cars, which then idle for 10 minutes, captures the particulate matter (PM) released by the car. The color of the sock darkens according to the amount of PM released, which varies by the car's age. Before they conduct the investigation, the fictional researchers hypothesize that the age of the car will not affect the amount of PM released. Students are told to "draw a conclusion" from data presented both in a table and in a bar graph. Consider the following student's explanation (spelling and grammar intact):

Pre: If the sock was black the car·was old. If the sock was dark gray then the car was aver-age. If the sock was gray the car was new.

Post: A conclusion would be that the older the car, the more pollution it would give off. The average car gave out a little pollution (PM), and the new car gave off some, but not a lot of pollution (PM). The class's hypothesis was not right. The age of the car does affect the amount of particulate matter.

This example illustrates each of four patterns we see across students' explanations:
1. Students are writing longer and more detailed explanations.

2. Students are marshaling data as evidence rather than simply listing data.
3. Students are more likely to make generalizations from the data.
4. Students are developing greater facility with scientific discourse (Moje, et al. 2004).

Development is evident in this student's conceptual understanding and explanation writing. Her work illustrates the potential of focusing on the particular More Emphasis conditions that feature explanations, concept development, and deep understanding.

Evidence of Alignment Between *More Emphasis* Conditions and Student Learning

While the methods we have developed for teaching scientific explanations could seem more teacher directed than is called for by the *More Emphasis* conditions, it is our belief that students—even if they understand science concepts and inquiry processes—are more likely to be able to navigate scientific discourse when its structure and use are transparent. It is not part of most students' everyday sense of "explain" to *write* explanations, and it is certainly not part of their experience to write *scientific explanations*. The writing of scientific explanations is a complex task, and we continue to refine practices that are already working so that more of our students have not only access to but also competence with a discourse of science that might also serve them outside the science classroom. In addition, our students learn that scientific principles, or "what we know in science," can be supported or challenged based on evidence gathered not only by scientists in sophisticated laboratories but also by 12-year-olds in urban middle school classrooms.

Conclusion

Scientific explanations, as called for in the National Science Education Standards, enable students to synthesize their understanding and to communicate that understanding to others. The system we have developed includes teaching three components of a good scientific explanation: claim, evidence, and reasoning. Moreover, it requires systematic teaching and scaffolding: (a) developing a framework or general understanding of what *explanation* means, (b) generating and agreeing upon criteria for a good explanation, (c) teacher modeling, (d) student practice, teacher-modeled critique, (e) teacher feedback, (f) peer feedback, and (g) revision. Helping students understand the function and components of scientific explanations, and to construct explanations on their own, results in deeper understanding of science content, of science as an inquiry process, and of science literacy as they develop thinking and writing skills congruently. Teachers who were once frustrated because their students did not go beyond simple answers nonetheless believed that their students *could* go beyond simple answers. As a teacher/researcher team, we continue to work to refine this process, yet it is clear that what we have done thus far has made a difference in student learning. Any teacher who believes that his or her students *can* think and write beyond the level at which they currently perform is invited to see what happens when careful, systematic attention is paid to writing scientific explanations.

References

Blumenfeld, P. C. 1992. The task and the teacher: Enhancing student thoughtfulness in science. *Advances in Research on Teaching* 3: 81–114.

Collins, J. L., and G. V. Godinho. 1996. Help for struggling writers: Strategic instruction and social identity formation in high school. *Learning Disabilities Research and Practice* 11(3): 177–182.

Harris, C. J., K. L. McNeill, D. J. Lizotte, R. W. Marx, and J. Krajcik. Forthcoming. Usable assessments for teaching science content and inquiry standards. *Peers Matter* 1:1.

Harris, K. R. and S. Graham. 1992. Self-regulated strategy development: A part of the writing process. In *Promoting academic competence and literacy in schools*, eds. M. Pressley, K. R. Harris, and J. T. Guthrie, 277–309. San Diego: Academic Press.

Krajcik, J., P. C. Blumenfeld, R. W. Marx, K. M. Bass, and J. Fredricks. 1998. Inquiry in project-based science classrooms: Initial attempts by middle school students. *The Journal of the Learning Sciences* 7: 313–350.

McNeill, K. L., D. J. Lizotte, J. Krajcik, and R. W. Marx. Forthcoming. Supporting students' construction of scientific explanations by fading scaffolds in instructional materials.

Moje, E. B., D. Peek-Brown, L. M. Sutherland, R. W. Marx, P. Blumenfeld, and J. Krajcik. 2004. Explaining explanations: Developing scientific literacy in middle-school project-based science reforms. In *Bridging the gap: Improving literacy learning for preadolescent and adolescent learners in grades 4–12*, ed. D. Strickland and D. E. Alvermann, 227–251. NY: Teachers College Press.

National Research Council (NRC). 1996. *National science education standards*. Washington, DC: National Academy Press.

National Research Council (NRC). 2000. *Inquiry and the national science education standards: A guide for teaching and learning*. Washington, DC: National Academy Press.

Peker, D. and C. S. Wallace. 2003. *Students' scientific explanations: A review of the research*. Paper presented at the annual meeting of the National Association of Research in Science Teaching, Philadelphia, PA.

Sutherland, L. M., E. B. Moje, D. P. Brown, P. C. Blumenfeld, J. S. Krajcik, and R. W. Marx. 2003. *Making scientific explanations: The development of scientific literacy in project-based science classrooms*. Paper presented at the 53rd annual meeting of the National Reading Conference. Scottsdale, AZ.

Traveling the Inquiry Continuum:

Learning Through Teacher Action Research

Alyssia Martinez-Wilkinson
Brian Middle School
Omaha, Nebraska

Setting

The Omaha Public Schools (OPS) is the largest urban district in Nebraska. OPS serves over 45,000 students who constitute an ethnically diverse population. Bryan Middle School is one of nine middle schools in OPS and is located in a largely Hispanic portion of South Omaha. A diverse population of seventh- and eighth-grade students attends the school. For example, in September 2003, the school had a fall membership total of 919 students: 437 Caucasian, 364 Hispanic, 94 African American, 13 Native American, and 3 "Other." The mission of Bryan Middle School is to create an environment in which all students can achieve at their highest levels and can recognize and demonstrate respect for others. To achieve this mission, teachers and students are assigned to instructional teams for core curriculum and cooperative arts.

When I first began teaching middle school science, after graduating from Creighton University in 1999 with a bachelors degree in chemistry education, I had a very traditional approach. After a short time, I began to realize I wanted to challenge my students (and myself) more. So I experimented with the Banneker CEMS (Community of Excellence in Mathematics and Science) program.

Banneker 2000: CEMS is a National Science Foundation award for the Urban Systemic Program. CEMS is a professional development opportunity for math and science teachers to structure and implement a learning plan, resulting in a variety of professional development activities.

Through the CEMS professional development experience and my action research I focused on inquiry and more specifically on student achievement of inquiry skills and abilities. This chapter will focus on inquiry and how it doesn't happen instantly: it is a continuum of development of critical thinking and analytic skills. Inquiry should be an incremental process.

Standards and the Classroom

"Experiences in which students actually engage in scientific investigations provide the background for developing an understanding of the nature of scientific inquiry, and will also provide a foundation for appreciating the history of science." (NSTA 1996). Based on my readings for CEMS, I believe that if students conduct their own experiments it will lead to better understanding of the history of science and the heart of inquiry.

One initial reason that I chose to participate in Banneker CEMS was to earn 18 credit hours of graduate course work. I thought about how much it would increase my salary and how it would enhance my resume. I figured it would also impact my teaching but I had no idea of the extent to which it would affect me. I have grown so much and learned so many new things that I feel as if I am almost a different teacher. I had good labs and lessons before but now my approaches and strategies are so different that my students get much more from class—as demonstrated by results collected from my action research. I have better management skills, I ask better questions, and I give clearer instructions. I have converted the majority of my labs and activities according to inquiry-based models. I do a lot of the same things, just revised and more student-friendly. I characterize it as teaching "kicked up a notch."

This chapter addresses the More Emphases on Teaching Standards and the Content and Inquiry Standards from the National Science Education Standards (NSES). From the Teaching Standards more emphasis is placed on understanding and responding to individual student's interests, strengths, experiences, and needs. Using the knowledge gained through CEMS process I changed the way that I approached teaching science. I was more focused on student understanding and use of scientific knowledge, ideas, and inquiry process. I designed a laboratory experiment format that guided students in active and extended scientific inquiry. Through these unique experiences I continuously assessed students understanding.

From the Content and Inquiry Standards I placed more emphasis on understanding scientific concepts and information and developing abilities of inquiry. Instead of only reading from the textbook or completing the preprinted labs, I integrated more flexibility and student responsibility into their work. I felt that when implementing inquiry as instructional strategies, abilities, and ideas to be learned the students would gain the required knowledge in a new and more permanent way. This new format for the labs included activities that investigate and analyze science questions. Throughout this chapter the focus will be on doing more investigations in order to develop understanding, ability, values of inquiry, and knowledge of science content.

The Standards highlighted in this chapter:
1. Science Teaching Standards: A,B, C, D, E;
2. Professional Development Standards: A, B;

3. Assessment Standards: A, B, C, D, E; and
4. Science Content Standards: A, B, C, G.

Classroom Experiences

Prior to the CEMS experience, my teaching style was very structured, with traditional "cookbook" style labs. Since then, my classroom has been well organized, with a gamut of activities, because I believe that students who are actively engaged will behave better and achieve more. I employ a variety of instructional strategies to keep my students on their toes and focused on their learning activities. My classroom had a good sampling of students within the building, with 46% Caucasian, 39% Hispanic, 10% African American, 3% Native American and 2% Other.

"Learning science is something students do, not something that is done to them" (NRC 1996). In my teaching experience I have seen students expect to sit back passively and let science come to them, resulting in an often frustrating lack in both student participation and in motivation to perform laboratory experiments. Seventh-grade students should be able to complete their own experiments and draw conclusions from them.

Colleagues and administrators from the district have thrown the term *inquiry* around without explaining how to really incorporate it into the classroom. Science is a subject that should center on inquiry. "Inquiry is a multifaceted activity that involves making observations; posing questions; examining books and other sources of information to see what is already known; planning investigations; reviewing what is already known in light of experimental evidence; using tools to gather, analyze, and interpret data; proposing answers, explanations, and predictions; and communicating the results" (NRC 1996). If students are not engaged and participating in their education they do not acquire a true understanding of the concepts and curriculum. The Northwest Regional Educational Laboratory (NREL 2003) breaks down inquiry into four parts: Connect, Design, Investigate and Construct Meaning. Considering these four points, I wanted to create laboratory investigations that were more open-ended.

In my experience, I have noticed that students wanted to be spoon-fed labs and perform them as if they were recipes in a cookbook, perhaps as a consequence of the frequent use of worksheets in fifth- and sixth-grade science studies. My goal was to see my students actively participate and take responsibility for their education. This concern for the continued absence of student motivation and drive to think for themselves led me to focus my teaching activities on scientific inquiry. "Inquiry learning requires environments and experiences where students can confront new ideas, deepen their understandings, and learn to think logically and critically" (Sutton and Krueger 2001).

By taking a lead from the growing interest in "Do-It-Yourself" (DIY) home projects, a series of DIY laboratory experiments were developed and tested in my seventh-grade science class. The activities in the DIY laboratory experiments were designed with NREL's four points in mind, as well as with attention to current district and state standards. In these activities, students were responsible for the procedure, collection of data, data tables, and conclusion. The DIY laboratory experiments were student centered and required the students to create a lab wherein they tested the concept we were learning. "Good science inquiry involves learning through direct interactions with materials and phenomena. One important sign of inquiry is the relative level of control that the students have in determining various aspects of the learning experience" (Kluger-Bell 1991). I wanted to engage my students to a point where they could create and conduct their own experiments—a more direct way to measure student understanding and ability. The DIY laboratory experiments were challenging to students. In these experiments there were no set rules to follow. Perhaps for the first time in their academic careers, the students were required to create the lab report rather than just fill in the blanks. The students wanted me to explain directions over and

Table 1. Essential Features of Classroom Inquiry and Their Variations

Essential Feature	Variations			
	A	B	C	D
1) Learner engages in scientifically oriented questions	Learner poses a question	Learner selects among questions, poses new questions	Learner sharpens or clarifies question provided by teacher, materials, or other source	Learner engages in question provided by teacher, materials, or other source
2) Learner gives priority to **evidence** in responding to questions	Learner determines what constitutes evidence and collects it	Learner directed to collect certain data	Learner given data and asked to analyze	Learner given data and told how to analyze
3) Learner formulates **explanations** from evidence	Learner formulates explanation after summarizing evidence	Learner guided in process of formulating explanations from evidence	Learner given possible ways to use evidence to formulate explanation	Learner provided with evidence
4) Learner connects explanations to scientific knowledge	Learner independently examines other resources and forms the links to explanations	Learner directed toward areas and sources of scientific knowledge	Learner given possible connections	
5) Learner communicates and justifies explanations	Learner forms reasonable and logical argument to communicate explanations	Learner coached in development of communication	Learner provided broad guidelines to use sharper communication	Learner given steps and procedures for communication

More...Amount of learner Self-Direction ....Less
Less..................................... Amount of Direction from Teacher or Material .... More

(Adapted from Inquiry and the National Standards, 2000)

over again. They wanted to be told exactly what to do and took no initiative upon themselves. These DIY, open-ended laboratory experiments challenged students to increase their autonomy and motivation.

According to Marzano et al. (2001), "Making careful observations, developing explanations, and designing and carrying out experiments are complex processes, so students will need guidance and opportunities to practice." Moving students from the preprinted lab to the DIY laboratory experiments was very challenging, and done in incremental steps. Using the Essential Features of Classroom Inquiry and Their Variations (Table 1), I developed a process to move students along the inquiry continuum, focusing on less teacher direction and more student self-direction. This movement was not easy for my students or me, as the reversal of roles for teacher and student was uncharted territory. On my part, I had concerns about letting go of control and worried that students would not be able to step up and take more responsibility in their education. Yet as evidenced by my action research results, my students acquired the skills and abilities to do inquiry.

Skills gained in each experiment are organized in Table 2 to demonstrate the continual process whereby students move along the inquiry continuum. Each laboratory experiment can be adapted to allow for the potential differences in subject matter and area. Table 2 summarizes this approach. The time frame spanned the entire school year, with many more laboratory experiments conducted.

Table 2. Skills Gained in Each Experiment

Experiment	Skills Gained	Continuum Placement See Table 1 Essential Feature 1-5 Variations A-D
1) Tower Activity	1) Introduction to lab report 2) Components of lab report	1.D 2.B 3.C 4.C 5.D
2) Rainbow Lab	1) Review components of lab report 2. Collect and display data	1.D 2.B 3.B 4.C 5.C
3) DIY Density Experiment	1) Choose materials 2) Generate lab report	1.C 2.A 3.B 4.B 5.A
4) DIY Mystery Matter Experiment	1) Generate lab report 2) Determine procedure and analysis	1.B 2.A 3.A 4.B 5.A
5) DIY Exercise Experiment	1) Pose question 2) Communicate explanations	1.A 2.A 3.A 4.B 5.A

At the beginning of the year I had students complete an inquiry-based activity to introduce them to writing their own lab reports. In "The Tower" activity, students were given 50 cm of masking tape, a pair of scissors, two pieces of paper, and a meter stick. They were given directions to build the tallest freestanding tower. The first 10–15 minutes were for practice time, using the first piece of paper. Students called me over to their groups to show me their blueprint and to get permission to build with their second piece of paper. While working on their tower, students had to copy an outline of a lab report. The outline included group members, materials, predictions, data, observations, and a conclusion. After each heading, I included a sentence or two giving the students direction on what information went into each section. The lab report was assessed in two different ways: for the content of the lab report, and for group participation and cohesion.

The next step in moving students to the DIY level was to have them create their own data tables. I had students copy another outline of the lab report for the Rainbow Lab, but this time they selected the information that was necessary and created the tables to show the data. The Rainbow Lab required students to demonstrate knowledge of measuring liquid volumes with a graduated cylinder. The students were given three beakers of red, yellow, and blue colored water, a test tube rack with six test tubes, two graduated cylinders, and an eyedropper. The goal of the lab experiment was to follow the directions correctly and end up with six different colors of water with exact volumes. The students had to copy the outline, including group members, materials, predictions, observations and conclusions. The procedure was handed to the students on a separate piece of paper. Before they could begin the lab, they had to explain its purpose and show me their data table. Assessment for the Rainbow Lab was taken from two different sources. The lab report was graded with a major contribution to the total score from the student-generated data table. The other assessment piece measured the accuracy of their skill in using the graduated cylinder. To further familiarize students with creating their own data tables, they completed two similar labs on the volume of solid, regular shaped objects and irregular shaped objects. The only difference between the Rainbow Lab and these solid volume labs was that the latter were preprinted with the data tables omitted.

I then required the students to write their own procedures and carry out the steps that were necessary to complete an open-ended, DIY laboratory experiment. The first DIY laboratory experiment concerned the concept of density. The class completed a traditional lab with a set procedure, data table, and conclusion questions. The next day I asked students to bring two small objects from home, one regular shaped and one with an irregular shape. I also had an extra supply of items that I brought in case someone forgot their objects. I started a class discussion about density. I had them look at their objects and asked which ones would float and which would sink. I challenged them to prove to me their predictions in a scientific manner that could be repeated.

I introduced to students the idea of a DIY laboratory experiment. Some were excited about being able to start from scratch, make a lab report and communicate their results. Others were more hesitant and did not know where to begin. I talked them through the other labs that we had done in the beginning of the year where they were responsible for the lab report. I asked them to explain the different parts that needed to be included in the DIY laboratory experiment. Once students got started they worked hard and completed the lab report. There was another group of students that started the lab report but did not understand the procedure for finding density. By asking them to do the DIY laboratory experiment, I quickly found the students who did not understand the concept of density. While the other students worked on their reports, I met with the group of students who needed review. I explained what density was, how mass and volume are determined, and how density is calculated. Overall, I was very pleased with the DIY lab reports, considering that this was the first time the students had ever created one entirely on their own.

The next DIY laboratory experiment the students completed was a district assessment on inquiry. The students completed a Criterion Referenced Test (CRT) lab on Inquiry, standard 7-01. The CRT was the same as a DIY laboratory experiment. Students had to start with a blank paper and fill it out on their own. Each student was given five bags of known powders and an unknown. The students had to determine through chemical analysis what substance was in the unknown. The students enjoyed this lab. They had to demonstrate knowledge of chemical analysis and the scientific method. Students included a hypothesis, a descriptive procedure, a complete data table, and a well thought out and supported conclusion. This laboratory experiment was graded on a district level prescribed rubric.

The final DIY laboratory experiment that I had students conduct was a Bromthymol Blue experiment that dealt with respiration and breathing rates. Students had to generate their own lab, testing the effects of exercise on respiration. The students were given a preprinted lab to demonstrate the use of Bromthymol Blue solution, and then they completed a DIY lab to create an experiment on their own. In this DIY, students tested the effects of exercise. Again they started with a blank piece of paper and wrote a lab report. The students developed the entire procedure and decided on the variable. Students enjoyed the freedom and the creativity this DIY brought them.

Looking back over the starting point for my students through the final DIY experiment showed me the tremendous growth of my students and their definite movement across the inquiry continuum. The students took small steps and gradually gained the skills and abilities to complete an open-ended experiment. The gradual process of moving students away from the traditional lab reports to more inquiry-based and student-generated experiments was a major accomplishment felt by both the students and myself. I observed more confident and engaged students. They felt that they were in charge of their learning and were responsible for their education.

Three of the DIY laboratory experiments were completed during the school year. DIY was a new concept that I wanted to try out to see if students would benefit from taking on more responsibility for their learning. Many students had trouble starting their own lab reports. I found that some of my top students struggled with this level of autonomy. They had succeeded and even excelled in school by following directions and complying with teacher-given assignments. When they had to take initiative and write their own lab reports some found it very difficult. They wanted to fill in the blanks and answer preset questions. DIY laboratory experiments really impacted student achievement, as indicated by data results, and many students became more confident in doing science. The qualitative look at student work and the coding done gave proof of the improvement of inquiry skills and movement on the continuum.

Assessment

Assessment is crucial to understanding a student's grasp of any concept. I have learned that assessment is not a test at the end of the unit, but has many different forms. A unit test or CRT should be the final measure of a student's progress, not the first. Assessments can be very short and informal or large, in-depth activities. Short questions posed by the teacher, observations made during group work, listening to students during lab, student surveys, quizzes, tests, and CRTs are all examples of assessments. Effective teachers continually assess their students in many different ways.

"Methods of gathering evidence of student learning include observing students engaged in inquiry, asking probing questions, looking closely at evidence from class work, and giving special tasks to address student needs" (Sutton and Krueger 2001). To measure student impact with DIY laboratory experiments, I conducted an action research investigation on student learning. In my research, I collected data in myriad ways, leading to the triangulation of data to make sure that I had examined the use of open-ended DIY laboratory experiments from multiple perspectives. Instead of collecting data for all 152 of my students in science, I purposefully selected 10 students who represented the demographic makeup of the classes. I chose an equal representation of males and females, as sampled to reflect classroom ethnicity. Having the 10 sets of papers to carefully analyze made it easier for me to assess. These 10 students were my test group for all three types, as well as for all three rounds, of data collection.

The first type of data was collected through teacher records kept in my research journal, including student progress on the open-ended DIY laboratory experiments. The class completed preprinted labs that had set materials, procedures, and a very structured conclusion. Then they completed the open-ended, DIY laboratory experiments, which held students responsible for the procedure, data table, and conclusion/summary. I kept records and copies of their lab reports and made notes that showed their progress. I read through their summaries and coded the common themes in the lab reports.

The second source of data came from classroom observations. I created a data table (chapter appendix 1) that allowed me to examine how students spent their time during lab. Data were collected at the beginning of the lab as well as 10, 20, and 30 minutes into the lab, and also at the conclusion of the lab. The student was assigned a "+" or a "−" for yes or no in the following three areas: engaged and on task, working with materials, and working with group members. I collected the first round of data with a group of students after school. Round two and round three data was collected by a colleague who came in and recorded observations during class time.

Finally, to get student input I created surveys on student perceptions of the open-ended, DIY laboratory experiments (chapter appendix 2). I asked students about their understanding of the concepts surrounding the open-ended labs. The survey was given to the same selected group of 10 students, within three school days after completion of the lab. There were four questions, two on the preprinted labs and two on the open-ended labs. A final question was asked about which type of lab the students preferred, preprinted or open-ended. These data were collected three different times during the year. The content was different for each unit but the methods of data collection remained the same.

Round One Data Collection

A qualitative look at student work identified trends concerning student understanding of the key concepts of density. By examining the summaries, I could classify five main areas where students demonstrated understanding. Of the ten summaries examined:

1. Seven out of the ten students mentioned how to find mass and the use of a triple beam balance with some mention of the proper units of grams;
2. six out of the ten students understood the method for collecting and measuring the

volume for an object with an irregular shape using the water method of displacement;

3. seven of the ten students understood the method for measuring the volume of a regular shaped object by using the formula Volume = Length x Width x Height;

4. five of the ten students understood both mass and volume were needed to calculate density; and

5. six of the ten students showed understanding that different objects have different densities due to differences in size and mass.

This analysis showed that at least half of my students gained the expected information by demonstrating proficiency and inquiry skills on their own, using the DIY laboratory experiment. I wondered why so many of the students successfully completed the lab but had a difficult time writing about their findings. I believed that was in part due to the fact that seventh-grade students had never been expected to complete a laboratory experiment on their own. Experiments had always been prepared for them. They simply had to follow along and answer the questions. I felt that some of the students did not understand the important parts of the experiment so they could not effectively write about them in their summaries.

The second method of data collection was the use of a data table to determine how the students spent their time during the open-ended labs (see Appendix 1). I was very pleased with the results of the student autonomy and time management research. These data were very valuable to get a sense of who was on task and who was not. The students who were on task and engaged had all of the necessary information that I was looking for in their work. The students who were off task left out the majority of the required information. This validates my initial hypothesis that if students were more autonomous they would understand the concepts better, learn more, and become more motivated.

The final method of data collection came from the students. I created a Likert survey that asked the students about lab preference (preprinted or open-ended) and about their understanding of the concept of density using the preprinted or the open-ended lab. The students had to rate themselves on a scale of 1–5, 1 being not agree and 5 being highly agree. I also asked which lab they preferred, the preprinted or open-ended. The results are shown in Figure 1.

The results indicated an overwhelming response of eight out of ten preferring the preprinted lab. I expected the results to be very different. Only two out of the ten students preferred the open-ended, DIY lab. I conclude that this was due to the fact that this was the first time they were ever allowed to write a science report on their own and it required more work on their part. These data were contradictory to the scores received by the students on the lab. The majority of the students received a higher grade on the DIY laboratory experiment then on the preprinted lab. My perception of student work was also opposite from what the student input shows. I feel that the students really did a better job on the open-ended, DIY laboratory experiment. The open-ended labs were more work but I truly believe, as evidenced by higher scores on laboratory experiments, that the students understood the content more by using the open-ended inquiry-based lab.

Round Two Data Collection

A qualitative look at student work was again obtained by examining the summaries from a new DIY laboratory experiment, the Mystery Matter lab. I classified five main areas in which students demonstrated understanding. The five categories came from the CRT rubric graded on the Inquiry lab "Mystery Matter." Of the ten summaries examined:

1. Nine out of the ten students' work included the five steps of the scientific method: Problem, Hypothesis, Experimental Procedure, Data and Results, and Conclusion;
2. seven out of the ten students included a well defined hypothesis, which included the unknown letter and indication of their own hypothesis;
3. nine of the ten students correctly created, collected, and reported data in a data table;
4. eight of the ten students included a conclusion which related their experimental findings to their hypothesis; and
5. eight of the ten students scored proficient or advanced level on the CRT 7-03 Inquiry.

This analysis showed 80% of my students gained the required skills and abilities to thoroughly conduct an inquiry-based laboratory experiment on their CRT 7-01 Inquiry. I was very pleased with the second round of data. The students showed improvement and confidence in writing their own lab reports. My students from years past never scored so high on this CRT.

The second method of data collection involved the use of a data table to determine how the students spent their time during the open-ended Mystery Matter lab. The results are shown in Figure 2. I was

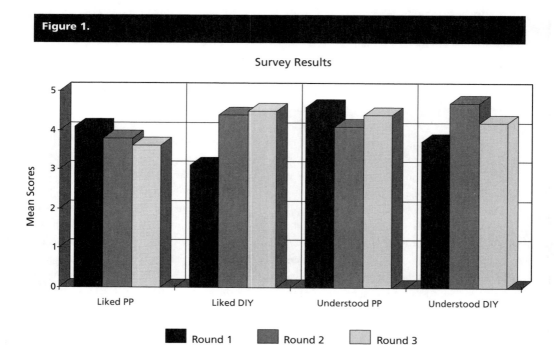

Figure 1.

Survey Results

still very pleased with the results on student autonomy and time management, which continued to show that student understanding comes from actual participation in the lab and that student participation is very important in understanding the required content. Those students who were actively engaged and working with their partners scored at the proficient or advanced level on their CRT.

The third method of data collection for the second round came from the students. The results are in Figure 1. The results of the question about preferred lab type indicated a response of five out of ten preferring the preprinted lab. These data indicate a more positive response than the first round but still only 50% of the students preferred the open-ended labs. I still struggled with this number. I strongly believed that the students learned so much more from the DIY laboratory experiment: their grades went up, they answered more of my questions about the lab, and they completed their lab report. I still felt that I needed to show them the benefits of their hard work. I wanted to be able to express to them how much more advanced they were than my former seventh-grade students. I had the students compare their preprinted lab to the DIY. One student told me the "DIY lab was harder because I really had to understand the Mystery Matter lab." Another student said, "I want you to tell me what to do." I explained to the class that if they wrote a lab report then I could see how much information they knew and understood. I told them it was possible to do a preprinted lab and still not understand the concept behind the lab. I felt that this explanation helped them see the value of the DIY laboratory experiments. I knew that requiring students to write their own lab reports was challenging but the students' work showed me that it helped students understand the content.

Figure 2.

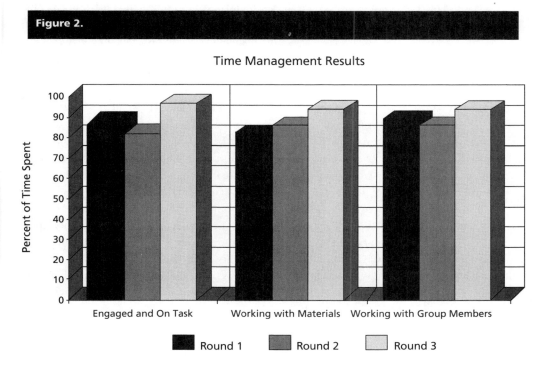

Time Management Results

Round Three Data Collection

Another qualitative look at student work was completed. This DIY activity had students write their own report about exercise and the effects of respiration. I coded their summaries in five categories. Of the ten summaries examined:

1. Nine out of the ten students' work included the five steps of the scientific method: Title, Problem, Procedure, Data, and Summary;
2. ten out of the ten students' work included a well defined problem;
3. ten out of the ten students correctly created, collected and reported data in a table;
4. eight of the ten students' conclusions clearly demonstrated understanding of the color change with the indicator Bromthymol Blue and the presence of carbon dioxide; and
5. eight of the ten students included a conclusion that related their experimental findings.

The two categories that dealt with the problem and data table had a 100% completion rate. This indicated that the students understood what was expected in their lab report and completed it successfully. Having an 80% completion rate on the students' conclusion also showed the impact of the DIY laboratory experiment.

The second method of data collection for the third round involved the use of the data table (appendix 1) to determine how students spent their time during the DIY Exercise lab. Figure 2 shows the results. During this final round of data collection, I felt an overwhelming sense of accomplishment. The students were on task and more engaged than I had seen them all year long. I realized that the DIY activities were making a positive impact in my science classroom.

The third method of data collection for the last round of data was the same Likert survey. The results are in Figure 1. The question regarding which type of lab the student preferred showed a response of 70% preferring the DIY laboratory experiment. I felt that this response indicated positive perceptions about the DIY labs. The preprinted labs require less effort from the student and a passive approach to an experiment. To have 70% of my students choosing the more difficult lab shows that there are real benefits from making them write their own lab report.

Another assessment came from the district on measuring student achievement. OPS changed from the end of the year benchmarks to standards-driven CRTs. These CRTs are instrumentally important to schools because of the No Child Left Behind Act and the new guidelines for Adequate Yearly Progress (AYP). They are also used in the state STARS reporting for school accreditation. Last year my students did fairly well with all the standards with the exception of the inquiry standard. I had almost 40% of my students scoring at the beginning or progressing level. This distressed me and was another factor in determining my focus for the Banneker CEMS project and my Action Research. This year I had 85% of my students score at the proficient or advanced level on their inquiry standard. I only had 7 students out of my 152 total students score a beginning level on their CRT 7-01. This alone was a great indicator of my success integrating inquiry into my classroom. Another indicator of success from my CRT data showed that only 11 students out of the 152 did not make AYP with an average score of at least 2.51 on their total battery for the CRTs. I was thrilled and believe that I am going in the right direction.

Discussion

Throughout this research process I saw many positive gains from the perspectives of both teacher and student. As a teacher, I saw students' achievement in higher CRT scores, in laboratory experiment scores, and in better behavior in the lab. From a student standpoint, I saw less frustration and more "I can" attitudes. The students were not waiting for me to start the lab; they knew what needed to be done and began to do it.

The survey results also showed positive growth from the students. The mean score for the DIY laboratory experiments went from 3.1 to 4.5. Figure 1 shows the trends for all three rounds. The fact the students' mean score went down on the preprinted labs and up on the DIY showed how the DIY laboratory experiments helped them understand the concept.

When I coded the summaries for common themes and understanding of the lab, I found that my students learned how to write as well as organize and complete a summary on their own. These incoming seventh-grade students had barely seen science experiments, much less had practice with lab reports. To have my students accomplish this was a major achievement.

Implications and Conclusion

This research indicated improvement in students' inquiry skills and abilities. Introduction of inquiry and having students complete open-ended labs definitely impacted student learning and achievement. By starting at the beginning of the year with an introduction to the DIY concept, students increased their ability to generate and conduct an experiment on their own. Conducting DIY laboratory experiments increased student motivation and autonomy in lab.

Moving students along the inquiry continuum is a slow but steady process. I still incorporate other teaching strategies that are tried and true. Middle level philosophies and strategies still have value and are used in my classroom. I suggest that a DIY laboratory experiment be added as a final check by the teacher to ensure student understanding. Incorporating more inquiry into a classroom can be an easy-to-follow path, adaptable to fit into any science program. Students need to be introduced to inquiry and have multiple opportunities to practice. Students should be at the proficient level of understanding and inquiry ability, not just able to repeat facts. I will continue to travel the inquiry continuum with each new set of students to become better scientists.

References

Bybee, R. W. 2002. Scientific inquiry, student learning, and the science curriculum. In *Learning science and the science of learning*, ed. R. W. Bybee, 25–35. Arlington, VA: National Science Teachers Association.

Clough, M. P. The nature of science: Understanding how the "game" of science is played. *The Clearing House* 74 (September/October): 13–17.

Connecticut State Board of Education. Open-ended, problem-solving activities: A description. In *Connecticut Academic Performance Test (CAPT) Second Generation Science Handbook*. *http://shs.westport.k12. ct.us/mjvl/science/capt/handbook/open_ended_description.htm*

Haury, D. L. 1993. Teaching science through inquiry. ERIC/CSMEE Digest. Columbus, OH: ERIC Clearinghouse for Science Mathematics and Environmental Education.

Kluger-Bell, B. 1999. Recognizing inquiry: Comparing three hands-on teaching techniques. In *Inquiry: Thoughts, views, and strategies for the K–5 classroom*. Arlington, VA: National Science Foundation.

Marzano, R. J., J. S. Norford, D. E. Paynter, D. J. Pickering, B. B. Gaddy. 2001. *A handbook for classroom instruction that works*. Alexandria, VA: Association for Supervision and Curriculum Development.

National Research Council (NRC). 1996. *National science education standards*. Washington, DC: National Academy Press.

National Research Council (NRC). 2000. *Inquiry and the national science education standards: A guide for teaching and learning*. Washington DC: National Academy Press.

Northwest Regional Educational Laboratory. 2003. *Teaching strategies. www.nwrel.org/msec/science_inq/ strategies.html*

Sutton, J., and A. Krueger. (Eds.). 2001. *EDThoughts: What we know about science teaching and learning*. Aurora, CO: Mid-continent Research for Education and Learning.

Weinburgh, M. 2003. A leg (or three) to stand on. *Science and Children* 40 (March): 28–30.

Appendix 1. Data Table for Assessment

Teacher _____ Date _____

Assignment: _____

Please mark "+" means yes, "–" means no.

	Student					Student					Student				
	A	B	C	D		A	B	C	D		A	B	C	D	
Beginning of activity															
10 minutes into activity															
20 minutes into activity															
30 minutes into activity															
End of the activity															
	Student engaged and on task.					Student working with lab materials.					Student working with group members.				

Collected by _____.

Appendix 2.

Open-Ended Lab Survey

Please read each question and rank yourself on a scale of 1–5 with 1 being not agree and 5 being very highly agree.

1)	I like the standard preprinted lab with the procedures and data tables already done.	1	2	3	4	5
2)	I like the open-ended DIY labs when I can make the data tables.	1	2	3	4	5
3)	I understand the concept for the lab with the standard preprinted lab.	1	2	3	4	5
4)	I understand the concept for the lab with the open-ended DIY lab.	1	2	3	4	5
5)	Which do you prefer? (Circle one.)	Preprinted Lab			DIY Lab	

Modeling: Naturally Selecting an Effective Teaching Method

Karen Mesmer
Baraboo Middle School
Baraboo, Wisconsin

Setting

The middle-level curriculum for evolution described below was taught and evaluated at a small, rural, public Midwestern middle school. The enrollment at the school is approximately 750 students. The majority of students in the school are Caucasian with a small population of Native American students. About 25% are low-income students.

More Emphasis Review

The middle school level curriculum for evolution we will examine incorporates many aspects of the *More Emphasis* conditions from the National Science Education Standards (NSES). In regard to Teaching Standards, those standards most evident include (a) focusing on student understanding and use of scientific knowledge, ideas and inquiry processes; (b) guiding students in active and extended scientific inquiry; and (c) providing opportunities for scientific discussion and debate among students. Assessment Standards that are integrated into the curriculum are: (a) assessing rich, well-structured knowledge, (b) assessing scientific understanding and reasoning, and (c) assessing to learn what students do understand. Content and inquiry standards that are addressed consist of (a) understanding scientific concepts and developing abilities of inquiry; (b) learning subject matter disciplines in the context of inquiry; (c) studying a few fundamental science concepts; (d) implementing inquiry as strategies, abilities and ideas to be learned; (e) activities that investigate and analyze science questions; (f) investigations over extended periods of time; (g) science as argument and explanation; (h) communicating science explanations; and (i) groups of students often analyzing and synthesizing data after defending conclusions.

Teacher, Students, and Classroom

The curriculum has been taught with one teacher in five different seventh-grade science classes. There are usually 20–25 students of mixed abilities per class. I have taught for 22 years, mostly at the middle school level. I recently completed my PhD at the University of Wisconsin-Madison; the topic of my dissertation was "Student Learning of Evolution and the Natural Selection Model," using this curriculum.

Using Modeling to Teach Evolution: The MUSE Curriculum

In order to teach evolution successfully, we must teach how evolutionary biologists conduct their inquiries and how concepts are used within the discipline. Taking this into account, together with research on student misconceptions, a curriculum and instruction project (comprised of university researchers and high school teachers) developed a model-based inquiry curriculum in evolutionary biology—the MUSE (Modeling for Understanding in Science Education) Project at the University of Wisconsin-Madison. This curriculum has resulted in student understanding of evolution at the high school level (Passmore, Stewart, and Mesmer 2001).

The MUSE project's focus on modeling helps students to make connections between classroom experiences and the reasoning patterns biologists use to solve evolutionary problems (Passmore and Stewart 2001, 2002). The students are asked to develop causal models, employ them, and then revise them when the data does not fit the existing model. A causal model is a set of ideas that describes a natural process. A causal model made of objects and the processes in which they are involved can be mentally "run," given certain constraints, to explain or predict natural phenomena (Passmore and Stewart 2002). More specifically, the students are asked to assess models to see if they can explain the data at hand, make predictions, and decide whether the model fits with other accepted models. In other words, students work together like a professional scientific community by offering evidence in support of claims.

The model that is central in evolution is Charles Darwin's model of natural selection. This model stresses that, within certain environments, some genetic variations in individuals increase the likelihood that they will survive to produce more offspring on average than individuals who possess some other variation for the trait. Since variations are inherited, the offspring of the individuals who produce more offspring are more likely to possess that advantageous variation as well.

Philosopher of science Phillip Kitcher states that Darwinian explanations "trace the successive modifications of a lineage of organisms from generation to generation in terms of various factors, most notably that of natural selection" (Kitcher 1993, p. 20–21). A Darwinian explanation would consist of several components:

1. A description of the trait at some time in the past, including the variations in the population

2. A description of the selective advantage (which variation survives and reproduces better and why)
3. Evidence that the trait is inherited from the parents
4. An analysis of how the species changed over many generations, including the variations in the present population.

These components highlight the major points of the natural selection model and demonstrate the ways it can be used to trace a trait through time in a population. In the MUSE curriculum students develop Darwinian explanations as they apply the natural selection model to given instances in the natural world.

Application of the MUSE Curriculum to Middle School

Because of the success of the MUSE evolution curriculum at the high school level, I revised the MUSE evolution curriculum for seventh graders, retaining the same emphases as in the original curriculum, but making it more accessible to middle school students. The emphasis is on using the natural selection model with three data-rich cases to construct Darwinian explanations for specific biological phenomena. Data-rich cases present realistic readings and data that introduce phenomena and are used by students to build Darwinian explanations. The students use the readings and data on phenomena included in the cases to formulate explanations of how the phenomena occurred. Each piece of evidence in these cases outlines at least one of the natural selection model's components, and students need to weave these together to construct explanations for the phenomenon. These data-rich cases provide the opportunity to use the natural selection model to understand evolution in a sophisticated way. Students solve problems similar to that of evolutionary biologists since they are reconstructing the sequence of historical events and using models to explain the evolutionary change. This curriculum is consistent with the NSES and Benchmarks ideas about teaching students both the major ideas in a discipline and the discipline's problem-solving methods.

The Evolution Unit

The six-week unit offered students a chance to employ Darwin's model of natural selection, to develop explanations linking the model with historical reconstructions, and to practice new reasoning patterns. Figure 1 contains a timeline that shows each activity in the evolution unit in the order that it is taught.

The first goal of the unit is to introduce students to one of the important models in evolutionary biology, the Darwinian model of natural selection. Another goal is to have them use this model in realistic ways by developing historical reconstructions and explanations of phenomena. A third goal is for students to be able to assess each other's knowledge claims and arguments.

At the beginning of the unit, before any instruction takes place, the students write an explanation of how the Galapagos tortoises on Hood Island came to have a saddleback shell. They are shown pictures of the tortoises as background to help them with the task. The students' explana-

Figure 1. Timeline for the Evolution Unit

1. Tortoise Pretest
2. Cartoon Activity
3. Lamarck Reading
4. Darwin Reading, Darwin's Evidence, Darwinian Model
5. Two Models Comparison
6. Timeline
7. Endless Variety
8. Moths
9. How Genes Work With Evolution—Darwinian explanation written about this as a class
10. Simulating Evolution—Darwinian explanation written about this as a class
11. Galapagos Slides
12. "What Darwin Never Saw" video—Darwinian explanation written about this as a class
13. Case 1: Seed Case
14. Case 2: Bird Case
15. Case 3: Iguana Case
16. Posttest

tions serve as the pretest on what they understand at the beginning of the unit. On the final exam for the unit, students are asked to analyze this pretest in light of the Darwinian model components and to explain what they would now include. These two tests form a basis for comparing what the students knew prior to the evolution unit and what they have learned from completing it.

Following the pretest, students arrange a series of cartoon pictures that include characters from Three Little Pigs and Little Red Riding Hood. Their task is to try to construct a storyline to explain the pictures. Each group is asked to tell their story to the rest of the class, who then critique it. The students see that data "between" pictures in the story is missing and that they can infer what happened in between. Because they already know the storylines, they bring prior knowledge and beliefs to the task, such as "the wolf is big and bad." They also may use the storylines from these two stories as a basis for their reconstruction and try to mesh the two stories together. From this activity students learn the differences among observations, inferences based on observations, and the prior knowledge and beliefs that underlie those inferences. In other words, the students are enacting a similar process to the one scientists use when employing historical reconstructions to study evolution.

The evolution unit also builds on a lesson from earlier in the year: scientists sometimes use the same data to draw different conclusions, creating controversy. After looking at sample controversial issues in science, students are asked to make claims about the structure inside of a closed box. Students learn that a model must be realistic, explanatory, used for prediction, and consistent with other ideas and models. The black box activity and instruction on how to examine claims gives students opportunities to look at each other's knowledge claims and to argue as evolutionary biologists do.

During the next week, students examine the assumptions of Jean-Baptiste Lamarck's model of use inheritance and Darwin's model of natural selection. These two models offer an explanation for the diversity of life on Earth and incorporate different metaphysical assumptions. After reading about Lamarck and Darwin, students look at brief synopses of concepts and evidence from Darwin's *The Origin of Species by Natural Selection* (1859). These include an old Earth, fossils, embryology, ocean islands, variation, artificial selection, vestigial organs, homologous structures, succession of types, representative types, adaptations, and classification. Students also read a sample Darwinian explanation for the change in pincer size in crabs. While doing this reading, students are asked to examine both the Darwinian model and its assumptions.

One reason for considering both Lamarck and Darwin is to confront common misconceptions that students hold about evolution. For example, Lamarck's ideas about use, disuse, and needs-based evolution are similar to ideas often held by students. By looking at Lamarck's model, students see that it is an inadequate explanation since a "need" for some feature does not result in the feature appearing. For example, students examine the idea that "needing" to be taller to reach a shelf in their room will not make them taller.

The students frequently bring up the idea of divine intervention at this time. They will often say that God made all the living things on Earth just like they are today. I discuss the idea of natural and supernatural explanations. We have established earlier in the year that natural explanations are the only ones used in science, since they can be tested and examined empirically. The idea of God creating species is not a part of science and can be judged as falling outside of science. I point out that other areas of science do not invoke God as an explanation for phenomena. When we are looking for the cause of a new human disease, scientists do not consider the idea that God made people ill. Natural explanations such as bacteria, a virus, a protist or an environmental agent are examined, just as they should be in biological evolution. The vast majority of students seem to agree with this idea.

Another common misconception involves time. Students often do not understand the significance of deep time 4.5 billion years) for biological evolution. A timeline activity illustrates to students that the Earth is very old and that there could potentially be time for hundreds of thousands or even millions of generations of each species. An old Earth is evidence that there was time for change to happen in populations even if only a slight change occurred in each generation.

Figure 2 illustrates the elements of the Darwinian model of natural selection.

Figure 2. A Summary of the First Chapter of the Origin of Species by Charles Darwin, 1859. This is the Darwinian model.

1. Organisms produce more offspring than are able to survive.
2. Since resources are limited, there is a struggle among individuals for survival.
3. Variation exists among individuals of the same species.
4. Some of this variation has a genetic basis (is inherited).
5. Some variations individuals possess increase the likelihood that they will survive to produce more offspring (on average) than individuals who possess some other variation for the trait.
6. Since variations are inherited, the offspring of the individuals that produce more offspring are more likely to possess that advantageous variation as well.

Each component of the Darwinian model (population, variation, selective advantage, survival, heredity, and reproduction) is presented within the context of an activity. Four activities are used to introduce the components. The components are presented one or two at a time, building on those already learned. For example, in the activity "Endless Variety," students look at populations of mealworms and humans for variation. They find characteristics of mealworms that vary from individual to individual. Students also record data about the eye color, hair color, gender, and height of their classmates. This activity introduces the idea of continuous variation, since after graphing the heights of their classmates, students see a wide variation on a continuous curve from the shortest to the tallest student in the class.

The second activity, "Moths," introduces the concept of selective advantage and also incorporates the concepts of variation and population learned earlier. Students have four different variations of paper moths: black, white, colored, and black-and-white. They scatter them on pieces of black-and-white newspaper and one student acts as a bird picking up ("eating") as many of the moths as he or she can in a specified period of time. The students change the background to colored comic newspaper in the next round and students see that the selective advantage of camouflage in one environment may not be the same when the environment changes.

"How Genes Work With Evolution" concentrates on the concept of heritability while also incorporating variation, population, selective advantage, and survival. Red and white beans represent genes in a population of a fictitious creature. Offspring are born from the parents with these genes and those offspring with two genes for white coloration resulting in a white phenotype are more likely to die before they reproduce. Data are taken for four generations and students observe the change in the number of red and white genes over that period of time. This illustrates that genes are involved in selective advantage and survival. Those with the genes that confer a selective advantage have a better chance of surviving than those with genes that do not offer a selective advantage.

We then write a Darwinian explanation to account for the change over time. The complete Darwinian explanation used in this class includes the components in Figure 3.

Figure 3: Components That Should Be Incorporated Into Every Darwinian Explanation.

1. A description of the trait at some time in the past including the variations in the population.

2. A description of the selective advantage (how that trait helps that individual have a better chance to survive than others of the same species).

3. Which variation survives and reproduces better and why.

4. Evidence that the trait is inherited from the parents (genes).

5. How the species changed over many generations, including the variations in the population in the present.

The next class activity is a video about Peter and Rosemary Grant's work with finches on the Galapagos Islands, which documents natural selection in finch beaks over a 25 year time span and ties together all the components of natural selection. From the information given in the video, the class writes Darwinian explanations for what happened to the size of the finchs' beaks both in a drought and in El Niño conditions.

During the remainder of the unit students examine three case studies at length. Each case takes approximately four or five 50-minute class periods to complete. The cases give students background information on a particular organism and an opportunity to read about or to "collect" data about each of the Darwinian model components for that organism. Students need to be able to recognize these components and weave them into an historical narrative about the change in a specified trait in the organism over time. This process helps them learn how evolutionary biologists solve problems, and how to support their argument with appropriate evidence.

The first case examines the change in the spine number and thickness of the seed coat in different populations of a hypothetical Galapagos Islands plant species. The materials given to the students include descriptions of the ancestral population, natural history information about the three populations as they are today, information on predators, and the data from several experiments. All of these materials help students see that the trait is heritable and not just subject to environmental effects. Half of the research teams write a Darwinian explanation for the number of seed spines. The other research teams do the same for seed coat thickness. Students produce posters outlining their explanations and then present the posters to other research groups for critique.

The second case gives students an opportunity to collect their own data on the selective advantage of "Galapagos Origami Birds." The "birds" are two looped strips of paper, paper-clipped to either end of a straw. The traits that vary in this activity are the circumference and the width of the loop ("wing"). An ancestral population (made by the teacher) includes birds with variations of these traits. Students then start with one of the members of the ancestral population and use a die and a coin to determine which variations get passed on by genes to the three birds in the next generation. Students construct those birds and see that each of the offspring is different from the others. They then fly them across the room. The most successful "bird" is the one that can fly the farthest, since it is able to reach the widely scattered springs better than other birds can. Its characteristics are passed on through its genes to the next generation. The genes of the other two birds in the next generation are determined by a toss of the die and coin. This activity continues for eight generations. Using the class average data, the students choose one of the traits that changed and write a Darwinian explanation of how it changed over time.

The third case pertains to real organisms—the marine and land iguanas of the Galapagos Islands and the black iguanas of the South American mainland. The iguana case offers students an opportunity to demonstrate their ability to use the Darwinian model when dealing with the issue of speciation. The selective advantage of the characteristics studied in this case is more realistic because it is not as obvious as it was in the previous two cases. Also, students look at more than one trait, since in many speciation events a change has occurred in more than a single trait.

Students begin by reading about the natural history of the three iguana species, with a focus on the characteristics connected with food acquisition: teeth, shape of the snout, and tail. They also look at pictures of the iguanas and read about the Galapagos Islands' geographic history, the results from DNA studies, the fact that iguanas "raft" on the ocean, the El Niño effect on Galapagos Islands inhabitants, and the marine and land iguana fossils. From this evidence they are asked to develop a Darwinian explanation for how either the land or the marine iguana originated.

A final exam completes the course work. The exam asks students to critique their answer from the pretest on Galapagos tortoises and to create a complete Darwinian explanation for a novel phenomenon. Students are also asked how various components of the Darwinian model relate to each other.

Research on the Effectiveness of Modeling for Teaching Natural Selection

For my PhD research, I collected and analyzed data on the effectiveness of teaching natural selection in the manner described above. I collected written data from the pretest and the posttest and all of the case studies. I also interviewed 10 students three different times, asking them to (a) identify the components of a Darwinian explanation in an explanation that was already written, (b) explain the significance of each component and the relationship between them, and finally (c) solve a novel evolutionary problem. In the last task, students read the natural history of a fictitious creature, chose a trait and an environmental change, and constructed a Darwinian explanation about how the trait would change over time in the population.

Tables 1–3 are summaries of my data, outlining what students knew about each component of the natural selection model (population, variation, selective advantage, survival, heredity, and reproduction) at the beginning of the evolution unit and what they knew at the end. The pre-instruction answers were taken from their pretest and the post-instruction responses were from the third interview where students solved the evolutionary problem described above.

Table 1. This table is a summary of the responses including the components of initial and final population and past and present variation in the pretest on the Galapagos tortoise and the Darwinian explanation during interview 3 for the interview students (n =10.) Each component was evaluated as to whether it was complete (C), partial or partially correct (P), incorrect (I), not included (NI), or implied (IM.)

Pop. Initial	Pop. Initial	Pop. Final	Pop. Final	Variation Past	Variation Past	Variation Present	Variation Present
Pre Inst.	Post Inst.	Pre Inst.	Post Inst.	Pre Inst.	Post Inst.	Pre Inst.	Post Inst.
C = 0	C = 10	C = 0	C = 10	C = 0	C = 8	C = 0	C = 8
NI = 8	NI = 0	NI = 9	NI = 0	NI = 8	NI = 0	NI = 7	NI = 1
P = 1	P = 0	P = 1	P = 0	P = 2	P = 2	P = 3	P = 0
IM = 1	I = 0	I = 0	I = 0	I = 0	I = 0	I = 0	I = 1

Table 2. This table is a summary of the responses including the components of selective advantage, survival, heredity and reproduction in the pretest on the Galapagos tortoise and the Darwinian explanation during interview 3 for the interview students (n=10.) Each component was evaluated as to whether it was complete (C), partial or partially correct (P), incorrect (I), not included (NI), added during the interview and correct (AC), added during the interview and partial or implied (IM.)

Selective Advantage	Selective Advantage	Survival	Survival	Heredity	Heredity	Reproduction	Reproduction
Pre-Instruction	Post Instruction	Pre Instruction	Post Instruction	Pre-Instruction	Post Instruction	Pre-Instruction	Post Instruction
C = 0 NI = 6 P = 4 I = 0	C = 10 NI = 0 P = 0 I = 0	C = 2 NI = 7 P = 1 I = 0	C = 9 NI = 1 P = 0 I = 0	C = 0 NI = 5 P = 1 I = 4	C = 9 NI = 0 P = 0 I = 1	C = 0 NI = 6 P = 1 I = 3	C = 7 NI = 1 P = 0 I = 0 IM = 2

Table 3. This table is a summary of the number of complete responses pre-instruction compared with the number of complete responses post-instruction.

	# of Complete Answers	Total Possible Answers	Percentage
Pre-Instruction	3	60	5
Post-Instruction	71	80	88.8

From these results, a modeling approach combined with data-rich cases is shown to be an effective curriculum approach in this area. The number of complete answers increased significantly, from 5% to 88.8%. Students learned not only about natural selection, but also how inquiry in this field is done. Considering that research has found that learning about natural selection is difficult for students, these results are encouraging. The majority of the interview students in this study could not only identify components of the natural selection model, but also explain the significance of the components and their relationship to one another, and, most importantly, use those ideas to solve problems similar to those of evolutionary biologists.

References

American Association for the Advancement of Science. 1993. *Benchmarks for science literacy*. New York: Oxford University Press.

Darwin, C. 1859. *The origin of species by natural selection*. (first edition). London: John Murray: facsimile reprint (1979). New York: Avenel Books.

Kitcher, P. 1993. *The advancement of science: Science without legend, objectivity without illusions*. New York: Oxford University Press.

National Research Council (NRC). 1996. *National science education standards*. Washington, DC: National Academy Press.

Passmore, C., and J. Stewart. 2001. A course in evolutionary biology: Engaging students in the "practice" of evolution. *Bio Quest Notes* 11(2): 5–11.

Passmore, C. and J. Stewart. 2002. A modeling approach to teaching evolutionary biology in high schools. *Journal of Research in Science Teaching* 39(3): 185–204.

Passmore, C., J. Stewart, and K. Mesmer. 2001. High school students' understanding and reasoning with Darwin's natural selection model. Paper presented at the annual meeting of NARST, St. Louis, MO, March 25–28.

Unlocking the National Science Education Standards With IMaST

Marilyn K. Morey, Richard E. Satchwell,
Franzie L. Loepp
Illinois State University
Normal, Illinois

Tracy Hornyak, Jim Pilla
Great Meadows Middle School
Great Meadows, New Jersey

Setting

reat Meadows is a rural community located 35 miles northwest of Newark, New Jersey, and 29 miles from Allentown, Pennsylvania; it has a population of 2,303. There are 496 students enrolled at Great Meadows Regional Middle School and the average class size is 25. Great Meadows Regional Middle School uses a team of science, technology education, and mathematics teachers to implement the Integrated Mathematics, Science, and Technology (IMaST) project. We will examine the IMaST project as it was applied at Great Meadows Regional Middle School, one of many program schools across the country.

The National Science Foundation funded the IMaST project for three consecutive developmental cycles, from 1992 through 2002, to design an integrated middle school curriculum. The professionals engaged in the IMaST project have learned many things about designing and implementing standards-based curricula.

As a developmental research project, the IMaST developed 16 standards-based curriculum modules that comprise a three-year program for science, technology education, and mathematics. During each three-year developmental cycle, master teachers selected to design, write, and test the materials created a unique program to facilitate the national standards for science, technology education, and mathematics. This chapter highlights the program and specifically addresses the *More Emphasis* facets highlighted in the National Science Education Standards (NSES) (NRC 1996).

The *More Emphasis* goals were addressed through the help of a number of dedicated personnel, school districts, and communities throughout the United States. Each developmental cycle tested the materials to ensure the program's adaptability as a model curriculum for meeting state and national standards for science, technology education, and mathematics. The IMaST modules for each grade level were tested in a variety of venues, ranging from some of the nation's poorest districts to some of its most affluent. Thirty schools in twenty different states have tested IMaST curricula for at least one year. The program was tested by self-contained teachers as well as by teams in science, technology, mathematics, language arts, and social studies from coast to coast. The resultant curriculum is being published by RonJon Publishing, located in Denton, Texas; it can be reviewed at their Internet site: *www.ronjonpublishing.com/imast.htm*.

With Goals in Mind

Constant attention was focused on the national standards as well as the domain-specific content and process knowledge for all three disciplines (math, science, technology) throughout the development of IMaST. Correlation matrices helped to track the connections made to the national standards. By focusing on the NSES, the curriculum maintains the spirit of the goals of science education.

The IMaST curriculum addresses the goals of the NSES by providing opportunities for students to (a) discover a wide range of scientific and mathematical patterns in the natural world; (b) apply knowledge as they develop and investigate their own questions; (c) work as communities of learners debating and communicating ideas to arrive at evidence-based conclusions; (d) develop the habits of mind used by scientists; and (e) make connections to real-world contexts and careers.

Clearly, IMaST addresses the goals that underlie the NSES. Specific examples throughout the next section illustrate how IMaST supports the *More Emphasis* facets identified in the content and Inquiry, Assessment, Professional Development, and Teaching Standards (NRC, 1996). The examples used to support our efforts to address the *More Emphasis* criteria are taken directly from one of our exemplar schools in New Jersey.

Strengths of IMaST That Support *More Emphasis*

The IMaST program has many strengths and unique characteristics, however, for the purposes of this paper, the authors will focus on the following features:

1. The program is the only middle-level program that integrates mathematics, science, and technology with connections to language arts and social studies.
2. The program provides a framework for students to learn how to inquire, problem solve, and design.
3. Multiple and varied methods of authentic assessment are utilized throughout the curriculum.
4. Materials are developed by teachers, then enhanced and formatted by a team of curriculum specialists.

5. The program focuses on developing a community of learners made up of students and teachers.

Each unique IMaST characteristic will be described detailing how the curriculum aligns with the *More Emphasis* vision highlighted in the NSES. Each of the following sections is organized by standards. First, a brief description of the unique IMaST feature that addresses that standard is presented. The *More Emphasis* aspect encompassed in the IMaST curriculum follows the description. Examples, supplied by our exemplary school team, provide authentic evidence from the field of how IMaST is addressing the areas of *More Emphasis*.

Content and Inquiry Standards

IMaST is a unique three-year, middle school curriculum that integrates contents and processes of science, technology, and mathematics disciplines. While other curricula use a variety of approaches to help students make connections across one or more disciplines, these connections are often implicit, uneven, and not fully realized by students. The IMaST curriculum, on the other hand, is a fully integrated curriculum that explicitly assimilates concepts from more than one discipline, designed to focus, equally, on science, technology, and mathematics. In addition, IMaST connects to the language arts and social studies disciplines by including multiple profiles of typical careers related to the curriculum content, as well as additional articles titled *Making Connections* that relate to social, environmental, or global issues.

By making explicit connections within and across disciplines, the IMaST curriculum does not separate science knowledge from other knowledge. Science content is integrated with other ways of knowing and doing.

Evidence from the field: As reported by a Great Meadows School teacher, "Our students, while using the Patterns of Mobility module, explore the concept of mobility from the perspectives of science, technology, and mathematics while designing and building string puppets to correct proportions. This gives our students an interesting context for learning about parts of the body (fingers, wrist, elbows, shoulders, toes, ankles, knees, hips, etc.) and how they function. After their puppets are constructed, they are dressed like characters from a novel read in language arts and are used to support oral presentations of biographies and autobiographies."

The Patterns Below Us module allows students in social studies to explore the history of mining while the Patterns Around Us model provides opportunities for students to link the study of the water cycle with methods used by ancient Greeks and Romans to purify water. Students in our exemplary school also integrate computer technology skills to develop spreadsheets, report and display data, conduct research on the internet, communicate their ideas, develop time lines, and incorporate digital photos into reports.

A second unique feature of the IMaST curriculum is the framework that it provides students so that they learn to conduct inquiries, solve problems and design solutions. The IMaST curriculum provides a toolkit for developing abilities of inquiry, problem solving and design. There is considerable emphasis on (a) gathering evidence and recording data, (b) managing ideas and information, and (c) communicating student ideas and explanations. Furthermore, students learn that problem solving is not a linear stepwise process with one correct outcome. The IMaST curriculum has derived a generalized problem-solving model that students use throughout the course of learning. This model has five components: Define, Assess, Plan, Implement, and Communicate, and is referred to by its acronym—DAPIC.

When engaged in the DAPIC model, students (a) define the problem to determine what they want to know; (b) assess the problem to determine what they need to know; (c) plan how the team will accomplish the task and determine what resources will be needed; (d) implement their plans; and, (e) draw conclusions and defend their data analysis. The instructional framework presented in each module supports the DAPIC methodology and provides many opportunities for students to investigate and analyze questions, plan an approach to inquiry, and use evidence and strategies to develop or revise an explanation.

The theme for each IMaST module provides the structured context for the development of fundamental science, technology, and mathematics concepts as well as the acquisition of *process skills* while reflecting common goals. Every module begins with a challenge—an integrated activity that introduces the module's objectives and key concepts. This is followed by a series of science, technology, and mathematics activities set in four-phase learning cycles (*Exploring the Idea*, *Getting the Idea*, *Applying the Idea*, and *Expanding the Idea*). Research indicates that students learn best when they are encouraged to construct their own knowledge of the world around them (Colburn 1998; Lawson, Abraham, and Renner 1989). The learning cycle stems from the constructivist learning theory and allows important concept development to take place in a structured venue. Some investigations initiated in the learning cycles are carried out over an extended period as suggested by the *More Emphasis* standards. Each module ends with an End of Module Assessment that requires students to apply results of their explorations and scientific explanations to a new problem.

Evidence from the field: The teacher at Great Meadows, who was responsible for organizing this year's science fair, was pleasantly surprised by the increased student interest in participating in the science fair and found the level of thinking to be considerably higher than in past years. Great Meadows faculty attribute this to the students' experience with the inquiry approach of the IMaST program.

Teachers at Great Meadows have reported a considerable increase in student-initiated questions, and an increase in creative and divergent thinking as students design alternative solutions to problems. In Patterns Above Us, students design various methods to purify water samples and in Patterns Within Us, students learn about working within a set of restrictions and constraints as they design their own microscope. A variety of process skills are used in each learning cycle, which is a much better representation of scientific inquiry than learning and using skills in isolation. Great Meadows teachers credit the inquiry approach used in IMaST for the increasing number of students now basing decisions on evidence and their ability to defend those decisions.

Assessment Standards

The NSES recommend multiple and varied methods of assessment with a focus on authentic assessments, the idea being that evidence from such assessments should yield a more accurate picture of what students know and can do, beyond memorizing facts. Assessments should reflect what is valued and addressed in the science classroom and align with the goals and objectives of the science curriculum.

The IMaST program uses several assessment strategies. Teachers are encouraged to use a variety of informal, formative assessments while students are in the process of completing activities. Students may be defining a problem, designing a problem solution, gathering data, building models, measuring, or using any number of process skills as they apply content knowledge to a problem-based situation. During these activities, teachers can read individual student portfolio entries, hold small- and large-group discussions, question students as they work on their group activities and observe students as they implement their plans to solve a problem.

In addition to suggestions for ongoing assessment, the IMaST teacher's edition, includes End-of-Module assessments to check students' scientific understanding and reasoning of key concepts as well as the technology and mathematics knowledge gained in the module. The End-of-Module assessments include a group activity designed to assess the concepts and processes from science, technology, and mathematics. During this assessment, students are required to write a comprehensive paragraph describing the key concepts in the module and support them with specific journal entries (e.g., planning documents, graphs, and charts). The teacher's resource binder includes a DAPIC Student Self-Assessment and DAPIC Teacher Assessment, which provides a rubric for students to self-assess and for the teacher to assess each student's ability to use of the DAPIC problem-solving strategy. In addition, the teacher's resource binder includes a Team Growth Rubric that students use to assess both their own and their team's ability and opportunity to work together.

Evidence from the field: According to our team of exemplary teachers, the authentic assessments from the IMaST curriculum provide a context for their students to connect their understanding. They admit that before IMaST, students were given isolated mathematics and science tests that focused on memorization, with no personal student connection to the data. One exemplary teacher recalled an episode during the Patterns of Mobility module, when a student was self-assessing the proportion aspect of his mobility puppet design and realized there was a part that was out of proportion to the rest of the puppet. Another student's number sense became apparent when he reevaluated a decimal answer while determining flow rate in gallons per minute as part of the Patterns Around Us module. This was instantly corrected by the student when his answer was displayed as an outlier to the rest of the class data. The importance of proper decimal placement became apparent.

In the Patterns Within Us module, students determine the percentage chance of who the parents of a lost puppy could be. Students have to apply their understanding of Punnett Squares and dominant and recessive genes. Assessments like this clearly reflect the authentic learning activities in each module.

Professional Development Standards

Building professional capability for science teaching and learning should be a continuous process, from preservice education throughout a teaching career. Educators need to raise their collective level of science literacy in order to effectively develop, refine, and implement new approaches to teaching, assessment, and curriculum (NRC 1996; AAAS 2001). According to the NSES, teacher professional development should include learning science, knowledge of science teaching, learning to teach science, and knowledge and skills for lifelong learning. (NRC 1996).

One of the unique features and strengths of IMaST is that teachers were involved in its original design, development, extensive piloting, revision, and field-testing. A Project Team made up of a director, two co-directors, and a project coordinator, worked very closely with curriculum specialists and a design team, both made up of master classroom teachers. The IMaST team worked together to develop an integrated theme-based curriculum, driven by standards-based objectives, delivered through learning cycle activities, and measured through authentic student assessments.

Professional development focusing on inquiry into teaching and learning, integration of theory and practice, and learning science through investigation and inquiry was continuous throughout the curriculum design and development. Throughout the process, the emphasis was on collegial and collaborative learning that recognized the teachers as intellectual, reflective practitioners and producers of knowledge about teaching. Knowledge gained throughout this process was incorporated into the curriculum.

The IMaST curriculum is designed to be taught by a team of teachers, one from each of the three disciplines, who plan the instruction to facilitate integration and make changes to the program to accommodate the learning needs of students. This situation can cause positive professional growth as the team works together to "combine their knowledge of mathematics, science and technology with their knowledge of teaching" (Satchwell and Loepp 2004). The curriculum is implemented best if the team of teachers has a common planning time to help coordinate the instruction and integration and the sharing of equipment and supplies.

Evidence from the field: During field-testing it was found that shifting to the IMaST curriculum prompted more collaboration among members of the school community, including school administrators, teachers, and parents. This occurred at many field-test sites with local curriculum meetings attended by parents, district curriculum coordinators, and superintendents. In some cases, parents and teachers from surrounding schools have come to IMaST schools to observe IMaST implementation. Parents from this exemplary school are making presentations in the school that support the concepts presented in the IMaST curriculum. Teachers implementing IMaST have made presentations to school boards, district curriculum meetings, and school improvement meetings at other school districts and they see themselves as facilitators of change. With IMaST, it appears that the idea of a collegial professional community begins to expand and work toward long-term coherent planning increases. According to a group of teachers and administrators from Great Meadows, the topics in IMaST are such that it is easy to gain internal and external support and expertise. At Great Meadows Middle School, where the sixth-grade curriculum was field-tested, the school has budgeted for an expansion of IMaST to the seventh- and eighth-grade levels.

Teaching Standards

The National Science Education Standards for teaching focus on the systemic nature of teaching. Teachers are expected to develop, facilitate, and assess short and long-term inquiry lessons for their students. They should also be able to design and manage the learning environment to support inquiry-based learning. Teachers should model scientific inquiry by developing a community of learners within the classroom and by participating in the larger community of learners within the school science program.

The IMaST curriculum emphasizes teaming by teachers as well as students. Teachers work as teams to prepare instructional plans, share equipment and materials, and share the responsibility for student learning. The professional development materials and the teacher's edition contain information to help teachers prepare their students for teamwork.

The sixth-grade Tools for Learning module introduces students to the concept of teamwork and provides opportunities for students to work together toward common goals. These initial experiences help to set up the classroom as a *community of learners* in which students cooperate and share responsibility for learning. As students work to design and build a "race car," set up the racecourse, determine rules of conduct, set up their "pit" teams and carry out the competition, the need for teamwork quickly becomes apparent. After the first race trial, using evidence from the car's and the team's performance, improvements to the design of the car are made. Students must discuss their ideas; drawing upon their knowledge of science, mathematics, and technological design as they inquire into which improvements will be most effective. It is not unusual for some heated debates to develop among the students as they try to reach consensus on their plan of action.

In the Expanding the Idea phase of each learning cycle, there are opportunities for the teachers and the students to select and adapt the curriculum by using the ideas presented there or by pursuing their own paths for extending/expanding learning. This section of each learning cycle includes a number of avenues that students, with some guidance from teachers, can choose to pursue. Selection of activities may depend on student interest, accessibility of materials, and time available.

As discussed in the section on assessment, there are many opportunities built into the IMaST program for teachers to continuously assess student understanding. The focus is not only of summative, end-of-learning cycle and end-of-module assessment, but also on formative, continual ongoing assessment of student understanding. The IMaST curriculum includes activities with varying lengths of time, providing opportunities for teachers to guide students in extended scientific inquiry.

Evidence from the field: When describing how students' interests are considered in the IMaST program, teachers from one exemplary site report that "students' interests and strengths come to the forefront…as they meet requirements but within their own level of interest." During the Expanding the Idea phase of each learning cycle, students apply their creativity, organizational skills, curiosity, artistic skills, and design abilities as they pursue one of the Expanding the Ideas activities or research a career-related topic. As a follow-up to her experience with the Patterns Within Us module, one student brought in a full-size framed poster that she designed to explain the various blood types and the clumping caused by incompatible blood. Other students share their learning and inform their peers with presentations they have created using computer-based presentation programs, displays incorporating digital photographs, video productions, and a variety of other graphic displays.

The computer technology teacher at one of our exemplary sites worked with IMaST students to develop web pages on which students posted their work, showing the students using DAPIC and completing other activities. The environmental education teacher supported the concepts learned in the Patterns of Mobility module by applying that knowledge to the migration of the monarch butterfly to Mexico and to the movement of invertebrate and vertebrate animals.

The Evidence Is In

The IMaST modules align very well with the eight areas of the NSES. Each of the seventh- and eighth-grade modules align with all eight content categories and each of the sixth-grade modules align with at least five of the categories. A complete chart of the alignment with science, technology, and mathematics content standards can be reviewed on the IMaST website: *www.ilstu. edu/depts/cemast/programs/imast/content_standards.shtml*.

The external evaluator for the IMaST program conducted several on-site visits and interviewed IMaST teachers and students. According to the evaluator (Mouw 2002), interviews confirmed the apparent high level of student motivation observed during his site visits. Furthermore, students seemed to sense the uniqueness of IMaST and were able to verbalize the integrated nature of the curriculum. Quotes from Mouw's interviews with IMaST students, shown in Table 1, capture students' insights about the program.

Table 1. Selected Student Responses When Asked, "How is IMaST different and how do you have to study differently with IMaST?"

Student	Quote from interview question
A.	"It's all mixed together, it's great."
B.	"We get numbers by collecting data, we don't just have to practice anymore."
C.	"You put your mind to it rather than just putting it on a page."
D.	"You need to figure out the answer, you have to be logical."

When interviewing IMaST field-test teachers, Mouw (2002) asked about the impact that IMaST was having on student motivation, initiative, skill development, academic preparation, and cognitive integration. Table 2 shows the mean response to these questions on a scale of 1 (high) to 5 (low). In addition to the comments captured during student interviews, Mouw provides the teacher comments shown in Table 3.

Table 2. Mean Scores of Teacher Responses to Selected Questions

IMaST Impact	N	Mean
Motivation	19	1.7
Initiative	19	2.0
Skill development	19	2.1
Academic preparation	19	2.1
Cognitive integration	19	1.6

Table 3. Selected Teacher Responses When Asked, "Compared to other curricula with which you are familiar, what is the impact of IMaST on student motivation, student initiative, skill development, academic preparation, and cognitive integration?"

Teacher	Quote from interview question
A.	"The kids really get into it, in some cases they would go beyond the assignments."
B.	"Students get such a sense of ownership."
C.	"The students understand what they are doing—that makes their learning so much more effective."
D.	"They'll be better prepared for high school than with any other curriculum."
E.	"I expect IMaST will help students to compete academically at any level."
F.	"I love that aspect [integration], the way it fits together and with reality."

Achievement of IMaST students was also measured using the mathematics and science subtests of the TerraNova Multiple Assessment. These tests were administered to the sixth-grade IMaST students and an appropriate comparison group as a pretest in the fall and a posttest in the spring. The results of the TerraNova science subtest indicate a statistically significant ($F = 13.22$, $p = .0003$) difference between the means of the comparison and IMaST groups on the science posttest performance. The results indicate that IMaST students performed better on the posttest than those students who did not experience IMaST. Both groups gained from pre- to posttests; however, IMaST students' scores increased more than the comparison students' scores.

In addition to the TerraNova testing, a test comprised of released items from the science subtest of the Third International Mathematics and Science Study (TIMSS) was administered to 293 IMaST students and a comparison group of 246 traditional students (Satchwell and Loepp 2004). The results of the analysis of covariance for the science subtest indicate that the IMaST students performed better in science *process* than in science *knowing*, with a slightly opposite effect for the traditional group, with an F-value for the Group Effect indicating an overall difference between the groups across subtests. The IMaST group appeared to perform better on the TIMSS science subtest than did their traditional peers, especially on the science Process subscale.

The curiosity of a field test school in Michigan led them to follow IMaST students from their school into two different high schools. The data indicate that IMaST students earned a higher GPA than non-IMaST graduates from their school. In addition, the IMaST students reported they felt better prepared for high school than did the students who were not enrolled in IMaST (Satchwell and Loepp 2004) .

There was some concern among the IMaST development team that the unique aspect of an integrated approach to learning might be too challenging to students. What if students found IMaST to be so different or so challenging that it would make students feel less confident of their ability to succeed in mathematics, science and technology? A curriculum that would negatively impact students' beliefs that they can succeed in science would not be acceptable. To address this concern, a modified Morgan-Jinks Student Efficacy Scale was administered to IMaST and non-IMaST comparison students at the sixth-grade field test sites. This scale contains three subscales for *talent*, *context*, and *effort*. The results indicate no statistically significant difference between the groups on all scales from pre- to post-assessments. While it might have been optimistic to expect great increases in the IMaST students' beliefs about their academic efficacy, the fact that IMaST did not have a negative impact on student beliefs is considered a positive aspect of the curriculum.

Assuming that the TerraNova subtests and the TIMSS subtests effectively assess student understanding of process and content in science, it is fair to say that IMaST has a positive impact on student achievement in science. The student performance on these well-known and respected assessment instruments lends great support to the qualitative data gathered throughout the three years of field testing for each of the IMaST modules. Examples taken directly from each of the modules and from field test site visit reports provide evidence to show how the goals and *More Emphases* aspects of the standards are being addressed. However, the real evidence of success is the higher-level student interest in science, and the increased student motivation to learn science—resulting in greater academic achievement in science.

The Key, the Lock, and Standards

In this chapter, we have addressed the *More Emphasis* facets for the Content, Inquiry, Assessment, Teaching, and Professional Development Standards. We have also provided considerable evidence of the effectiveness of the IMaST curriculum. It was not our intent to make it sound as though implementation of the IMaST curriculum is a simple recipe for science teaching and learning. The teachers who commit to teaching the integrated and inquiry-based IMaST curriculum are risk takers. The teaming approach, the work of gathering and organizing materials, the planning time, the surrender of some control of the classroom—these are all challenges faced by teachers and schools implementing any truly standards-based integrated curriculum. However, in "standards-based schools," the teachers should not be alone in facing these challenges. While the teacher may be the key to effectively unlocking a new curriculum, the lock they are trying to open is often frozen by a lack of program and system support. A more effective implementation of standards-based science curricula will likely occur in schools that are striving to meet all the standards, including program and system standards for science education.

References

American Association for the Advancement of Science. 2001. *Designs for science literacy.* New York: Oxford University Press.

American Association for the Advancement of Science. 1993. *Benchmarks for science literacy.* New York: Oxford University Press.

Colburn, A. 1998. *Constructivism and science teaching.* Fastback, 435. Bloomington, IN: Phi Delta Kappa Educational Foundation.

International Technology Education Association. 2000. *Standards for technological literacy: Content for the study of technology.* Reston, VA: Author.

Lawson, A., Abraham, M. and Renner, J. 1989. *A theory of instruction: Using the learning cycle to teach science concepts and thinking skills.* Columbus, OH: The National Association for Research in Science Teaching.

Morey, M. Forthcoming. Integrated Mathematics, Science and Technology and Student Academic Efficacy.

Mouw, J. 2002. Final report for the project. Integrated Mathematics, Science and Technology, IMaST Plus.

National Council of Teachers of Mathematics. 2000. *Principles and standards for school mathematics.* Reston, VA: Author.

National Research Council (NRC). 1996. *National science education standards.* Washington, DC: National Academy Press.

Satchwell, R. and Loepp, F. 2004. Designing and implementing an integrated mathematics, science and technology curriculum for the middle school. *Journal of Industrial Teacher Education* 39(3).

Authors' Note

Morey is a co-director for the Integrated Mathematics, Science, and Technology (IMaST) project and assistant professor in the Curriculum and Instruction Department at Illinois State University, Normal, Illinois. Satchwell is the IMaST project coordinator and Loepp is an emeritus distinguished professor and IMaST director. Satchwell and Loepp are at the Center for Mathematics, Science, and Technology at Illinois State University, Normal, Illinois.

Hornyak is a master mathematics teacher and Pilla is a master science teacher implementing the IMaST curriculum at Great Meadows Middle School in Great Meadows, New Jersey.

This manuscript is based on work supported by the National Science Foundation under Grant # 9819002. The Government has certain rights in this material. Any opinions, findings, and conclusions or recommendations expressed in this material are those of the authors and do not necessarily reflect the views of the National Science Foundation.

Achieving a Vision of Inquiry:

Rigorous, Engaging Curriculum and Instruction

Barbara Nagle, Manisha Hariani
University of California, Berkeley

Marcelle Siegel
University of California, San Francisco

Setting

The changing emphases of the National Science Education Standards (NRC 1996) have spurred many school districts to reinvent their science programs. New curricula developed by NSF-funded programs have been at the core of some districts' comprehensive plans to reform science education through changing emphases in content, teaching, and assessment. Lemon Grove, California, and Charleston, South Carolina, provide two examples of districts that have developed and followed a comprehensive plan for the reform of science education through changes in curriculum, assessment, and instructional practices.

The Lemon Grove School District (LGSD) serves 4,600 students in grades K–8. Although Lemon Grove is a small city that is partly urban and partly suburban in character, it is part of the much larger San Diego metropolitan area. The student population is diverse, with approximately 36% Hispanic, 29% white, 24% African American, 4% Asian, 4% Filipino, and 3% other groups. The population also includes approximately 18% English Language Learners (7.8% English Proficient ELL). Over 50% of the students are receiving either free or reduced price meals.

Charleston County School District (CCSD) is the second largest school district in South Carolina, serving approximately 45,000 K–12 students in 13 middle schools. The district is 88% urban and 12% rural, with a student population of approximately 59% African American, 39% white, and 2% other. Approximately 2% of students are English Language Learners and 53% percent of the children are eligible for free or reduced-price meals.

More Emphasis on Inquiry

Although Charleston and Lemon Grove are quite different in size, geographic location, and student population, both have used inquiry-based science as a focus for changing emphases related to content, teaching, and assessment. The overarching vision of the Lemon Grove School District strategic plan for science is to "provide developmentally appropriate, inquiry-based science experiences so that all students will have a foundation in scientific principles." This vision places inquiry at the forefront of Lemon Grove's science program. The strategic plan, developed in 2000, included specific goals to develop a district-wide inquiry-based science program, prepare all science teachers to facilitate inquiry-based science, implement a comprehensive approach to assessment, and provide administrative and community support for inquiry-based science. Through a National Science Foundation Local Systemic Change grant, Charleston County School District has created Project Inquiry in order to prepare teachers to implement the rigorous new science curriculum they have adopted in Grades K–8. Project Inquiry provides an extensive professional development program that supports teachers as they shift emphases toward inquiry-based instruction and the use of authentic assessment to inform instruction. The ultimate goal of both districts is to improve student achievement in science. Figure 1 illustrates some of the key elements of the changing emphases suggested in the NSES and addressed in LGSD and CCSD.

Exemplary Classrooms

Samantha Swann and Helen Copeland teach seventh-grade life science at Lemon Grove Middle School, one of two middle schools in the Lemon Grove School District (LGSD). Lemon Grove Middle School's demographics reflect those of the district in general. A unique feature of the district is a strong technology component, including a district-wide intranet and the presence of one computer for every two students throughout the district. Patrick Shell and Tina Kleindt teach seventh-grade life science at West Ashley Middle School and Laing Middle School in Charleston. West Ashley Middle School's demographic profile is similar to the district profile. Laing Middle School's students are 60% white, 36% African American and 2% other. Approximately 34% of the students at Laing Middle School receive subsidized meals. The schools in both districts have a strong focus on literacy through science. The schools in both districts have a strong focus on literacy through science.

Unique program features

In order to achieve their goals, both districts developed detailed plans that included a number of specific objectives. For example, in order to progress toward an inquiry-based curriculum, LGSD identified essential learnings and reviewed and recommended instructional materials based on the National Science Resources Center (NSRC) Evaluation Criteria for Curriculum Materials. Both districts used state and national standards as they searched for science curriculum materials that focus on inquiry and the relationships among scientific and other disciplines in order to achieve an increased emphasis on learning subject matter in the context of inquiry, technology, science in personal and societal perspectives. Once the core curriculum materials had been identified,

Figure 1. Curriculum, Instruction, and Assessment Triangle: More Emphasis On. . .

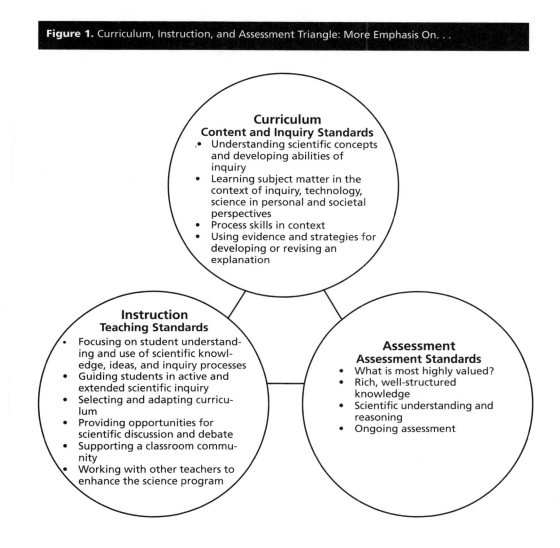

Curriculum
Content and Inquiry Standards
- Understanding scientific concepts and developing abilities of inquiry
- Learning subject matter in the context of inquiry, technology, science in personal and societal perspectives
- Process skills in context
- Using evidence and strategies for developing or revising an explanation

Instruction
Teaching Standards
- Focusing on student understanding and use of scientific knowledge, ideas, and inquiry processes
- Guiding students in active and extended scientific inquiry
- Selecting and adapting curriculum
- Providing opportunities for scientific discussion and debate
- Supporting a classroom community
- Working with other teachers to enhance the science program

Assessment
Assessment Standards
- What is most highly valued?
- Rich, well-structured knowledge
- Scientific understanding and reasoning
- Ongoing assessment

teachers worked to adapt them to their local settings.

The instructional reform efforts of teachers involved in Lemon Grove Middle School were catalyzed by two experiences: their participation in the NSRC's Leadership and Assistance for Science Education Reform (LASER) Project and their participation as a field-test center for Science Education for Public Understanding Program (SEPUP) middle school courses. The LASER Project resulted in the development of a group of teacher leaders at each school, while the field-testing gave teachers an opportunity to pilot, evaluate, and contribute to new curriculum. In CCSD, Project Inquiry provided elementary and middle school Teachers with 135 hours or more of professional development through a variety of activities such as graduate courses, science content institutes, science curriculum training, assessment institutes and inquiry institutes. Four district-level science resource teachers and a lead science teacher in each school facilitated professional development activities. Through Project Inquiry, seventh-grade teachers worked together to develop story lines and curriculum unit maps to identify key areas for emphasis district-wide. These maps are available on the science and health curriculum page of CCSD's website (*www. ccsdschools.com*) and show how teachers related each unit of the middle school program to specific inquiry skills and content.

Professional development is a cornerstone of science education reform in both districts. The professional development programs prepare teachers to use the new curriculum, the authentic assessments, and the instructional strategies described below in order to achieve the changing emphases of the NSES.

Curriculum

Lemon Grove and Charleston have chosen to use innovative science curriculum materials that focus on inquiry and the relationships among scientific (and other) disciplines as one of the main agents for change. For example, both districts use SEPUP's Science and Life Issues as the core of the seventh-grade life science program. Science and Life Issues was developed by the Science Education for Public Understanding Program (SEPUP) at the Lawrence Hall of Science, University of California, Berkeley. Like many other NSF-funded curricula, Science and Life Issues addresses the National Research Council's essential features of classroom scientific inquiry. In particular, it supports the goal that "learners give priority to evidence, which allows them to develop and evaluate explanations that address scientifically oriented questions" (NRC 2000). Both school districts chose the program because of its issue-oriented, guided inquiry approach, in which students participate in investigations, discussion, and debate about scientific ideas and decisions about personal and community issues that require an understanding of scientific evidence and principles. The program also includes a research-based embedded assessment system and extensive support for changing instructional practices. Carol Tempel, CCSD math, science and technology coordinator at the time the materials were selected, reported that the curriculum was chosen because "the content was focused on the national and state standards, inquiry is embedded in the activities, activities address all learning styles and promote the use of research-based, effective instructional strategies."

The course was developed to provide an issue-oriented approach to teaching life science related to the NSES. Both districts have adapted the program to meet additional state standards and district goals. LGSD includes additional units that address California standards that are not emphasized in Science and Life Issues, and CCSD teaches most of the course in seventh grade and the Ecology and Evolution units in eighth grade, to correlate with the South Carolina standards.

The program uses an approach that SEPUP refers to as issue-oriented science (Thier and Nagle 1994), in which students learn to understand and use scientific evidence, assess risks and benefits, ask questions, and make decisions based on scientific evidence and approaches to problem solving. The course uses a guided-inquiry approach to instruction, in which students experience "sequenced investigations that engage students by posing problems that have meaning for them and that also develop students' knowledge and skills in an academically sound and rigorous way" (Thier 2001). This typically involves a question or problem that is interesting to students, followed by investigations of scientific principles that contribute to understanding the problem and an opportunity to make a decision related to the problem. For example, the first unit of the Science and Life Issues course, titled "Studying People Scientifically," introduces scientific methods and processes in the context of questions related to human variation and health. Consistent with the guided-inquiry approach, students are first introduced to models of good experimental design and then design and conduct their own investigations. Students learn about aspects of experimental design such as reproducibility, multiple trials, control of variables, sample size and composition, quantitative and qualitative data, and ethical considerations in the context of investigations of human variation, as well as simulations of clinical trials to determine the safety and effectiveness of medications. The unit concludes with an opportunity for students to apply what they have learned, when they analyze four funding proposals to conduct clinical trials and choose which proposal to fund, based on criteria such as experimental design, importance, and ethical considerations. This unit relates to the *More Emphasis* recommendations of the NSES by providing opportunities for students to develop abilities of inquiry and learn subject matter in the context of inquiry and science in personal and societal perspectives. They use process skills in the context of learning about variation among humans and evaluating the safety of medications. As the course continues, students have more opportunities to use these process skills when they design experiments related to key concepts in human physiology and plant genetics.

Assessment System

Understanding concepts and using inquiry skills are key elements of the course's assessment system, developed through a collaborative effort with the Berkeley Evaluation and Assessment Research Group at the Graduate School of Education, UC Berkeley (Wilson and Sloane 2000). This authentic, embedded system was developed with the goal of assessing rich, well-structured knowledge and scientific reasoning. The assessment system includes the following components:

1. SEPUP variables describe the areas in which student learning is assessed through both formative and summative assessments. The current variables in Science and Life Issues are Understanding Concepts (UC), Analyzing Data (AD), Designing Investigations (DI), Evidence and Trade-offs (ET), Communication of Scientific Information (CM), with subvariables on organization and technical aspects of writing, and Group Interaction (GI), with subvariables on role performance/participation and shared opportunity.

2. Assessment tasks embedded in the instructional activities provide opportunities for teachers and students to monitor students' understanding of key concepts and ability to use process skills to investigate scientific questions and demonstrate their understanding.

3. Scoring guides, specific to each of the SEPUP variables, establish criteria for assessing levels of student performance.

4. Assessment blueprints provide an overview of the points in instruction where assessments are embedded.

5. Assessment moderation, a process through which teachers meet to discuss student papers and achieve consensus on student scores.

6. Exemplars of student answers that have been scored and moderated illustrate performance at the different levels of the scoring guides.

For teachers in Lemon Grove and Charleston, the embedded assessment system is a major component of their effort and has been a focus of professional development efforts. Samantha Swann of Lemon Grove Middle School has observed that the system has "guided teachers from strictly end-of-unit testing for summative assessment to using formative assessment to guide instruction and to using alternative methods of summative assessment." Rodney Moore, science coordinator of CCSD notes, "teachers are using the formative assessments to inform them of students' progress." In both districts, teachers are moving from what is easy to test to focusing on what is important to assess. Both districts have focused on professional development to support teachers in using the new and challenging assessment methods. They start out gradually, gaining experience with the curriculum the first year, and adding in the assessment system with additional professional development over the next year or two of implementation. The assessment system requires extended answers and products from students, with an emphasis on the writing required for students to express their understandings and ideas fully. This has been incorporated into district goals for literacy.

Teaching

Lemon Grove's strategic plan for implementing inquiry-based science in grades K–8 included a mission: for students to appreciate, recognize, and communicate about scientific applications in everyday life, consistent with the NSES in personal and societal perspectives. Teachers interpreted this mission as a call to enhance learning through engaging, rigorous curriculum and instruction. In their classrooms, they have integrated the new curriculum and assessment with the district's use of instructional technology and focus on literacy.

Lemon Grove's connected intranet learning community, called LemonLINK, connects students' homes, the school, and city facilities, providing equitable access to information technology to all district students. Students and their families can access both the internet and school resources from home, allowing easy communication as well as completion of school assignments, which can be submitted to teachers electronically. The effective use of instructional technology has continued as a cornerstone of the district's plan to improve student learning in all subjects. District-wide, there is one computer for every two students. This year, as part of an experimental effort, some science classes have one computer for every student. In some cases, the computers remain in the classroom, but in two of Samantha Swann's sixth-grade classrooms, every student has a thin client tablet that can be taken home in the evening. She takes advantage of the technology in numerous ways; she uses spreadsheets for students from all of her classes to share and analyze data; posts the scoring rubrics and exemplars of her students' work for students and parents; and provides one-minute videos of classroom results for students to review when they work on assignments and lab reports at home.

In Charleston, Tina Kleindt finds that science in the seventh grade is a unique experience. "Students operate much like real scientists, designing and conducting investigations and analyzing their data…. Students like the activities and how involved they are in the class. One of my students would enthusiastically greet meet with 'What are we going to do today?'" The Charleston teachers find that this has changed students' focus from memorizing answers in bold text from the book to thinking more about what they are learning and generating their own answers.

The reform of science education in CCSD and LGSD is part of a larger effort to improve student literacy and numeracy throughout the district and is closely connected to the curriculum and assessment system. Teacher leaders facilitated staff development sessions on effective use of notebooks, including strategies for enhancing literacy through science, and in authentic assessment strategies. In CCSD, teachers have developed literature connections to the science curriculum, and reinforce them through including them in the students' science notebook entries. In LGSD, science teachers collaborate with teachers of other subjects. For example, they work with English teachers to assign and score student work to improve student writing, especially persuasive writing. As a result, the SEPUP Communication of Scientific Information and Evidence and Trade-offs variables are a focus of the Lemon Grove Middle School science program. In addition, the assessment items and rubrics are used to prepare for the LGSD writing assessment. Teachers in CCSD and LGSD share the scoring guides with students and use them as the basis for feedback to students, for peer and self-review, and for revision.

Evidence of Change

Classroom and district-wide assessment efforts provide evidence that the changing emphases in curriculum, instruction, and assessment are having the desired effect. At the classroom level, teachers have observed dramatic improvements in students' notebooks and work on the embedded assessments. In particular, there are great improvements in students' ability to express their ideas in writing. Helen Copeland has observed that the assessment approach helps students to present evidence to support their ideas and opinions and to build their inquiry skills over time. Samantha Swann, who has been teaching the program for five years, has found that students in her classes begin the year performing at level 1, or mostly incorrect and incomplete, on the four-point assessment rubrics. Over the course of the year, the quality of student work improves until most are consistently doing work at level 3, complete and correct. She finds that "Students are engaged and passionate to do well on the embedded assessments as they are being guided to ask meaningful questions, use their inquiry skills to answer them, and then apply what they have discovered to investigate and solve new problems."

This type of growth only occurs when the curriculum, instruction, and assessment system are working together to achieve more emphasis on inquiry, higher-level thinking, and collecting evidence about what is most important to learn. Earlier research showed that student gains greatly improved when the curriculum is used with the assessment system (Wilson and Sloane 2000). When the assessment system is used, gains have varied from approximately 0.5 to 1.0 units, with students typically making gains from level 1 to level 2 or from low level 2 to level 3. Teachers who use the assessment system and scoring rubrics regularly find that the system changes the character of the classroom and greatly improves students' understanding of criteria for good performance (Siegelm, Hynds, Siciliano, and Nagle, forthcoming). In Lemon Grove and Charleston middle schools, students participate in numerous embedded assessment activities that require them to (a) develop procedures for investigations, (b) analyze their results, (c) explain scientific phenomena, and (d) write persuasive essays explaining how scientific evidence informs their decisions about personal and societal issues. Embedding inquiry skills and core science concepts in the day-today assessment emphasizes their importance to students. They use the scoring rubrics frequently for peer and self-assessment. Teachers help students clarify the scoring rubrics and make them student-friendly. Discussions of the scoring rubrics and of criteria for good work are part of everyday life in the science classroom. In CCSD, teachers use the Group Interaction variable to support classroom community. In LGSD, teachers use the variables and scoring rubrics as part of the district writing assessments for persuasive and technical writing. Thus the assessment system is fully embedded in the curriculum and classroom instruction.

LGSD and CCSD are working with SEPUP in a national study to investigate the impact of Science and Life Issues on student learning. Pretest/posttest results from a 2002–2003 pilot study are currently being analyzed. The test includes multiple-choice items intended to sample a broad range of content, short answer items related to content and process, and extended items related to the SEPUP variables. These items were carefully developed and pilot-tested in 2000–2001 to correlate with the course curriculum and the NSES in life science, inquiry, and science in personal and social perspectives. Preliminary analysis indicates improvement from pre- to posttest on each item type. For example, on 10 of the short answers (scored 0–2), the mean improvement was 0.4 points ($p = 0.0018$, $n = 27$ matched cases for these items, out of 320 students' pretests and posttests on four randomly distributed test forms). Improvement for the extended items scored with the SEPUP rubrics (scored 0–4) ranges from approximately 0.3 to approximately 0.9, depending on the item and variable assessed. A rigorous technical analysis of these items, as well as the multiple-choice items (using Rasch modeling from item response theory), is underway.

One concern expressed by some teachers and administrators is that spending so much time on issue-oriented science, extended inquiry, and time-consuming embedded assessments may in some way shortchange students by depriving them of content breadth and that this in turn may affect students' performance on standardized tests. The experiences of Lemon Grove suggest that when science education reform is part of an overall plan to improve curriculum, assessment, and instruction, these fears are unfounded. In March 2002, the California Department of Education selected Lemon Grove Middle School as recipient of the California Title I Achieving Schools Award. Their overall Academic Performance Index is 5 out of 10, yet when compared to similar schools, they score an impressive 10. Their Stanford 9 (SAT 9) scores in both reading and mathematics have improved steadily over the period from 2000 to 2002 in all three middle school grades. For example, in 2000, 45% of students scored at or above the 50th percentile. By 2002, approximately 53% achieved or exceeded the 50th percentile. Similar increases in percentage of students scoring at or above the 50th percentile were also observed in mathematics. CCSD, which is at an earlier stage in their implementation of the new program, is conducting a seventh-grade outcome study to investigate classroom practice and student achievement.

The accomplishments of LGSD and CCSD, as illustrated by the seventh-grade classrooms at Lemon Grove Middle School in LGSD and Laing Middle School and West Ashley Middle School in CCSD, are based on their commitment to improving learning through new curriculum and assessment materials in a context that provides support for teachers to develop their teaching and to change their classrooms.

References

National Research Council (NRC). 2000. *Inquiry and the national science education standards: A guide for teaching and learning.* Washington, DC: National Academy Press.

National Research Council. (NRC). 1996. *National science education standards.* Washington, DC: National Academy Press.

Roberts, L., and M. Wilson. 1998. Evaluating the effects of an integrated assessment system: Changing teachers' practices and improving student achievement in science. Paper presented at the annual meeting of the American Educational Research Association, San Diego, CA.

Siegel, M. A., P. Hynds, M. Siciliano, and B. Nagle. Forthcoming. Using rubrics to foster meaningful learning. *PEERS (Practical Experience and Educational Research) Matter.* Arlington, VA: Joint publication of NSTA and NARST.

Science Education for Public Understanding Program (SEPUP). 2000. Science and life issues. Ronkonkoma, NY: Lab-Aids.

Thier, H.D. 2001. *Developing inquiry-based science materials: A guide for educators.* New York: Teachers College Press.

Thier, H. D. and B. Nagle. 1994. Developing a model for issue-oriented science. In *STS education: International perspectives on reform*, eds. J. Solomon and G. Aikenhead, 75–83. New York: Teachers College Press.

Wilson, M., and K. Sloane. 2000. From principles to practice: An embedded assessment system. *Applied measurement in education,* 13 (2): 181–208.

Wilson, M., K. Sloane, L. Roberts, and R. Henke. 1995. *SEPUP course I, issues, evidence and you: Achievement evidence from the pilot implementation.* CA: University of California, Berkeley, BEAR Report Series, SA-95-1.

Adapting the JASON Project
Real Science. Real Time. Real Learning.

Warren Phillips
Plymouth Community Intermediate School
Plymouth, Massachusetts

Setting

The Plymouth Public School System is located on the south shore of Massachusetts. It has 8,754 students enrolled within 10 elementary schools, 2 middle schools, and 2 high schools. The students (6% minority and 94% white) live in households with a median income of $54,677 and many parents commute to Boston. The average per pupil expenditure is $6,755, compared to the state average of $6,779. It is a fast-growing community with many new housing developments and a lot of available land.

Plymouth Community Intermediate School (PCIS) is the older of two middle schools of equal size. Despite its age (30 years old), it has a relatively new appearance and includes a television studio and a planetarium. Despite its student enrollment of 1,500, PCIS has incorporated a small-school environment by dividing into four equal-sized "houses," each with its own housemaster and guidance counselor. Within the houses are teams of teachers; fifth- and sixth-grade classes have two-teacher teams with 50 students. Seventh- and eighth-grade classes have five-teacher teams with about 115 students.

Our science curriculum has been adapted and developed to incorporate the best features of available resources. We believe that it is the only online K–12 curriculum (available at *www.plymouth/schools/Science/index.htm*) on the web to date. This allows us to personalize individual lessons to our unique environment, such as incorporating planetarium lessons, web lessons, and television technology. Also, the school is surrounded by town forest, and is located near historic

Plymouth, the ocean, a nuclear plant, and Cape Cod National Seashore. These lessons are aligned with the state and national standards by teachers, who write the curriculum and post it on the website under the guidance of Nick Micozzi, our science curriculum supervisor. The JASON Project—funded by the JASON Foundation for Education and named after Greek myth of Jason and the Argonauts—is adapted as part of the 5–8 curriculum and involves four weeks of lessons that use our environment and compare it to another environment in a different part of the world each year. This comparison provides students with a global perspective for environmental issues as well as local applications.

I am a seventh-grade teacher on the "Red Team" at PCIS. I was selected as Disney's Outstanding Middle School Teacher in 2004 and TIME for Kids magazine's Teacher of the Year in 2002. I am National Board certified and have master's degrees in instructional technology and teaching physical sciences. I am a JASON-certified trainer and attend the JASON conference in Milwaukee each year. I also have produced an award-winning website entitled Mr. Phillips's Science Home Page (*http://wphillips.com*). My schedule consists of five classes of 23 students and an additional class in Television Technology with 10 students. My classroom is set up with two sinks, several fish tanks, six computers and a GrowLab for plants. A virtual tour is available at *http://wphillips.com/classroom.htm*.

Adapting and Integrating the Curriculum

In classroom lessons, our team uses authentic theme-based learning revolving around the JASON Project, a multidisciplinary curriculum involving real science studies and comparing them to local studies performed by students. Bob Ballard, who is one of the host researchers, began it. The JASON Project includes an interactive website (available at *http://jasonproject.org*), live broadcasts, and a paper curriculum with teacher's guide, videos, and many other resources. While adapting and teaching these lessons, we incorporate brain-based learning (Jensen 2000) to provide students with unforgettable learning experiences. Our instructional strategies engage students using Marcia Tate's brain-based learning strategies (Tate 2003). Last year, the JASON Project traveled to the rainforest of Panama. I introduced it by reading *The Great Kapok Tree* (Cherry 2000) from my "story bench." This led into a discussion and debate on human uses of natural resources. As a class, we came up with the potential value of using these resources as opposed to preserving them. The class also compared the valuable resource of the rainforest to the Plymouth Town Forest, adjacent to the school. Each student constructed a JASON Journal using an oaktag cover and plain paper inserts. They were encouraged to create their own cover, using crayons, clip art, magazine pictures, etc. The cover design also included 10 or more facts about the JASON Project adventure. Inside the journal, students keep field notes, measurements, reflections, drawings, and test results. The JASON Project includes a prologue video, introducing main concepts, which students viewed. Each student visited the JASON website next to learn more about the scientists involved. They were given an assignment to "adopt" one of the scientists, writing about their interests and a short bio.

My classes went to the computer lab and the students constructed a web page field guide using FrontPage, picking one animal to study. Some students picked rainforest animals, while others picked animals from the Plymouth vernal pools. The web pages included scientific names, fun facts, habitats, bibliographies and background information. Students also produced original drawings, which were digitally photographed and included on the web pages. Other students from around the country who are involved with the JASON Project use these published web pages. Additionally, the artwork and written descriptions were used in collaboration with the Vernal Pool Association's Poster Outreach Project (*http://vernalpool.org/ed5-pp1.html*). These professionally designed posters, assembled by Leo Kenney (1996), are entitled "Rainforest Animals" and "Plymouth Vernal Pool Animals" They have been distributed to other teachers, the Plymouth Town Hall, libraries, schools and public buildings. Later, in class, we discussed the food webs and foods chains for each environment and recorded the information in our JASON Journals.

As students became familiar with rainforest animals, the Red Team teachers decided to construct a rainforest in a large hallway area out of used carpet tubes and 2 x 4 supports. These tubes represented the trees, and our students and teachers began to "build" the forest in many after-school sessions. Students covered the walls in rolled paper and painted the trees and walls. In science class, we researched various rainforest trees and found their scientific names. Then, we made a leaf template for each tree and began to mass-produce leaves for each tree. The trees were given plaques with scientific names and information about each one. Meanwhile, the reading teacher assigned stories about the rainforest. The geography teacher taught lessons about various rainforests of the world and students drew and cut out animals to place in the new environment. The math teacher taught proportions. The students brought in stuffed animals to complement the scenery. A river was made out of blue paper and cellophane. Finally, a rainforest cassette tape played noises of the rainforest while a mist from a ceiling pump sprayer (hidden in the suspended ceiling) surprised visiting guests. A "scavenger hunt" question sheet was prepared and distributed to visiting classrooms from around the school.

After web pages were constructed, we began to do pre-field studies in science class in anticipation of a Cook's Pond field trip. These pre-field lessons included mini-labs set up at stations around the room. Students worked in groups to determine sediment analysis, weather conditions, temperature, water clarity, density, salinity, pH, current speed, dissolved oxygen, and invertebrate populations. Students went from station to station over a period of three days and recorded their findings in their JASON Journals. Afterwards, we reviewed the data and reflected on the importance of the activity. I then began preparing students for the trip to Cook's Pond. We did similar tests while there. Additionally, the language arts teacher conducted a writing reflection and the geography teacher used a GPS unit to determine exact location. The math teacher determined the slope of the beach area. The reading teacher conducted a scavenger hunt for species using a "pond life" field guide. Students went from teacher to teacher doing pond-related activities for the entire day. This was team teaching and experiential learning at its finest!

On the JASON website, we learned about the Panama Canal. We studied the canal's importance to worldwide travel, its history, and how it works. The JASON website has "Digital Labs," which are excellent interactive lessons promoting science concepts. Although there are too many to use and too little time, we used Your Panama Canal Adventure, Race to Reforest: Battling the Fast Growing Grass, EDS Virtual Canopy Walkway, and Rainforests: You Compare. They allow students to work at their own pace in an interactive, engaging lesson. Students recorded their results in their JASON Journal. Another website, The Panama Canal: How Iit Works, (*www. pancanal.com/eng/general/howitworks/index.html*), demonstrated the reasons for having a canal and the technology behind it. These excellent lessons reinforce technology's importance in educating the students of today.

Now it was time to visit our local canal, the Cape Cod Canal. I arranged for a field trip for the entire team on a Cape Cod Canal cruise. The boat took us up and down the entire length of the canal while students were informed of its history, technology, and general significance. In conjunction with this activity, I invited a canal ranger to do a television interview in our TV studio. As a TV Technology teacher, I have a crew of Red Team students trained in the use of our television studio. Besides doing a weekly PCIS news show, we periodically invite guests to enhance our curriculum. These guest shows are done in front of a live studio audience of seventh graders. TV Technology students run the cameras, soundboard, computer, and switchboard; they also construct the credits. One student does the interview, followed by questions from the audience. Public Science Lessons (PSLs) are used for commercial breaks. These PSLs were constructed by students during a Summer Science Camp session. The entire production is edited by students and then placed on the local cable Channel 14 for viewing by the Plymouth public of 40,000 households. Besides providing good public relations for the school, TV shows serve as authentic lessons and educate the public!

We began studying the rainforest habitat with lessons from the JASON paper curriculum. For example, we constructed a simple device called a "penetrometer" to determine the strength of leaves. Using a small 8 oz. cup, I glued a golf tee to the bottom. A 10 x 20 cm piece of cardboard was folded in half (so that it was 10 × 10 cm) and a 1 cm circular hole drilled in the middle. Any leaf could be placed in between the folds. Then the golf tee was placed on top of the leaf. Water was added to the cup until the leaf was penetrated. The amount of water was recorded, which provided concrete objective data to be recorded by students in their JASON Journals. The same experiments were conducted by JASON researchers in their environment in the Panama rainforest. Students could then compare their local data to that of the rainforest.

Part of the JASON experience is a live broadcast that takes place at the end of January. During the day, satellite broadcasts from Panama showed students, scientists, and researchers at work. Their experiments mimicked some of the experiments we did in the classroom (such as the penetrometer activity). Students see their adopted scientists and get to know their personalities. This live broadcast reinforces their authentic learning experiences.

In order to provide instructional strategies for all types of learners, I wrote a JASON song to the tune of "Blow the Man Down," as follows:

Bob Ballard's exploring the earth and the sea
Along with JASON and me.
Discovering treasures and learning a lot
Making me feel like a true Argonaut!

With JASON we study outside of our school
Observ-ing is really cool!
With science equipment and telepresence
We can explore the ocean sea vents!

Each year when we travel to new habitats
We learn all kinds of facts
About the environment and how to conserve
This tiny planet we're trying to preserve.

The Panama rainforest ecology
In JASON XV we'll be
Studying species unique to this place
Biodiversity is commonplace!

Bob Ballard's exploring the earth and the sea
Along with JASON and me.
Discovering treasures and learning a lot
Making me feel like a true Argonaut!

I have noticed that music contributes both to learning and to a good environment for learning. I play the guitar, and use this song each year, changing the words slightly to adapt to the JASON expedition. I also wrote this song about the rainforest, which is sung to the tune of Britney Spears's "Baby One More Time":

Tropical rainforest   Bio-diver-sity
Half the Earth's species thrive there
But in the rainforest   human activities
Threaten their survival
The habitat is shrinking
And one quarter of the forest is gone. It's wrong!

Chorus:
Slash and burn activity
Clearing land and killing trees
The plants and animals are disappearing
Look at the signs…
Save the forests while there's time!

From the canopy to the understory
It's humid and it's hot there

The floor is dark – and surprisingly bare
The light is blocked from up above
Macaws, iguanas, snakes....
And tons of other species can thrive – It's Alive!

These and other songs have turned out to be very successful in teaching concepts to students. The songs we sing introduce vocabulary, reinforce concepts, and encourage environmentalism. They are also very popular with other teachers at various workshops.

The Museum of Science in Boston, Massachusetts has an omnitheater, which was showing an 180° movie entitled *Jane Goodall's Chimpanzees*. I felt this was a perfect opportunity to reinforce environmental concepts, as well as a chance to watch and learn from a world-famous scientist. The entire Red Team visited the science museum. Many students saw practical applications of their science lessons and the effect that a lifetime of hard work can have on others. Immediately after the movie, I sat students down in a quiet area of the museum to write their reflections in their JASON Journals. Of course, we were also able to visit the museum exhibits that apply hands-on experiences to teach science concepts.

Because I am heavily involved in technology, the JASON Project called and asked if I would be interested in a live teleconference with Bob Ballard. This was in conjunction with his upcoming television special, *Return to the Titanic*. I pounced on this opportunity. This would provide students with a culminating activity beyond belief! We quickly installed the necessary software and tested the teleconference with the JASON technologists. My students would be in the audience of our TV studio. Bob Ballard was aboard a ship at the Titanic site. The broadcast worked flawlessly. The Red Team students were able to ask questions for about a half-hour, and Bob answered them directly while students viewed him on a large screen. This was a personal highlight of my teaching career.

In past years, I have done other activities in conjunction with the JASON Project. Two notable ideas that work well included constructing a quilt and adopting a partner classroom. In the Quilt Project, each student creates a square of quilt that represents their local environment. These quilt squares are shared with other schools around the country that are also studying the JASON Project and students then assemble a quilt that has squares from all around the country. This can be accomplished with the help of a consumer education (sewing) teacher. In addition, I have found other classroom teachers willing to set up ePals—a way to connect classrooms around the world via the internet (see *www.epals.com/index.tpl* for more information). While this can be potentially dangerous, if parental permissions are obtained and a website is used to screen content, it can be done with mutual benefit (Phillips 2001).

Assessment

The students were assessed according to rubrics provided by the teacher. The JASON Journal included many different lessons and the rubric reflected this.

Mr. Phillips

Jason Journal Rubric

Name _____

Class: _____

Apollo 1

| Total Score | |

Elements	Point Values					Score
Cover (in color, with facts and a full heading)	2 Not much information, or inaccurate.	4 Incomplete, confusing or inaccurate	6 Some new information, but incomplete.	8 Cover is good and nearly complete.	10 Cover is complete and well presented.	
Tropical Forest Ecosystem	4 Not much information, or inaccurate.	8 Incomplete, confusing or inaccurate	12 Some new information, but incomplete.	16 Information is good and nearly complete.	20 Information is complete and well presented.	
Prologue video	2 Not much information, or inaccurate.	4 Incomplete, confusing or inaccurate	6 Some new information, but incomplete.	8 Information is good and nearly complete.	10 Information is complete and well presented.	
Reflections Wild Chimpanzee	2 Not much information, or inaccurate.	4 Incomplete, confusing or inaccurate	6 Some new information, but incomplete.	8 Information is good and nearly complete.	10 Information is complete and well presented.	
My Favorite Exhibit Science Museum	2 Not much information, or inaccurate.	4 Incomplete, confusing or inaccurate	6 Some new information, but incomplete.	8 Information is good and nearly complete.	10 Information is complete and well presented.	
Adopt a Scientist	2 Not much information, or inaccurate.	4 Incomplete, confusing or inaccurate	6 Some new information, but incomplete.	8 Information is good and nearly complete.	10 Information is complete and well presented.	
Digital Labs (Race to Reforest and the Big Top)	2 Not much information, or inaccurate.	4 Incomplete, confusing or inaccurate	6 Some new information, but incomplete.	8 Information is good and nearly complete.	10 Information is complete and well presented.	
Digital Labs (Tour the Virtual Canopy Walkway)	4 Not much information, or inaccurate.	8 Incomplete, confusing or inaccurate	12 Some new information, but incomplete.	16 Information is good and nearly complete.	20 Information is complete and well presented.	
Baseline Study/ Field Tests	4 Not much information, or inaccurate.	8 Incomplete, confusing or inaccurate	12 Some new information, but incomplete.	16 Information is good and nearly complete.	20 Information is complete and well presented.	
How the Broadcast Works	2 Not much information, or inaccurate.	4 Incomplete, confusing or inaccurate	6 Some new information, but incomplete.	8 Information is good and nearly complete.	10 Information is complete and well presented.	
JASON Live notes	2 Not much information, or inaccurate.	4 Incomplete, confusing or inaccurate	6 Some new information, but incomplete.	8 Information is good and nearly complete.	10 Information is complete and well presented.	
Field Guide Notes and Sensory writing	2 Not much information, or inaccurate.	4 Incomplete, confusing or inaccurate	6 Some new information, but incomplete.	8 Information is good and nearly complete.	10 Information is complete and well presented.	

As part of a Master's thesis, I surveyed students on their attitudes toward computer use in the JASON Project. I also surveyed the students on their level of comfort using computers before and after completing the JASON project. Tables 1 and 2 indicate their responses:

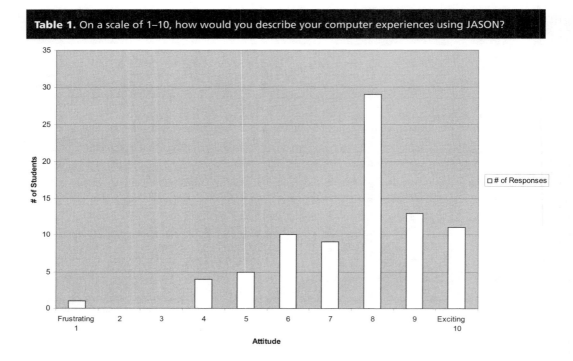

Table 1. On a scale of 1–10, how would you describe your computer experiences using JASON?

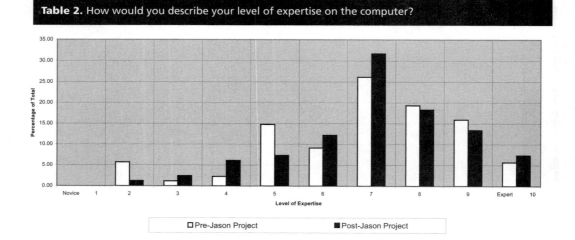

Table 2. How would you describe your level of expertise on the computer?

The JASON Academy also offers a variety of professional development courses for teachers in conjunction with the project. At the conclusion, teachers reported that the courses gave them more access to resources and produced an increased interest in science content (Penuel 2004). Table 3 shows how teachers rated courses (on a scale from 1–3) with respect to gains on selected professional development goals.

Table 3. Professional Development Course Ratings*

Four different JASON Academy online professional development courses were offered in fall 2001. At the conclusion of the courses, participants ranked their progress, on a scale of 1–3 (with 3 being the highest), in the following areas:

Area of Development	Ranking (1–3)
Access to new resources	2.64
Increased interest in topic	2.60
Expanded teaching techniques	2.39
Increased confidence	2.31
New professional contacts	2.29
Increased comfort with the internet	2.26

*From Penuel, W. 2004. *JASON academy formative evaluation: Summary of findings.* SRI International.

Conclusion

The JASON Curriculum, when adapted to the Plymouth online curriculum, addresses the *More Emphasis* section of the NSES. It guides students in active and extended scientific inquiry and allows teachers to work together to enhance the science program. It also provides more emphasis on assessing highly valued environmental concerns, scientific reasoning, and ongoing assessment using the JASON Journal. For Content Standards, it provides more emphasis on conducting investigations over a period of time, synthesizing data, and defending conclusions. The Poster Project and TV show provide public communication of student ideas and information to classmates, the school, and the community. The Professional Development standards give more emphasis to integrating theory and practice in school settings, providing long-term coherent plans, and using staff developers as facilitators, consultants, and planners.

The wide spectrum of activities described in this chapter is intended to immerse the students in science. I firmly believe in emotional, experiential learning using multiple intelligences. I try to use a wide range of teaching tools whenever a student question arises. I like to be able to answer their questions with a spontaneous response that includes specific demonstrations, songs, and stories that will cement their facts, ideas, and scientific concepts, creating unforgettable brain-based learning experiences.

References

Cherry, L. 2000. *The great kapok tree: A tale of the Amazon rain forest.* New York: Voyager Books.

Jensen, E. 2000. *Brain-based learning: The new science of teaching and training.* San Diego, CA: The Brain Store.

Kenney, L. P., ed. 1996. *Diving into wicked big puddles.* Reading, MA: Vernal Pool Association, Reading Memorial High School.

Penuel, W. 2004. *JASON academy formative evaluation: Summary of findings.* Menlo Park, CA: SRI International.

Phillips, W. 2001. The impact of establishing e-pals in conjunction with the JASON project action research. Paper submitted to Bridgewater State College.

Tate, M. 2003. *Worksheets don't grow dendrites: 20 instructional strategies that engage the brain.* Thousand Oaks, CA: Corwin Press.

"Re-Inventing" Science Instruction:

Inquiry-Based Instruction in a Fifth/Sixth-Grade Classroom

Melissa Rooney
Arlington Heights Elementary School

Deborah L. Hanuscin
University of Missouri-Columbia

Setting

f the 14 elementary schools in the Monroe County Community Schools Corporation, Arlington Heights Elementary is one of the smallest and oldest, serving a predominantly white student population of 300, grades K–6. The composition of the student body is reflective of the socioeconomic conditions in south-central Indiana; approximately one-third of students qualify for free or reduced lunch. Located in Bloomington, Indiana, the school has benefited from partnerships with Indiana University. Among these partnerships is the Learning Science by Inquiry professional development program. Beginning in 2001, faculty at Arlington Heights had the opportunity to participate in monthly workshops designed to improve their abilities in teaching science in ways consistent with recent reforms.

I decided to join Learning Science by Inquiry in the second year of the program, when I took on the responsibility of teaching science in a sixth-grade classroom. I was motivated by my dissatisfaction with relying on the textbook for instruction. Much as the National Science Education Standards (NSES) (NRC 1996)have described, this more traditional textbook instruction left much to be desired in terms of motivating students and promoting their conceptual understanding of the content. The Standards indicate less emphasis should be placed on these more traditional approaches, including (a) knowing "facts and information"; (b) studying subject matter disciplines for their own sake; (c) separating science knowledge and process; (d) covering many science topics; (e) conducting brief, single-class period investigations; (f) developing process skills out of context;

and (g) students communicating their ideas and conclusions to the teacher only (NRC 1996, p. 113). By participating in this professional development program, I was hoping to (a) improve my instruction in science; (b) put more emphasis on having my students understand scientific concepts and develop their inquiry abilities; (c) learn science in the context of inquiry, technology, history, and social perspectives; (d) develop an understanding of the nature of science; (e) integrate and develop their content knowledge through application of science processes; (f) study fundamental science concepts in depth by conducting investigations over extended periods of time; and (g) help students communicate their work and ideas within the classroom community to their peers (NRC, p. 113).

After having participated in the professional development program for the past two years, my instruction has greatly changed. I feel confident in my abilities to adapt more traditional lessons and textbook activities to teaching science as inquiry. I've been able to move beyond the idea of *the* scientific method to helping my students understand the diverse ways in which scientists go about their work. My purpose for sharing my experiences in this monograph is to help other teachers like me, who may be less confident in teaching science than they are teaching other subjects, to help them see the value in what the Standards envision for their students, and to find ways to make changes in their own teaching.

This is my fourth year in the classroom. As the teacher in a full-inclusion classroom of 26 students, split between fifth and sixth grades, I find one of my biggest challenges is planning instruction to meet the diverse needs, interests, and abilities of my students. Exploring science-technology-society topics within my science curriculum allowed me to meet this challenge. In this chapter, I will describe the unit I created for use in my classroom, and how features selected for *More Emphasis* in the Standards are reflected in the unit.

An Example of Inquiry Science: Inventions

The unit focused on the theme of *Invention,* which referred to both inventive thought and the products created through invention. In addition to the text series adopted by my district, the resources I used in this unit included a set of nonfiction books that engaged students in all areas of inventions, inventors and machines. I found the following books to be useful in my teaching, highly interesting to my students, and well suited to the diverse reading abilities in my classroom: *The New Way Things Work*; *Eyewitness Books: Invention*; *So You Want to be an Inventor*; *What A Great Idea: Inventions that Changed the World*; and *Accidents May Happen: Fifty Inventions Discovered by Mistake*. The approach I used reflects the greater emphasis on learning subject matter disciplines in the context of technology, and the history and nature of science, rather than studying subject matter disciplines for their own sake.

The Standards emphasize that students should understand science as a human endeavor, in which "women and men of various social and ethnic backgrounds—and with diverse interests, talents, qualities, and motivations—engage in the activities of science, engineering, and related fields" (NRC 1996, p. 170). Additionally, "studying some of these individuals provides further understanding of scientific inquiry, science as a human endeavor, the nature of science, and the relationship between science and society" (p. 171). We began our investigation of science and technology from a historical angle, with students conducting an in-depth inquiry into individuals they considered "inventors." Students developed research projects that revolved around their own interests and questions concerning the inventions and inventors they selected.

Students' investigations spanned a broad spectrum, ranging from Marie Curie and Thomas Edison to more contemporary creators of inventions, including the Rubik's Cube, Gatorade, and Post-It notes. The choices made by peers triggered a discussion of the relative value of particular inventions to society in comparison to others. For example, a student who selected Marie Curie (someone who, in her mind, made significant contributions to society) questioned her classmate's choice to investigate the inventor of Gatorade. This debate highlighted the ways in which "social needs and values influence the direction of technological development" (NRC 1996, p. 169) as well as the diverse social and personal perspectives held by different individuals.

The *NSTA Position Statement on the Nature of Science* (2000) states that, "no single, universal, step-by-step scientific method captures the complexity of doing science." During their research, I asked students to specifically focus on how their inventor or scientist used various scientific processes; this question served as a springboard for classroom discussions about the processes students used in the context of our classroom, and how their activities reflect the nature of science and technology. By sharing the variety of ways that scientists, engineers, and others go about their work, students could dispel the myth that characterizations such as "*the* scientific method" adequately portray scientific and technological endeavors. Additionally, they could begin to develop an understanding of the similarities and differences between scientific inquiry and technological design. While "scientists propose explanations for questions about the natural world, engineers propose solutions relating to human problems, needs and aspirations" (NRC 1996, p. 166).

According to the Standards, "societal changes often inspire questions for scientific research" (NRC, p.169) and, similarly, technological design. This experience also invited students to examine how their inventor was inspired by, and in turn, affected society. To share the products of their research, students created posters and presented them to their classmates in an open forum. This public communication of student ideas and work to classmates reflects the shift in emphasis away from private communication of student work to the teacher alone. The poster session led to discussions of how particular inventions and inventors have the ability to change our society in many ways. Students demonstrated their understanding of both the positive and negative effects that certain inventions had on our society and our quality of life, or as stated in the Standards that "the effect of science on society is neither entirely beneficial nor entirely detrimental" (NRC 1996, p. 169).

The second phase of the unit engaged students in the process of inquiry. Consistent with the areas identified in the Standards for *More Emphasis*, I wanted students to enhance their knowledge and understanding of simple machines by allowing them to study fundamental concepts by conducting in-depth investigations of each machine over an extended period of time. This related to the issue of breadth versus depth in the teaching of science. One of the most beneficial aspects of the inquiry approaches I learned through my professional development has been the realization that devoting an extended period of time to these investigations is necessary to allow students to develop their interests in a particular topic. Before, I would have thought that students would have grown bored or been ready to move on to the next thing, but what I found was that the longer that we were involved in the unit, the more I felt students became engaged in the topic. I really felt they began to develop the big picture in respect to connections among the concepts, as well as applications to their daily lives. The following sections describe the investigations that students participated in for each simple machine studied.

In the initial design of the unit, I envisioned presenting students with a guided inquiry, or question concerning a particular simple machine, in addition to appropriate materials for them to explore and investigate. I did not give students a set of directions for following a particular method. As I had anticipated, I observed that students developed their own ideas of how to explore and investigate each machine. While they worked, I was available to guide students with questions such as "What would happen if you moved the fulcrum?" or "How does the way in which you arrange the pulleys influence the amount of effort you need to exert?" and provide additional materials they required.

Levers

During the first investigation, students explored the three different classes of levers, focusing on

the concepts of effort, fulcrum, and load. Students were given yardsticks (levers), clay and film canisters (fulcrums), and washers (loads) to begin their investigations. (Their own effort was used to raise the load.) I wanted students to recognize the connection between the placement of the fulcrum, and the amount of effort needed in relationship to the load. As a teacher, it was interesting to stand back and watch as students explored with these very basic materials; each had his or her own way of approaching the investigation. Some were concerned immediately

with balance and the placement of the load, while others focused more on the placement of the fulcrum.

After they had sufficient time to explore, we came together as a large group to discuss what the students had observed. This type of discussion, involving students diagramming different levers on the board, provided a place for them to share their ideas, observations, and inferences with their peers, and to

thus learn from them. After this discussion and reinforcement of content knowledge, students were allowed more time to explore with their lever materials. Students began replacing the washers with other items, such as textbooks, to see what impact this would have. The freedom to change and integrate new materials into the investigation gave students the opportunity to enhance their own abilities of inquiry.

Pulleys

For this portion of the unit, students explored using pulley kits, similar to Legos, which our school had purchased for use in our science lab. After a brief class discussion that consisted of introducing students to pulleys and brainstorming examples of everyday objects that used pulleys, the students broke up into small groups to begin constructing pulley systems using the kit materials. After groups had explored a single configuration, I asked students to think of other ways they could use the same materials to build a different type of pulley system. Throughout their investigation, I listened to many groups discuss numerous types of pulley configurations and how they could be used to reduce the amount of effort they needed to exert in order to raise different objects. It seemed as though their hands-on experience with the pulleys was able to spark their ideas of how pulleys function, and how they could be used to accomplish various forms of work in our lives. This investigation supported students in developing abilities of technological design (Content Standard E), specifically in identifying the trade-offs in using pulleys in one configuration versus another.

Wheel and Axle

For this portion of the unit, I asked students to bring in household items that included use of the wheel and axle (size appropriate). Some examples of wheel and axle items that were investigated by students were: toy cars, door knobs, and old wagon wheels. With permission from parents, students were able to take apart these items to investigate the concept of wheel and axle. This allowed students to learn the subject matter through their own processes of investigation, rather than being told the information by the teacher.

After the initial investigation, students participated in combining both a wheel and axle and pulley system in the construction of a "paper pinwheel." Teams were assigned the task of developing a way to raise a load using wind power as the effort. Because of their initial investigations with these two simple machines, students were able to translate their understandings to developing solutions to this problem with much success.

Inclined Planes, Wedges, and Screws

Because of the relationships between inclined planes, wedges and screws, students spent time investigating these three simple machines as a group, rather than singly. Students examined everyday examples of these three simple machines, such as hardware screws, light bulbs, bottle caps, doorstops, wheelchair ramps, stairs, etc. As in our earlier explorations, students had become skilled at identifying where these machines were used in everyday life. This is an important part of understanding science and technology in society (Content Standard E). Students came to realize ways that their quality of life was influenced by the products of technology.

At the beginning of this portion of the unit, students seemed unclear about the initial commonalities among these three simple machines; however, after hands-on investigations and examinations of these machines, students became more confident in their similarities. As a way to help students organize their understandings of the relationships between these items, I had students construct a three-circle Venn diagram.

Unit Assessment

Assessment of student learning outcomes took place on an ongoing basis. Throughout the unit investigations, students collected the work they created—these included drawings of different types of levers with labels of concepts and ideas, such as (a) the placement of the fulcrum, effort, and load, along with their observations of different levers; (b) sketches of pulley systems and notes about the effect of the configuration on the effort required to lift the load; (c) diagrams of their invented products that used simple machines, along with descriptions of how they worked; and (d) Venn diagrams of their ideas about similarities and differences between inclined planes, screws, and wedges.

As students brought in their own household items illustrating various simple machines and included these in their investigations, they added information about these examples along with their work in a *Simple Machines Portfolio.* The portfolio served as a tool for students to organize their ideas and keep track of their work, as well as their thought processes. The portfolios also served as a tool for the teacher to document and assess students' developing understandings of the structure and function of simple machines, and their ability to recognize their applications in the world around them.

Prior to the investigations, the portfolios provided a place for students to reflect on their prior knowledge concerning a particular simple machine and to write a technical description of how they thought each machine functioned. Students were also asked to brainstorm examples at this time. During the investigations, the portfolio provided a place for the students to write about their investigations, including questions they developed, observations they made, and eventually their inferences and understandings of simple machines that evolved throughout the study. The portfolio was also used as a type of "science scrapbook," as students were asked to find pictures of each specific simple machine in action. They found pictures of simple machines in magazines, newspapers, and on the internet, which were then placed in their portfolios. The scrapbook portion of the unit allowed students to bridge connections between their content knowledge of scientific concepts and their real world applications. Along with this, students included a log of Daily Doings With Simple Machines in their portfolio, where they recorded their own personal daily uses of simple machines at home, at school and on the go.

The portfolio also served as a tool for students to use in communicating their ideas to others, not just to the teacher or themselves. Throughout the unit, students met in small groups to share their portfolios and discuss the applications and realities of simple machines in our society. These small-group meetings allowed students to engage in conversations about social perspectives concerning the uses of simple machines, as well as communicate their work and ideas within the unit to their classroom peers. The idea of sharing ideas, observations, and findings in a group, or in a public setting supports the *More Emphasis* idea proposed by the Standards. Instead of communicating their ideas only to the teacher in a more private forum, the students are exposed to the ideas and findings of their classmates as well, which leads to the formation of further ideas and knowledge. Within these small-group conversations, students talked about the results of their investigations, including the similarities and differences that were found among groups. Students were also able to compare the data that they collected within these investigations. The portfolios served as a conversation starter, helping students to remember their observations and encouraging them to explore the observations of their group members. It also allowed students to compare their pictures of each simple machine that students collected in their portfolios, helping students to recognize other objects that fell under each simple machine category. Similarly, the sharing of students' Daily Doings With Simple Machines also allowed them to recognize additional simple machines they use in their daily lives that they possibly hadn't thought of on their own. I also observed students discussing the various questions they had posed throughout their investigations with the simple machines. This aspect of their discussion supports learning in the context of inquiry in that it encourages students to ask further questions within a unit.

Overall, I found the simple machines portfolio to be a successful tool in assessing student learning throughout the unit. In reviewing the students' portfolios, I was able to conclude that all students were able to demonstrate a strong understanding of simple machines—specifically, examples of each type of machine and how these simple machines are a valuable tool in our everyday lives. Many students were able to demonstrate their further knowledge by accurately describing the parts and functions of each machine. Using the portfolio was beneficial in this respect, because it allowed me to see the diverse ways in which my students communicated their ideas. I learned that while some students were not as strong at getting their ideas across in writing, their strength in drawing the simple machines clearly communicated their mastery of the concepts. Other students showed a particular strength in recognizing simple machines in our daily lives and how they are able to make our lives and jobs more effective. The portfolios and group discussions allowed students to share their strengths within simple machines, which furthered the learning and knowledge of everyone within the group.

Summary

I believe this unit was able to support the Standards in terms of learning subject matter in the context of inquiry. It allowed students to consider science in light of personal and social perspectives, in addition to the history and nature of science. The length of the unit allowed students the opportunity to investigate a particular topic over an extended period of time, which extended the depth of their learning. The experiences and investigations provided in this unit also allowed for students to develop an understanding of scientific concepts, while enhancing their abilities of inquiry as well. As I reflect on how I *may* have taught this unit before my experiences with the Learning Science by Inquiry program, I am certain that the unit would have been characterized by the *Less Emphasis* conditions outlined in the Standards. Through my experiences and professional growth within this program, I feel more confident in my abilities to teach and conduct science through inquiry, focusing on the *More Emphasis* conditions, which ultimately provides a much richer science curriculum for my students.

References

Bender, L., and D. King. 2000. *Eyewitness books: Invention.* New York: DK Publishing.

Jones, C. F., and J. O'Brien. 1996. *Accidents may happen: Fifty inventions discovered by mistake.* New York: Bantam Doubleday Dell Books for Young Readers.

Macaulay, D., and N. Ardley. 1998. *The new way things work.* Boston, MA: Houghton Mifflin Company.

National Research Council. (NRC). 1996. *National science education standards.* Washington, DC: National Academy Press.

National Science Teachers Association. 2000. NSTA position statement on the nature of science. In *NSTA handbook.* Arlington, VA: Author.

St. George, J., and D. Small. 2002. *So you want to be an inventor.* New York: Philomel Books.

Tomecek, S., and D. Stuckenschneider. 2003. *What a great idea: Inventions that changed the world.* New York: Scholastic.

What Do We Get to Do Today?

The Middle School Full Option Science System Program

Terry Shaw
University of California, Berkeley

Setting

The Oklahoma City Public Schools (OKCPS) is the second largest school district in the state of Oklahoma with approximately 40,000 students in 60 elementary schools, 10 middle schools, and 9 comprehensive high schools. The student body in the district is 30% Caucasian, 37% African American, 25% Hispanic, and 8% Other. Twenty-three percent have limited English proficiency. Eighty percent receive free or reduced lunch. The graduation rate is 92%.

In 2000, the district received a five-year National Science Foundation (NSF) Urban Systemic Project grant to improve science and math instruction. The 2003–2004 school year was the third in which the Full Option Science System (FOSS) Earth History and Diversity of Life courses were used in the middle schools. Two teachers at Roosevelt Middle School piloted the Populations and Ecosystems course for implementation the following year. Currently, students in 70% of the classrooms in Oklahoma City are experiencing one of the FOSS courses. However, due to administrative decisions, teacher turnover, and changes in teaching assignments, many teachers have not had training for the particular course they are teaching. Oklahoma does not have middle school certification. Approximately half of the middle school teachers in the district are elementary certified and half are certified in secondary science.

Teacher, Student Body, and the Nature of the Classroom

Roosevelt Middle School has approximately 900 students, 60% being Hispanic, 21% Caucasian, 9% African American, and 10% Other. Ninety-five percent of the students receive free or reduced lunch. Brenda Tilley, the science teacher piloting the Populations and Ecosystems course for Oklahoma City, is elementary certified and has taught for six years, this being her third year of middle school science. She has received professional development for the Diversity of Life course, but has not received training for Populations and Ecosystems. Her classroom is an attractively decorated, inviting room with ample space for the approximately 25 students in each of her five classes. Students work in groups of three or four at tables. There is one computer, two outlets, no sinks or running water, and no other modifications for teaching science.

Features of FOSS that address the four National Science Education Standards (NSES) Goals

Goal 1: Produce students who can experience the richness and excitement of knowing about and understanding the natural world (NRC 1996, p. 13).

Throughout all of the FOSS courses, students are engaged in asking questions, making careful observations, identifying discrepancies, designing investigations, gathering and interpreting data, generating evidence, building models to explain results, and defending their conclusions. A deep understanding of science concepts is built through this process of collecting and discussing the meaning of data. Students then use what was learned in an expanded context, either later in the course, or by local applications such as interpreting local rock formations or analyzing household chemical reactions.

Goal 2: Produce students who can use scientific processes and principles in making personal decisions.

Connections are frequently made between the FOSS course content and the world of the middle school student. Whether it is making decisions based on weather data, weighing the trade-offs between human needs and ecosystem sustainability, or understanding the human safety issues involving seat belts and air bags, students are encouraged to apply what they have learned to their daily decisions.

Goal 3: Produce students who can engage intelligently in public discourse and debate about matters of scientific and technological concern.

While working in their collaborative groups, students are encouraged to question, brainstorm, compare data, discuss the validity of their findings, and use their data to reach and defend evidence-based conclusions. Also, students are frequently asked to reflect on the development of their own conceptual understanding and the quality of their work. Numerous assessment tools provide teachers with the information needed to make instructional decisions and keep constant tabs on individual and group concept development.

Goal 4: Produce students who can increase their economic productivity using the knowledge, understanding, and skills of the scientifically literate person in their careers.

Throughout the FOSS courses, students assume the role of scientists involved in highly engaging, conceptually rich investigations. What better way to help students become scientifically literate, independent learners who are ready for the Information Age?

Unique Features of Middle School FOSS

The Middle School Full Option Science System (FOSS 6–8) is comprised of nine courses, each requiring approximately one-third of a year to teach. There are three life science courses: Diversity of Life, Populations and Ecosystems, and Human Brain and Senses; three physical science courses: Electronics, Force and Motion, and Chemical Interactions (spring 2006); and three Earth science courses: Planetary Science, Earth History, and Weather and Water. FOSS and the NSES (NRC 1996) share a commitment to

1. reduce the number of topics to be taught;
2. allow students time to explore and learn important ideas well;
3. have students use the process of inquiry to gather information about the natural world;
4. sequence thinking processes and ideas so that they are developmentally appropriate;
5. create assessments that provide teachers with feedback for instructional decision making and students with feedback on their learning;
6. integrate technologies in a way that extends and enhances the learning experience; and
7. support teachers as intellectual, reflective, constantly improving professionals.

The features that make FOSS unique among middle school science curriculum offerings are: thorough development of concepts, level of inquiry, developmental appropriateness, a comprehensive assessment model, and use of technology,

Thorough Development of Concepts

The emphasis in all of the FOSS courses is to have students develop a deep understanding of central science concepts over time in an engaging context. The concepts learned in one investigation are applied when solving problems and studying related situations in subsequent investigations. For example, two of the many concepts developed in Populations and Ecosystems are reproductive potential and limiting factor. As with all major concepts in FOSS courses, students start with concrete experiences, gathering data before moving on to more abstract levels of the concept. By the end of the second day of the course, each group of students has observed adult milkweed bugs, built a large zip bag habitat, and introduced a male and a female bug into their new home. The following class period comments can be heard throughout the room.

"Look! Our bugs are mating!"

"One of ours is sucking water out of the paper towel and the other one has its proboscis stuck in a sunflower seed. Do they suck the insides out of the seeds? That's so cool!"

When students walk in the door, they usually gravitate to their milkweed bug habitats to see if any changes have occurred. When there are significant changes, the class takes a few minutes to make formal observations. Over the next 7–10 days, excitement continues to build as students observe newly laid clutches of eggs and tiny nymphs as the eggs hatch. Students draw the habitats, and record the location and number of egg clutches, the number of eggs

Figure 1. Students with milkweed bug habitat.

in a clutch, the number of eggs that hatch, and the length of time required for each new development.

About a week after the students record the first nymphs in their habitat, they make some alarming observations.

S1: Mrs. Tilley, there are spiders in our bag! How did they get in there?

S2: The bottom of our bag has tiny dead bugs all over it! What killed them?

As several other students also notice the "spiders" and "dead bugs" in their habitats, Mrs. Tilley, the teacher, moves from group to group and asking questions.

Mrs. T: Are the spiders alive?

S3: No.

Mrs. T: Why do you think they are spiders?

S3: Look at them, they're dead spiders!

Mrs. T: How many legs do they have?

After a pause while several students examine the "spiders" more closely with hand lenses, "They have six legs."

S4: Then they aren't spiders. Spiders have eight legs; insects have six.

S2: See, I told you they were dead bugs, but what killed them?

Mrs. T: How many live bugs do you have compared to the number you had before?

After a pause while several students count, "Our habitat has about the same number."

S2: So does ours. That doesn't make sense. How could so many die and we still have the same number of living bugs?"

After pondering this mystery, students are given an article to read on the life cycle of the milkweed bug. The class expresses a great deal of relief when they learn that the "spiders" and "dead bugs" were actually exoskeletons that were shed when the nymphs molted.

The milkweed bug habitats are observed for a few minutes each week to monitor the changes in the bugs and record the time it takes for them to pass through each stage as they mature into adults and begin to mate. When students have collected information about the complete milkweed bug life cycle, they calculate the theoretical reproductive potential of a single pair of milkweed bugs for one year. The number is astronomical! What keeps the population of milkweed bugs from overrunning the classroom? Students brainstorm all the variables that might limit the population size of the bugs. Using the CD-ROM (described later), students conduct virtual experiments on milkweed bug reproduction. By changing one variable at a time, they determine how each variable affects the size of the population. This is followed by a reading assignment on how limiting factors manifest themselves in various situations.

This instructional sequence, sometimes called a learning cycle, is typical of all FOSS courses. Students in Populations and Ecosystems became engaged by observing an intriguing living organism. They then explore the characteristics of the bugs and collect data. During the concept development stage, students make sense of their data, generating and reinforcing major scientific ideas: organism, population, life cycle, reproductive potential and limiting factor. Vocabulary is introduced as students need precise language for concepts they have already formed. Next is the expansion-of-the-idea stage, when the concepts are expanded and applied to new situations. In this case, students used the concepts they had learned to complete the computer simulation of milkweed bug reproduction, while the reading on limiting factors expanded these ideas to other situations. Reading assignments in FOSS are given after students have made observations and acquired enough experience to make the reading meaningful.

In the second investigation of the Populations and Ecosystems course, students construct terraria and aquaria. Students introduce various plants, earthworms, isopods, and slugs into their terraria. They place Elodea, Lemna, Gammarus, tubifex worms, aquatic snails, and guppies in their aquaria. Over the next few weeks they observe the life cycles of several of these organisms, studying food chains and food webs. In making their observations and collecting data, students develop a working knowledge of concepts such as life cycle, individual, population, community, ecosystem, biotic, abiotic, producer, consumer, decomposer, and trophic level. All of these concepts are learned and developed in the same way that reproductive potential and limiting factor are learned—through observations, data collection, and application of the information in context over time.

Level of Inquiry

In the first course in the FOSS life science strand for middle school, Diversity of Life, students begin by wrestling with the concepts of living and nonliving. This is not a simple exercise, because most middle school students believe that if something occurs naturally and moves by itself, it is alive. In order to challenge their ideas, pairs of students are asked to classify the objects in pictures as living or nonliving

Figure 2. Students with terrarium.

and explain their reasons. If they cannot agree, the picture goes in tan undecided pile. Discussions like the following are common:

> *S1: A tree is nonliving.*

> *S2: But it IS living! It moves!*

> *S1: No, it doesn't! That's just the wind moving it.*

> *S2: Oh, I guess you're right.*
Or:

> *S3: The Sun is alive, because it moves, and everything needs it to stay alive.*

By the end of the activity, there are usually more pictures in the undecided pile, in either the living or nonliving pile. For the next few days, students are involved in several guided-inquiry activities that include the concepts of living and nonliving, focusing students' thinking on a set of characteristics shared by all living things. Throughout the course, these concepts are revisited numerous times in different contexts, helping students internalize the shared characteristics of all living organisms. Consistent, repeated exposure to these core ideas in biology will, in time, move students away from their misconceptions (Driver, Squires, Rushworth, and Wood-Robinson 1994).

As the Diversity of Life course progresses, the investigations become less teacher centered and more student centered. Many of the investigations in FOSS courses are designed to stimulate predictable questions, which become the impetus for the next investigation. Thus, from the students' perspective, the course is driven by their questions.

Toward the end of the Diversity of Life course, students are making observations independently, framing questions, and designing experiments. For example, after observing the Madagascar hissing cockroach, students typically ask questions about its food and habitat preferences and what its native habitat is like. They then design experiments to answer these questions, decide what constitutes evidence, compare their results with other groups, and investigate discrepancies in results. Students move from guided inquiry at the beginning of Diversity of Life to independent, open inquiry (NRC 2000, p. 29) toward the end. One of the central goals of all FOSS courses is to help students develop the skills they need to become independent learners and interpreters of the natural world.

Developmental Appropriateness

FOSS investigations are carefully designed so that the thinking processes and science content are appropriate for the students' level of cognitive development. As one middle school teacher stated, "Those FOSS people seem to have figured out exactly what my kids can learn." More information on The Thinking Behind FOSS is available at *www.deltaeducation.com/foss/thinking.html*.

FOSS has organized thinking processes as well as content into a developmental sequence related to cognitive development. Although students possess the capacity to use all the scientific thinking processes to some degree throughout their lives, some processes are more powerful at certain ages. Most middle school students are in the late concrete stage of cognitive development, with some beginning the transition to early formal thought. At this time, their capacity to understand ideas that are remote in time and space improves. The FOSS middle school courses take advantage of these expanding skills in inferential logic (Lowery 1998; Restak and Grubin 2001). Students make inferences about the principles that govern the activities in the natural world and the importance of the results of their investigations. For example, the students use information from their experiments with the Madagascar hissing cockroaches and from observations of structure and behavior, to infer what the native habitat of the cockroach would be. Middle school students delight in activities that require this type of high-level inferential logic (Shayer and Adey 1981).

A Comprehensive Assessment Model

Three overarching goals assessed throughout the FOSS program are (a) science content, (b) conducting investigations, and (c) building explanations. The instructional design and the FOSS assessment model are interconnected to closely monitor student progress in these goal areas. For example, during an early investigation in the Diversity of Life course, students learn that all life requires water. Later in the course, they place a stalk of celery in a vial of water. By the next day, much of the water is gone. Students usually conclude that the water went into the celery. They design and conduct an experiment to test this idea (conducting investigations). They discover, however, that little, if any, of the missing water is in the celery. Further investigation suggests that the water moved through the celery instead of accumulating in it (building explanations). Students also observe the vascular system of the celery that transports the water. A reading assignment explains the importance of transpiration in moving water and nutrients throughout the plant (science content). Student sheets, lab reports, teacher checklists, end-of-investigation exams, and formative assessment tools are used to continually assess all three of the major learning goals throughout the course.

FOSS makes an important distinction between formative and summative assessment. Different forms of formative assessment are embedded throughout the instructional materials and are frequently indistinguishable from the normal classroom activities. These tools give the teacher information about what students understand, what misconceptions they hold, and what they may be confused about while instruction is taking place, not after they have taken the test and it is too late. As one teacher aptly stated, "Formative assessment eliminates the surprises."

The FOSS formative assessment model facilitates the development of rich, well-structured knowledge. One type of formative assessment is the Quick Write, which provides insight into student understanding before they receive formal instruction. For example, in the Populations and Ecosystems course, students are asked, "Where does your body get the energy it needs in order to do all the things you do?" Most students will list sleep, water, and exercise as sources of energy in addition to food. After instruction, students revise their original response. These revised responses can then be used as summative assessments. Research shows that when students are asked to reflect on their thinking, and when teachers use the information gained from formative assessment to modify instruction, student achievement improves substantially (Black and William 1998).

Use of Technology

Another unique feature of middle school FOSS is the multimedia CD-ROMs that were developed for each FOSS course. The multimedia is an integral part of the instruction. The myriad resources on the CD include virtual experiments, virtual field trips, visual databases, instructional animations, and a simulated microscope, as well as teacher resources (such as lab technique videos), for procedures that may be unfamiliar. In addition, the CDs for the more recent courses are html-based so that numerous internet resources can be accessed directly from the CD. When the multimedia for earlier courses are revised, they will also be html based.

In addition to the CDs, other examples of technology used in the courses include multimeters in Electronics, microscopes and electronic balances in Diversity of Life, weather instruments in Weather and Water, and electronic carts to record time and motion data in Force and Motion.

The Teacher as an Intellectual, Reflective, Continually Improving Professional

Three of the biggest challenges teachers face in moving from a textbook-driven curriculum to an inquiry-based curriculum are: (a) content knowledge, (b) feeling comfortable with the student and materials management, and (c) having the questioning skills and teaching strategies to successfully lead inquiry investigations. This third challenge, moving from teaching by dispensing information to teaching by creating a rich, inquiry environment, and then asking probing questions, is the most difficult transition for most teachers to make.

The FOSS Teacher Guide provides strong support in all three of these areas. Each FOSS course consists of 8–10 investigations, most requiring four to seven class periods to complete. Each investigation begins with a section titled "Scientific and Historical Background" that includes the content information a teacher needs in order to successfully teach that investigation, as well as information about frequent student misconceptions. Next is a Getting Ready section that describes materials preparation and management. The Conducting the Investigation section provides the teacher with a step-by-step teaching outline, including key questions, common student responses, ideas for helping students transform their misconceptions, and suggestions for classroom management and assessment opportunities.

No matter what a teacher's background might be, the Teacher Guide provides him or her with the support needed to successfully teach the inquiry-based course. The FOSS Teacher Guide can be thought of as a high-quality, individualized, professional development program. When asked about the Teacher Guide, teachers typically make comments such as: "The guide is very specific and easy to follow." "I never would have thought of all those great questions to ask kids." "The assessment ideas have helped me understand a lot more about what students are thinking and where they are having problems." "The Teacher Guide, with its ideas for assessment and inquiry strategies, has caused me to think more about how to be an effective teacher than I ever have before."

Evidence of the Effectiveness of Middle School FOSS

Studies examining curricula that include the FOSS K–6 Program (which has been available for more than a decade) have shown improvements of the areas of (a) science achievement (Tempel 2003; Raghavan 2001), (b) achievement in writing and reading (Valadez and Freve 2002; Klentschy, Garrison, and 2001), and (c) narrowing the achievement gap (Kim, et al. 2001). A list of references on the effectiveness of the FOSS curriculum is available at *http://lhsfoss.org/scope/research/index.html*.

Because middle school FOSS is a continuation of the same learning philosophy, and is developed by many of the same science educators, one would expect the results to be similar to the FOSS K–6 data. However, the FOSS Middle School Program is so new (the first courses premiered in the fall of 2000 and the last of the nine courses is due out in 2006) that only two multiyear studies addressing student achievement are available. Those results are included below.

The Oklahoma City Public Schools (OKCPS) began including Earth History in eighth grade and Diversity of Life in seventh grade during the 2001–2002 school year. These courses replaced portions of the previously adopted curriculum. The graphs below (Figures 3a and 3b) show the increased achievement on the science portion of the Iowa Test of Basic Skills (ITBS) for students in FOSS classes as compared to students in classes where the teacher did not use FOSS (Garner

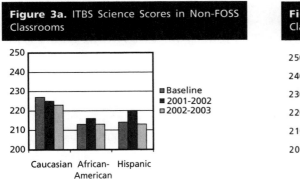

Figure 3a. ITBS Science Scores in Non-FOSS Classrooms

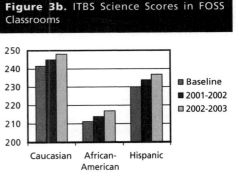

Figure 3b. ITBS Science Scores in FOSS Classrooms

2003). The OKCPS FOSS implementation requires teachers to complete 30 hours or more of formal training. During the 2002–2003 school year, approximately 50% of the seventh- and eighth-grade teachers had completed the training and used one of the FOSS courses in their class. The elementary curriculum is textbook centered.

The Oklahoma Priority Academic Student Skills (PASS) Test is a criterion-referenced test aligned with the Oklahoma science standards, which emphasize science processes as well as content. The science portion of the test is administered only at eighth grade in the middle schools. Data collected by OKCPS (Figure 4) shows that the more criterion-referenced professional development teachers received in standards-based instruction, the higher the student scores on the science portion of the test (Garner 2003). Teachers receiving fewer than 30 hours of professional development would not be using the FOSS materials.

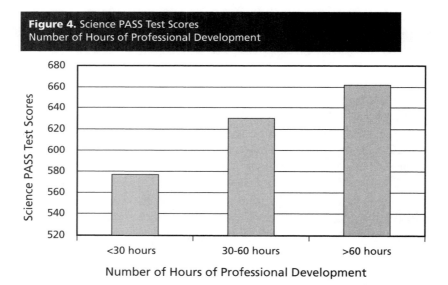

Figure 4. Science PASS Test Scores
Number of Hours of Professional Development

For the 2002 PASS Test, approximately 30% of the students had Earth History in the eighth grade as their only FOSS course and 70% received no FOSS instruction. For the 2003 test, approximately 15% of the eighth graders had experienced Diversity of Life in seventh and Earth History in eighth grade, 50% had one course or the other, and 35% did not have either course. The goal in the district is to have all classrooms using FOSS in the near future. Even with only partial implementation of the FOSS program, the graph in Figure 5 shows the narrowing of the science achievement gap on the eighth-grade Oklahoma PASS test from 2002 to 2003. The African American/Caucasian gap decreased by 5% and the Hispanic/Caucasian gap decreased by 13% (Garner 2003).

In a second study, one school in the Fayette County (Kentucky) Public Schools district adopted FOSS for their entire science curriculum starting in the 1999–2000 school year, using kits from the

Figure 5. Percent Satisfactory Scores on Science PASS Test

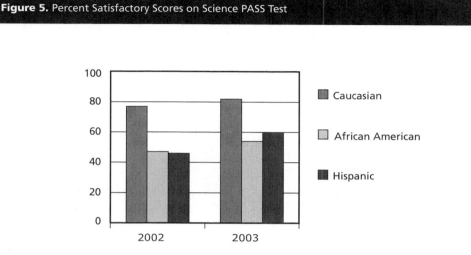

national trials. Figure 6 shows a comparison between Crawford Middle School and the district average scores for the 11 middle schools in the district (Kentucky Department of Education 2004). The graph shows the percentage point gains in the combined "Proficient" and "Distinguished" categories on the seventh-grade Kentucky Core Content Test (KCCT). Crawford Middle School was the only middle school using the FOSS materials. The elementary curriculum in the district was primarily FOSS K–6 and Science Curriculum Improvement Study (SCIS II).

Figure 6. Gains in Proficient and Distinguished Categories Between 1999 and 2003

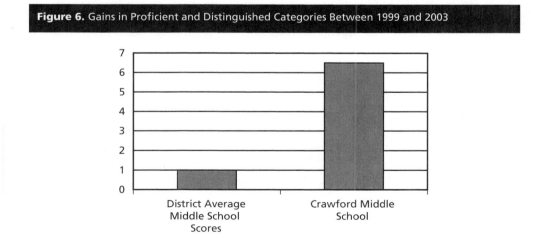

As impressive as the results from Fayette County Kentucky and Oklahoma City are, even more impressive is the level of involvement of students. They frequently come into class with comments such as, "What do we get to do today?" It is common for students to share thinking that happened outside science class. "I thought about what happened to that water in the celery last night, and I thought of a new experiment we could do," or "After the flower dissection yesterday, we went home and three of us started dissecting some of the flowers there. We found some flowers that weren't like the ones we had here." Students can be overheard in other classes or at lunch talking about the neat things that happened in science that day. Comments during class such as, "This is tight!" or students enthusiastically sharing their observations with those at another table are common.

David Garner (2004), the project director for the Oklahoma City USP, stated, "One thing that has impressed me about the FOSS curriculum is the inquiry and pedagogy skills that teachers learn while teaching it. The teachers then use these skills even if they are not teaching a FOSS unit."

Summary

With FOSS curriculum, students are introduced to content through exploration of and asking questions about their natural world. They develop science concepts and process skills as they work as scientists to collect and interpret data in order to explain what they have observed. Science concepts and process skills are reinforced and expanded as students use them in a variety of contexts over time. Assessment is seamlessly interwoven into the instruction, giving students and teachers frequent feedback on concept and process skill attainment. Intellectual demands of the FOSS curriculum are designed to match the students' level of cognitive development. When all of these essential ingredients are included in a content-rich, inherently interesting, inquiry-oriented curriculum, and when teachers receive appropriate professional development, student achievement improves significantly.

Shuler (2004) points out that several conditions are required for sustained systemic reform: (a) exemplary curriculum, (b) teacher professional development, (c) student and program assessment, (d) administrative and community support, and (e) materials support. The FOSS middle school curriculum provides the exemplary curriculum and the student assessment portions of this formula for success.

References

Black, P., and D. William. 1998. Inside the black box: Raising standards through classroom assessment. *Phi Delta Kappan* 80: 139–148.

Driver, R., A. Squires, P. Rushworth, and V. Wood-Robinson. 1994. *Making sense of secondary science.* London: Routledge.

Garner, D. 2003. *The new ERA: Eliminating random arrows. Year three annual report.* National Science Foundation Grant #ESR-0084836.

Garner, D. 2004. Personal communication. February 16, 2004.

Kentucky Department of Education. 2004. Data for Fayette County public schools. Available online at *http://max.kde.state.ky.us.*

Kim, J., L. Crasco, R. Smith, G. Johnson, A. Karantonis, and D. Leavitt. Academic excellence for all urban students. 2001. *www.systemic.com/pdfs/Booklet.pdf.*

Klentschy, M., L. Garrison, and O. M. Amaral. 2001. *Valle imperial project in science: four-year comparison of student achievement data 1995–1999. Research report.* National Science Foundation Grant #ESI-9731274.

Lowery, L. 1998. *The scientific thinking processes.* Berkeley: Graduate School of Education/Lawrence Hall of Science, University of California.

National Research Council (NRC). 2000. *Inquiry and the national education standards: A guide for teaching and learning.* Washington, DC: National Academy Press.

National Research Council (NRC). 1996. *The national science education standards.* Washington, DC: National Academy Press.

Raghavan, K. 2001. Student outcomes in a local systemic change project. *School Science and Mathematics Journal* 101: 417–426. Available online at *lsc-net.terc.edu/do.cfm/paper/7118/show/use_set-lsc_init*

Restak, R. and D. Grubin. 2001. *The secret life of the brain.* Washington, DC: Joseph Henry Press.

Shayer, M., and P. Adey. 1981. *Towards a science of science teaching.* London: Heinemann Educational Books.

Tempel, C. 2003. *Project inquiry: Effects of professional development on science achievement.* Charleston and Berkeley County schools study. May.

Valadez, J., and Y. Freve. 2002. *A preliminary summary of findings from a study of the effects of hands-on/inquiry-based instruction on SAT9 reading scores.* Available online at *http://sustainability2002.terc.edu/invoke.cfm/page/143*

ARIES:
Science as Discovery...
and Discovery as Science!

R. Bruce Ward
Harvard-Smithsonian Center for Astrophysics
Cambridge, Massachusetts

Janice Catledge
Alice Harte Elementary School
New Orleans, Lousiana

Kathy Price
Naaba Ani Elementary School
Bloomfield, New Mexico

Introduction

P roject ARIES, developed at the Harvard-Smithsonian Center for Astrophysics (CfA), beginning in 1991, was funded by the National Science Foundation (grants MDR 91-54113 and ESI 95-53845), with additional support from Harvard University and the Smithsonian Institution. ARIES is a modular, astronomy-based physical science curriculum for students in grades 3–8. The curriculum is informed by research done at the CfA's Science Education Department (SED) and elsewhere into the effect of prior ideas on student learning. ARIES provides classroom teachers with effective pedagogical strategies to help students construct new understandings of the natural world. Over a ten-year period, scientists and science educators at the SED developed explorations and materials for eight self-contained modules. Each module has numerous intercurricular and multicultural extensions. A companion project, Project SEDNet (NSF grants TE 9819459 and ES 0101958), provides professional development opportunities and support in regions around the nation, in collaboration with more than 25 Challenger Learning Centers (CLCs).

Settings

Each of the two coauthors whose classrooms are featured in this article has used ARIES modules for more than seven years. The Naaba Ani Elementary School is located in Bloomfield, New Mexico. Bloomfield is a rural, culturally diverse community in the northwest corner of New Mexico, an area commonly known as the Four Corners. Beginning in 1993 and following, Kathy Price piloted and field-tested six of the eight ARIES modules with fourth- and fifth-grade students. Naaba Ani Elementary School serves about 620 children in grades 3–5. The school houses nine or ten classes of each grade level. One other school in the district has two classes for each of these grades. The average class sizes over the last five years have been about 24 students.

The school district serves 21 small isolated localities within a 1,500 square mile area. Bloomfield's student population is 34% Native American (Navajo), 30% Hispanic, and 36% Anglo, reflecting the region's diversity. There are eight schools in the district, with about 3,200 K–12 students. During the past five years, the district's enrollment has dropped by 8% and the characteristics of the district's student population have shifted. There have been large declines in middle-class Anglo population and decreases in socioeconomic status. In 2002–2003, 62% of the students qualified for free and reduced-fee lunch, up 5% in the last five years. The Bloomfield School District home page is *www.bsin.k12.nm.us*.

The Alice M. Harte Elementary School is in New Orleans, Louisiana, one of the 81 elementary schools in this large, urban district. The New Orleans system serves about 75,000 K–12 students in its 134 individual schools. In Harte there are a little more than 700 students in kindergarten through sixth grade, with four classes at each grade level. The average class size at Harte is about 25 students. Nearly 40% of the students are African American, and 52% are white. The remaining students are Hispanic (4%), Asian American (3%), and Native American (1%). Thirty-five percent of the Harte students qualify for free or reduced-fee lunch. The Harte demographics do not fully reflect those of the overall New Orleans district, where about 92% of the students are African American and about 5% are white. Asian Americans, Hispanics, and other groups account for the remaining 3%–4% of the student population across the district.

From 1993 forward, coauthor Janice Catledge and a second teacher piloted and field-tested four ARIES modules with third and fourth graders at the Harte school. There is a sequence now where about half of the children complete one of the modules during the third grade and a second module in the fourth grade. Catledge team teaches with a colleague, but is responsible for all the science instruction in the two classes. Information about the Harte school is found at *www.nops. k12.la.us/SchoolWebs/Harte/default.htm*.

Changing the Emphases in Science Education

The blueprint for changing science education outlined in the National Science Education Standards (NSES) is both multilayered and extensively detailed. This blueprint provides both a destination, and a map to that destination, for those working to improve science education. Much of that mapping calls for changing emphases—from many of the current practices to exemplary models of teaching and learning that capture how science is done.

While the ARIES developers began their work in 1991, well in advance of the Standards, the curriculum mirrors in most every respect the call for changing emphases in the NSES Teaching, Professional Development, Assessment, and Content and Inquiry Standards. Student science journals (described below) are part of every module. Nearly all of the NSES teaching standards are integrated into the journal format, where the emphases are on deep understanding for each individual student, active and extended inquiry, and ongoing assessment of that understanding. The sequence of explorations in the student science journals reflects the shared sense of scientists and science educators have about the overall learning objectives in ARIES—that is, the objective in any given module is to help students deepen their understanding of one big idea, or at most two big ideas, in astronomy, space science, or physical science.

Teachers need to experience the science of ARIES as would their students, first in workshops, and later in the classrooms along with the students. SED staff believes it takes at least two years for most teachers to internalize key concepts in the department curricula. Workshops are then only the initial step in the type of professional development carried out by the SED and emphasized in the Standards. The profile of physical and space science education when developers began work on ARIES is revealing. Elementary and middle school teachers were less prepared to teach these sciences than all other sciences, had the lowest confidence in these domains, resulting in these science subjects being taught less than all the others (Nelson, Weiss, and Conway 1992; Weiss 1994). Yet the interest in these sciences, especially astronomy, was very high (NSTA 1990; Culotta 1990; Simpson and Oliver 1990). To help address the shortcomings identified in the studies, ARIES emphasizes investigatory learning for both students and teachers. The science of ARIES is inextricably intertwined with the exemplary, research-based pedagogy. As with students, ARIES teachers must reflect on their own learning, a necessary step so that they may also reflect on their teaching practices. In all these ways, ARIES reflects two *More Emphases* to the changes in professional development envisioned in the Standards.

The Standards call for less emphasis on easily measured, discrete science knowledge assessed by finding out what students do not know, and more emphasis on assessing rich, well-structured knowledge and science reasoning by determining what students do understand. ARIES emphasizes that on which the Standards place greater emphasis for student and teacher alike. Learning is seen as building new models of understanding, not borrowing the ideas of others. The student science journals become a daily record of that learning. Students are asked to make predictions, observations, and records of natural phenomena, using these steps to build new models for understanding the world. This new understanding is encapsulated in the final part of each exploration—an embedded assessment component—where the students write out or draw what they have come to know.

In ARIES and the Standards there is greater emphasis placed on conceptual understanding, inquiry, history and nature of science, extended investigations, and using evidence from nature to draw inferences about the world. Few subjects lend themselves so well to all these elements of good science as do astronomy and physical science. Some modules are designed to historically reflect the growth in understanding of the central themes. Each ARIES module is an exemplar for the nature of science, a feature emphasized in all the work of the SED. As noted here and elsewhere, modules are framed around only one or two major concepts, and do not emphasize facts and information that detract from deep understanding.

Teachers, Students, and Classrooms

Kathy Price has 26 years teaching experience in the Four Corners area of New Mexico. The majority of this time has been at Naaba Ani Elementary School. In 1993, Price was chosen, through competitive selection, to become a part of the Project ARIES teacher development team. Piloting and field-testing ARIES modules also included extensive formative and summative assessment, and comparison testing done as part of the project. Simultaneously, Price worked with a colleague to integrate ARIES into the curriculum, also preparing her colleague to teach the ARIES modules. Currently, she is the district's sole math/science specialist and her colleague is now the Naaba Ani ARIES teacher. Price spends the majority of her time on instructional coaching, mentoring, and conducting a variety of professional development initiatives for her district, surrounding districts, and at the state level. She has been a presenter for ARIES and other science sessions at numerous national and regional NSTA conventions. Since 1999, Price has served as one of the three instructors at Project SEDNet's two-week summer institutes, with responsibility for preparing CLC team members to become ARIES professional development leaders.

Over the past several years, Price has conducted a variety of ARIES-related professional development programs. San Juan Community College in nearby Farmington, New Mexico, received Eisenhower funds to promote Project ARIES; over 80 teachers benefited from these two-day workshops, which included teachers receiving the complete modules (*Exploring Light and Color* and *Exploring Energy*). For seven years, Price has taught a science methods course through the University of New Mexico and has incorporated ARIES into this preservice teachers course. She has also conducted ARIES workshops at the Challenger Learning Centers in Peoria, Arizona, and Tucson, Arizona.

In 1996, Janice Catledge received the Presidential Award for Mathematics and Science Teaching; she was the Louisiana awardee for elementary science. She has 23 years of teaching experience, mostly in the New Orleans region. Catledge joined ARIES in 1993 as part of the project's teacher development team. She piloted and field-tested four ARIES modules in the Harte school, participating as well in the project's formative and summative assessments, and in the comparison testing. In addition to her classroom responsibilities, Catledge has conducted a variety of ARIES-based professional development workshops in the New Orleans area, in part as outreach from the CLC in Baton Rouge, Louisiana. She has given numerous other workshops throughout the state, elsewhere in the East and Northeast, and at many national and regional NSTA conventions. She is a coauthor of the K–5 science curriculum guide for the New Orleans Parish Schools and currently serves on the state science testing committee. Catledge is also one of three Project SEDNet summer institute instructors. In recent years, she has made extensive trips to Japan, Australia, and Latin America, returning always with new astronomical and science enrichment activities for her students. She studied science instruction in Japan as a participant in the Fulbright Memorial Teacher Fund Program and monarch butterflies in Mexico.

The students in the fourth- and fifth-grade Naaba Ani ARIES classrooms generally reflect the ethnic diversity of the school district. However, a portion of the gifted student population of the school was placed in these two classrooms as part of the district's special education inclusion model. The Bloomfield school district has had an average mobility rate (students moving in and out of schools) of 25% for the last four years, but the mobility rate in the ARIES classrooms for the same period was less than 10%. As noted above, while diverse, the Harte classrooms do not mirror in every respect the overall student population patterns in the New Orleans schools.

All ARIES teachers use an approach that is discovery based, focused on a limited number of big ideas in astronomy, space science, or physical science, ideas such as the seasons, the motions of the Earth, light, color, or time. Each module features a sequence of explorations, 15–20 in number, with one, or at most two, conceptual goals. For example, in the module on time, the overall conceptual goal is that children will come away realizing that to find, tell, or keep time, one needs to construct apparatus that take advantage of repetitive patterns in nature. In the module on waves, the conceptual goal is to have children come to see that a wave is a model helpful in understanding phenomena of sound and (in part) light.

Program Description/Philosophy and Pedagogy of ARIES

The excitement of astronomy, solar system missions, and deep space exploration has become a staple for much of the public. In surveys done by the SED, nearly all students and teachers report being very interested in everything from comets to manned missions, from Hubble photos of stars forming to images of Earth from space. ARIES starts with this intrinsic interest in astronomy by students and teachers as an entrée to major themes, such as those mentioned previously as well as others such as motion, force, and energy. This includes the rising and setting of the Sun, the Moon's changing appearance or the gradual yet perceptual shift in seasons. ARIES uses students' everyday experiences and observations of these more common astronomical phenomena, accessible in any location, as the logical setting for constructing new models to understand the natural world.

The pedagogy of ARIES is embedded in all features of the curriculum, which includes explorations designed by scientists and teachers, student science journals, and a comprehensive teacher manual. Students build and use simple and affordable apparatus to actively investigate and observe a variety of patterns in nature, both indoors and outdoors. They use the ARIES Suntracker to trace the path and location of the Sun from week to week and season to season; they investigate the effects of the changing orientation of the Earth to the Sun in the ARIES astronomy lab; and they use an inexpensive ripple tank to observe and study wave patterns. From such investigations the students can build, test, and modify their models for understanding nature, and, most importantly, establish a firm foundation for later learning. For ARIES classrooms this is the primary learning objective—students draw on their observations to construct models for understanding nature's behavior, and then use these models to predict that behavior in new circumstances. ARIES teachers become skilled in listening and questioning, and are attentive to the students' needs to rethink ideas that are not compatible with their observations.

Program Description /Research Basis of ARIES

Since 1985, the CfA's Science Education Department (SED) has been documenting and studying students' misconceptions or prior ideas, which persist in spite of some of the very best science teaching. The department's work in this area is widely known through its Science Media Group's (SMG's) award-winning videotape *A Private Universe,* which documents the way misconceptions block deeper understanding. More recently, the SMG's *Minds of Our Own,* shown on public television, reinforced that research. As a result, the SED has designed its curricula around explorations and classroom teaching strategies to help students rethink their personal models of the natural world. Where these models are not supported by observation, it becomes necessary for students to rethink their ideas.

The SED has a deep interest in assessment, especially in finding ways to determine what students are able to do, or what they do know. To further that objective, the ARIES developers created *constructed-answer* questions for each module. These questions permit students to write out, or even draw, their answers. Such answers can be deeper and richer than with other assessment measures, providing a powerful means for teachers to determine what the students have come to know. The developers of ARIES also carried out a comparison assessment program, testing like numbers of ARIES and non-ARIES students studying the same astronomy themes. On 15 of the 17 test items, ARIES students significantly outperformed their non-ARIES colleagues.

Program Description/Curriculum and Professional Development

There are eight ARIES modules: *Exploring Time*; *Exploring Light and Color*; *Exploring the Earth in Motion*; *Exploring Energy*; *Exploring Motion and Forces*; *Exploring Waves*; *Exploring Moon and Stars*; and *Exploring Navigation*. For each module, there is a teacher manual with complete science and history background notes, tips for adult helpers, intercurricular extensions, and detailed assessment strategies which include a *constructed-answer* pretest/posttest with scoring rubrics. Student science journals are part of each module. The pedagogical approach of ARIES is carefully built into the student science journal. Each exploration begins with an elicitation of the student's prior ideas and their own original questions, followed in turn by the exploration itself and then a section for interpreting the results. This final section includes an embedded assessment prompt where students write on "what they know about" the exploration's science focus. While many of the take-home items constructed as part of ARIES can be made from supplies readily available in classrooms, some explorations require specialized materials, which are included in the apparatus bins for each module.

The SED directs a nationwide professional development program in collaboration with 25 Challenger Learning Centers (CLCs), located in 20 different states. Co-investigating with the SED is the Christa Corrigan McAuliffe CLC on the campus of Framingham State College. Known as Project SEDNet—for the Science Education Department Network—the goal of the program is to increase the quality and quantity of professional development in physical and space science for classroom teachers. The Project SEDNet website, listing the participating CLCs, is found at *www.christa.org/SEDNet/index.htm*. Teams composed of teachers and staff members from CLCs attend two 2-week summer institutes at the SED where they prepare as ARIES workshop leaders. Their preparation includes working through all the modules, as would students, led by the SEDNet leaders (including the co-authors) who model throughout a discovery approach to science teaching. Returning to their home CLCs, the teams provide a range of professional development options for teachers using one or more of the ARIES modules. This includes adoption workshops and one-day introductory seminars. The seminars are sponsored in conjunction with the ARIES publisher, Charlesbridge Publishing. Teachers using

ARIES modules receive continued support through CLC focus meetings as well as through the SEDNet e-mail network and website.

Featured Classrooms: Naaba Ani Elementary School

Beginning in 1993, Price and her colleague piloted and then field-tested six ARIES modules (*Exploring Time*, *Exploring Light and Color*, *Exploring Energy*, *Exploring the Earth in Motion*, *Exploring the Moon and Stars*, and *Exploring Waves*) in fourth- and fifth-grade classrooms. As the modules were published, they were integrated into one of several grades. *Exploring Time*, *Exploring Energy*, and *Exploring the Earth in Motion* are used in the fourth grade. The same cohort of students moves on to the fifth grade where the students work with *Exploring Light and Color* and *Exploring the Moon and Stars*. Most of these same students then move to the only middle school in the district and complete the *Exploring Motion and Forces* module during sixth grade.

There are three "official" science lessons per week averaging 45–60 minutes in duration. However, many of the ARIES activities—both the science explorations and the intercurricular extensions—are integrated into each week's lessons. Students work in learning teams of four or five at small tables. Teachers are readily able to manage materials by having students store any specialized ARIES apparatus in large plastic bins. Parents are welcome in the classrooms at any time to either observe or to help students construct apparatus or make observations. The ARIES classes in Naabi Ani and elsewhere are neither quiet nor passive, with the teachers at the center. Rather, students continually converse within and across groups when doing the explorations, asking questions of one another as they make recordings in their ARIES Science Journals. Questions such as "How come…?" or "What is happening…?" flow freely, often spilling over to the playgrounds, other classes, or the teachers' lounges. Many find their way into dinner conversations of both students and teachers.

Price and her colleague have woven the ARIES modules into broader 6–8 week thematic units used across the grade level. Fourth graders begin the year with the *Dig-It, an Adventure Into Archeology* theme. The ARIES *Exploring Time* module provides a perfect science match to this theme. The New Mexico sunshine creates a great setting for shadow explorations and the fall or autumnal equinox occurs during the time the module is being used. Moreover, students continue to take shadow readings even after completing the module. In particular, students take new shadow readings near the times of the winter solstice and the spring or vernal equinox. One year an enterprising class of fourth graders decided to create more wristwatch sundials during the *Exploring Time* module and sell them as a fundraiser. During recess, this class was busy on the playground helping a variety of students from all cultures orient their "watches" to find the time. Another year a very shy, quiet Navajo girl took the sundials home during vacation and continued to track the outdoor shadows throughout the summer on the reservation. In a recent conversation with Price, the same girl (now a senior in high school) recalled many of the ARIES explorations and other science-rich features of her schooling. She now plans a college career in science. Price has tracked many of her former students and finds a significant proportion of these students retain high interest in science through high school and beyond.

Exploring Energy is taught in conjunction with a second theme, *The Force Be With You*. This module links seamlessly with a social studies project that culminates in a classroom "trial" between fossil fuels and alternative energy sources. After completing the module, students take home a decorated two-liter bottle that can be converted into a windmill, watermill, or solar cooker. Eyes sparkle and the pride of ownership of the apparatus is evident. In ARIES it is expected that much of the apparatus constructed will be taken home by students for continued exploration. Students are thrilled that the "stuff" is actually theirs and often ask "Are you sure I can take this home? Can I make one for my [brother, sister, parent, friend]?"

The final classroom theme of the fourth-grade year is space related. During this time, *Exploring the Earth in Motion* is taught. The module begins by having students revisit some of the same shadow concepts they addressed at the start of the year. In *Exploring Time,* outdoor shadows are one of several naturally occurring patterns that can be used as a basis for finding time. In *Exploring the Earth in Motion,* outdoor shadows provide evidence for the changing region of the Earth's surface being illuminated by the Sun from day to day, forming the basis for future understanding of seasons. By revisiting and expanding the shadow activities, students and teachers alike are able to see how new models can be constructed for understanding the natural world through their shadow observations. Students also model many of their outdoor observations within the classroom using the ARIES astronomy lab, a unique feature in two of the curriculum's modules.

The fifth-grade year begins with the theme *Let Your Light Shine.* Students use the *Exploring Light and Color* module as their science resource at this time. The module includes a range of discovery activities to investigate light, color, lenses, refraction, and reflection. Almost without exception, some children doing the pinhole camera exploration (constructed with the ARIES light and color lab) are amazed to observe the inverted image inside the camera. "How come my pinhole camera isn't working? Everything is upside down, even when I turn it over! What's wrong?" Price, like all ARIES teachers, resists the impulse to respond directly, but rather has become very comfortable in helping children actively construct their own understanding of what they are observing or doing. In ARIES classrooms, teachers work to help students make sense of their observations through gentle questioning and shared learning.

Exploring the Moon and Stars is used in conjunction with the final fifth-grade theme, *Astronomy Adventures.* Students are able to model many of their indoor and outdoor astronomy observations in the school district's portable STARLAB planetarium. Price and her Naaba Ani's fifth-grade students were selected to be videotaped working with *Exploring the Moon and Stars* for an upcoming Annenberg/CPB professional development series, entitled *Essential Science.* This series is produced by the SED's Science Media Group.

The ARIES experience also transfers into the community. As an example, parents approach Price and her colleague at the community's only ballpark with questions about the astronomy and physical science being done in ARIES. The parents are curious about what they see their children bringing home and how best to respond to the children's questions. Project ARIES has also been featured successfully in the Bloomfield School district's ELL (English Language Learner) program. During the summer of 2003 Price conducted training with eight district teachers who then taught four different one-week summer adventure camps geared for 120 students in grades 1–6. This is the first time the district offered such a program. During these camps, students used the *Exploring Energy* module as their primary focus. A simpler journaling process and more help in preparing the waterwheels and windmills for the younger students were the only modifications made. Teachers, students, and parents were very enthusiastic about the camp, and it will be continued in summer 2004 pending funding.

ARIES teachers report they have become much better at asking questions and revisiting what they thought they knew. Price's experience is typical—pondering and thinking about the big ideas in science more than ever before. ARIES workshops force teachers to build up new understanding of the science in the modules rather than borrow another's understanding. In turn, the teachers model the same approach in the classroom. For experienced ARIES teachers this has become a transferable skill.

Featured Classrooms: Alice M. Harte Elementary School

Beginning in 1993 Catledge piloted and field-tested four ARIES modules (*Exploring Time*, *Exploring Light and Color*, *Exploring Energy*, and *Exploring the Earth in Motion*) with her Harte students. During the comparison-testing phase of the project, students from another Harte classroom, taught by a colleague, were part of the control group. That is, these students were also studying the same astronomy and physical science topics as in the ARIES classrooms, but with a different curriculum. Based in part on the results of the comparison testing, Catledge now teaches ARIES to two third-grade classes and two fourth-grade classes.

Catledge sees the same students for two successive years. For one quarter, she may teach language arts with the third-grade classes and science with the fourth-grade classes. During the next quarter, she will teach science to third graders. Each year the third-grade students complete *Exploring the Earth in Motion*, the ARIES module that develops a foundation for understanding seasons. These same students complete *Exploring Light and Color* in grade 4. Catledge's science classes at Harte are two hours in length, giving students opportunity to write down their predictions and an open-ended time to familiarize themselves with the apparatus. In addition, a longer science period gives students opportunity to think or work through some of their questions within the class time frame. As an example, when discussing compasses and compass directions, one student allowed that "north was the way you faced, and each way you faced was north." Asked to walk south he decided he would have to back up. He constructed his own compass from a bar magnet and compass rose and spent a long time indoors and outdoors investigating compass behavior. Writing later in his "What I know..." section in his science journal he noted that he had come to realize "there was something wrong with my first model since I found that I was able to walk south without backing up."

When doing ARIES explorations, Catledge has the students work around flat desks pushed together. Students work in pairs or in groups of four depending on the nature of the exploration. Most ARIES explorations are designed to be done by students working in pairs. Catledge keeps the third graders in pairs until they have become accustomed to group work. When working in groups of four, one of the students is responsible for getting and returning the materials. Every exploration in the ARIES science journals has a checklist to help students monitor the materials needed to complete the activity. While another student may take on a reporting role, all the students record their observations and readings in their science journals. In addition to the embedded assessments integrated into the science journals, Catledge uses hands-on activities to provide opportunity for her students to further demonstrate with the apparatus what they are able to do or have come to know. For example, students can model in the ARIES astronomy lab the way sunlight illuminates different portions of the Earth's surface for different periods from month to month, a prerequisite for eventually understanding seasons. Or in the light and color lab, the students can demonstrate the way the parallel beams of light are refracted when passing through a glass of water and the effect when two different colored beams of light are mixed.

Like most ARIES teachers, Catledge schedules evening star parties for her students and their families as a direct spin-off from the modules. Students prepare in advance by constructing their own star finders and the ARIES refracting telescope. She sees parental involvement as key to nurturing interest in science and astronomy with young children, and a wonderful setting for them to learn together. Catledge and parent helpers prepare astronomically connected refreshments, such as "Moon Cookies" or other "celestial-theme treats." ARIES teachers agree that adults find the experience every bit as thrilling as the students, and have the same questions and comments. In fact, many of the ARIES students know more about astronomy and space science than their parents. When looking at Saturn through a telescope for the first time, people of all ages will inevitably ask, "Is that real, or is it a picture?" Or if it is the Moon that is being observed the questions range from "Why are parts of it so dark?" to "Can we see where the people landed or any of the things they left behind on the surface?"

Members of the local astronomy club—many who recall that their own interest in space science began at the same age as the students—set up telescopes in the school yard for observing the Moon, stars and star fields, and any planets visible at the time of the party. The classes create their own "celestial bingo game." The card for the game has images of constellations, star clusters, the Moon, and double stars. Astronomy club members have their telescopes locked onto the features pictured on the cards, and as students and parents move from one viewing station to another, they complete the bingo game. Everyone practices naked eye astronomy and looks at the craters on the Moon using the ARIES telescopes. Many Harte students now ask for and receive telescopes and binoculars as gifts, and stargazing becomes a family affair as a result of the introduction to astronomy through ARIES. In some of the ARIES modules, an adult-level observing guide can be copied for use at home. The guide contains suggestions for finding directions and good viewing locations for both daytime and nighttime observing along with helpful hints about identifying key celestial markers. Additionally, the star parties at Harte demonstrate that it is possible to observe the heavens in urban settings without the benefit of dark skies.

Catledge finds the experience of teachers with ARIES differs little from that with students. When leading workshops she finds many teachers and even science specialists cannot reliably predict the pattern of outdoor shadows or model moon phases. Most do not know how the hours of daylight and darkness vary from one location to another, from season to season, nor how different colors mix to give new colors. Much of this is expected since few adults have had opportunity to investigate these concepts in depth. Catledge remarks that even "after only one day of work with ARIES explorations teachers begin to change their models" for understanding many of these concepts. Forced to create the moon phases as in *Exploring the Moon and Stars*, teachers who were "Earth-shadow people" begin to construct a model of the phenomena in keeping with scientists' understanding. Or working with the ARIES ripple tank, teachers are able to study the motion of transverse waves as one step in understanding how energy moves from one location to another.

Assessing the Effect

All fourth- and fifth- grade New Mexico students are tested in science. The data in Table 1 show the 2000–2003 average science scores of those Naaba Ani fourth- and fifth-grade students in the ARIES classrooms in comparison to the district and state scores. In all instances, the ARIES students had percentile scores significantly above the district and state averages.

Table 1. Science Test Scores for Fourth- and Fifth-Grade New Mexico Students: 2000–2003

National Percentile Scores in Science From Norm-Referenced Tests								
Spring test	2000		2001		2002			2003
Grade	4th	5th	4th	5th	4th	5th	4th	5th
ARIES Class/Naaba Ani	84%	92%	77%	83%	77%	78%	76%	81%
District/Naaba Ani	44%	43%	44%	50%	40%	44%	53%	38%
State	48%	50%	49%	50%	50%	47%	51%	49%

All students in the fourth grade in Louisiana take the Louisiana Education Assessment Program (LEAP) statewide assessment exam. Table 2 shows the test scores for the Harte students who have had two years of ARIES. Thirty percent scored at the advanced (highest) level and thirty-nine percent scored at the mastery (second highest) level. The ARIES students score higher than classmates from Harte, and higher than fourth graders across the New Orleans Parish and the state.

Table 2. Science Test Scores for Harte ARIES Students: 2003

Louisiana Education Assessment Program Scores: 2003*					
	Advanced	Mastery	Basic	Approaching Basic	Unsatisfactory
ARIES Students	30.0%	39.0%	18.0%	10.0%	3.0%
Harte	8.0%	19.0%	42.0%	25.0%	8.0%
Parish (District)	0.0%	3.0%	19.0%	44.0%	34.0%
State	2.0%	12.0%	37.0%	35.0%	13.0%

*Due to rounding, not all totals add up to 100%

By every measure, the test results from Naaba Ani and Harte are impressive. Since these data are not part of a controlled study it is impossible to definitively state what factors are at work. The ARIES curriculum is consistent with the vision in the Standards to emphasize fewer concepts, in-depth inquiry, authentic assessment, constructivist pedagogy, sustained professional development, and more. Teacher commitment, student demographics, administrative support, and other factors may well play a part. Yet to the degree ARIES reflects the blueprint for change in the Standards these results confirm the validity of that vision.

As noted earlier, the developers of ARIES carried out a comparison-testing study. It begins with the summative evaluation of 8,000 ARIES students as a baseline. Then in 1996–1997, the developers conducted a comparison study focused on three modules in 31 elementary and middle school classrooms. The study involved approximately 700 students in 15 classrooms using AR-IES materials and about the same number of students in 16 control classrooms. Students in the control classrooms covered the same major concepts as the ARIES students. All students in the two groups were tested on 17 different items, both before and after classroom instruction. The overall data show that ARIES students both significantly increased their conceptual understanding of the materials taught and significantly outperformed students in control classes where the same topics were taught without ARIES. The results from Naaba Ani and Harte are consistent with this earlier comparison study.

Summary

The road map and destination drawn in the Standards for changing science teaching and learning may seem unrealistic to many educators given the current nationwide focus on testing. On the other hand, there is a different lesson to be drawn from the Naaba Ani and Harte experiences for teachers faced with increasing demands on their time for test preparation. Both schools are ethnically diverse, one in a rural setting and the other part of a large urban district. These are not settings that traditionally have the highest test scores. The lesson here is that it is possible for children from all settings and of all abilities to experience science education at its best—particularly as defined by the NSES—and to also do very well on standardized tests.

As noted throughout, there is almost complete overlap between ARIES and the attributes of science education needing *More Emphasis* called for in the Standards. The curriculum is based on misconception research, focused on a limited number of major concepts, built around a pedagogy that requires both students and teachers to develop new models of the natural world, designed so the science is accessible to children through observation and discovery, and readily integrated into any school's program. The effects of these *More Emphases* are illustrated in the performance of the students in the Naaba Ani and Harte classrooms.

References

Culotta, E. 1990. Can science education be saved? *Science* 250 (4986): December 7.

Grossman, M. C., I. I. Shapiro, and R. B. Ward. 2000a. *Exploring light and color.* Watertown, MA: Charlesbridge Publishing.

Grossman, M. C., I. I. Shapiro, and R. B. Ward. 2000b. *Exploring the Earth in motion.* Watertown, MA: Charlesbridge Publishing.

Grossman, M. C., Riley-Black, I. I. Shapiro, and R. B. Ward. 2001. *Exploring energy.* Watertown, MA: Charlesbridge Publishing.

Grossman, M. C., R. S. Rothstein, I. I. Shapiro, and R. B. Ward. 2001. *Exploring waves*. Watertown, MA: Charlesbridge Publishing

Grossman, M. C., I. I. Shapiro, and R. B. Ward. 2001a. *Exploring motion and forces*. Watertown, MA: Charlesbridge Publishing.

Grossman, M. C., I. I. Shapiro, and R. B. Ward. 2001b. *Exploring time*. Watertown, MA: Charlesbridge Publishing.

Grossman, M. C., J. Peritz, I. I. Shapiro, and R. B. Ward. 2002. *Exploring the moon and stars*. Watertown, MA: Charlesbridge Publishing.

Grossman, M. C., J. Peritz, R. S. Rothstein, I. I. Shapiro, and R. B. Ward. 2003. *Exploring navigation*. Watertown, MA: Charlesbridge Publishing.

National Research Council. (NRC). 1996. *National science education standards*. Washington, DC: National Academy Press.

National Science Teachers Association (NSTA). 1990. *Science teachers speak out: The NSTA lead paper on science and technology education for the 21st century, a position paper*. Washington, DC: Author.

Nelson, B. H., I. R. Weiss, and L. E. Conway. 1992. *Science and mathematics education briefing book, volume 3*. Chapel Hill, NC: Horizon Research.

Simpson, R., and J. Oliver. 1990. A summary of major influences toward achievement in science among adolescent students. *Science Education* 74: 1–18.

Weiss, I. R. 1994. *A profile of science and mathematics education in the United States, 1993*. Chapel Hill, NC: Horizon Research.

Successes and Continuing Challenges:

Meeting the NSES Visions for Improving Science in Middle Schools

Robert E. Yager
Science Education Center
University of Iowa

T he authors and coauthors of the 15 chapters represent an intriguing set with respect to the type of schools, program foci, and their degree of alignment with the National Science Education Standards (NSES). Evidence for the success of the programs concerning their impact on students, schools, and communities proved the most difficult feature for many to identify and quantify. It was generally easier to describe a program than to establish its impact on students with scores and descriptive evidence from a variety of assessment efforts.

Noteworthy is the fact that many of the 15 exemplars did not arise in typical schools, especially in view of the over 16,000 public schools operating in the United States. Certainly it is easier to change and to implement the Standards in special schools with an atypical teaching force, and in communities with nearby colleges, special facilities, or funded projects from which to draw. Nonetheless, the 15 exemplars identified provide impressive information as to how the NSES can be (and are being) used to achieve the goals summarized at the end of each chapter in the Standards.

These 15 stories give evidence of the Standards' impact, along with important examples for others for improvements they might consider if they want to move in directions like those advanced by the hundreds of persons involved in preparing the Standards over a four-year period (1992–96). These were years of debate and consensus building, which resulted in the final versions of the National Standards.

The exemplars comprising this monograph have not made significant progress with respect to *all* the standards listed in the *More Emphasis* recommendations, which include 9 suggestions for needed changes in teaching, 14 features recommended for programs designed to prepare and/or provide continuing education projects for in-service teachers, 7 new directions for assessment efforts, and 17 new guidelines which focus on general content and those associated directly with inquiry. A full listing of all Less/More Emphasis recommendations can be found in Appendix 1.

More Emphasis in the Teaching Standards

The exemplary middle school programs all provided evidence of changes in teaching. Five of the nine *More Emphasis* conditions were judged as having been met in an exemplary manner. The remaining four standards were found to have been demonstrated by over half of the 15 exemplars.

By far the greatest need (at least as evidenced by the exemplars described in this monograph) was in the ninth feature (NSES, p. 52), namely, the teacher involved in "working with other teachers to enhance the total science program." Perhaps too often exemplary program teachers are individuals who do not affect the total school program as much as they should. Perhaps many of their colleagues do not share their dedication, their views toward the NSES visions, or their practice of inquiry as it exemplifies science as well as their teaching.

Other aspects of recommended changes in teaching where more progress is warranted focus on: (1) *Continually assessing student understanding.* Too often standard measures from other instructors were used; too infrequently students were asked to demonstrate their understanding by using the information and/or skills taught in new situations and contexts. (2) *Understanding and responding to individual student's interests, strengths, experiences, and needs.* Too often even the exciting programs come from unique situations, teacher planning and leadership, whole class activities, and content foci. (3) *Sharing responsibility for learning with students.* Many find such sharing difficult, since most teachers, parents, and administrators start with the assumption that this is primarily the teachers' chief responsibility. (4) *Supporting a classroom community with cooperation, shared responsibility, and respect.* Again, many of the exemplars had moved in this direction; in other cases there was little evidence that this condition had been fully met. Progress was reported in all areas, at least by some of the authors. However, these were the weakest areas noted after analyzing the analyses and conclusions of the 15 preceding chapters.

Most would still maintain that changes in teaching are the most critical needs if the reforms of the NSES are to be realized generally in classrooms around the world. The 15 programs described in this monograph have succeeded in showing how teaching can change, while also identifying some areas where continued attention is needed.

More Emphasis in the Professional Development Standards

An evaluation of the middle school programs in this monograph yields more information that progress is being made in implementing the Professional Development Standards. Nearly all reported that the following *More Emphasis* conditions recommended for the education of teachers were being met and working in an exemplary manner:

1. Inquiry into teaching and learning;
2. Learning science through investigation and inquiry;
3. Integration of science and teaching knowledge;
4. Integration of theory and practice in school settings;
5. Collegial and collaborative learning; and
6. Teacher as intellectual, reflective practitioner.

Three areas where significantly more attention is needed are

1. Staff developers as facilitators consultants and planners;
2. Teacher as source and facilitator of change; and
3. Teacher as producer of knowledge about teaching.

Five other areas were in evidence in some chapters, but missing in others:

1. Long-term coherent plans;
2. Mix of internal and external expertise;
3. Teacher as leader;
4. Teacher as member of collegial, professional communities; and
5. A wide variety of professional development activities.

More Emphasis in the Assessment Standards

The seven *More Emphasis* conditions envisioned to improve assessment practices were also used by the 15 exemplars for middle school. One of the seven conditions was mentioned as having been achieved by all the authors—assessing to learn what students do understand. Much progress has been accomplished in the following two areas:

1. Assessing what is most highly valued; and
2. Assessing scientific understanding and reasoning.

One area of the Assessment Standards was rarely considered or described as significant by any of the exemplars: the recommendation that teachers be involved in the development of external assessments. Perhaps external examination groups should seek out more teachers who are preparing such exams, and who are knowledgeable and skilled in meeting the NSES visions. Although certainly not as glaring a deficiency as the *More Emphasis* condition of "teacher involvement in external assessments," the NSES recommendation that teachers assess "opportunity to learn" lags behind among our exemplars.

Two areas where much is being done (while still leaving room for improvement) are "assessing rich, well-structured knowledge," and "students engaged in ongoing assessment of their work and that of others."

More Emphasis in the Content and Inquiry Standards

As might be expected, all of the exemplars reported significant progress concerning the NSES recommended *content* foci; 12 of the 17 *More Emphasis* conditions were mentioned and illustrated in all 15 reports; five were met in excess of 90% of the reports. These were

1. Understanding scientific concepts and developing abilities of inquiry;
2. Learning subject matter disciplines in the context of inquiry, technology, science in personal and social perspectives, and history and nature of science;
3. Integrating all aspects of science content;
4. Science as argument and explanation; and
5. Communicating science explanations.

Unlike some of the other monograph foci, two areas were definitely more in need of attention:

1. Doing more investigations in order to develop understanding, ability, values of inquiry and knowledge of science content; and
2. Applying the results of experiments to scientific arguments and explanations.

Meeting the *More Emphasis* conditions was in evidence in many of the programs in the following areas:

1. Using multiple process skills—manipulation, cognitive, procedural; and
2. Groups of students often analyzing and synthesizing data after defending conclusions.

Other content conditions of the NSES met in an exemplary way (but to a more limited degree), included

1. Studying a few fundamental science concepts;
2. Implementing inquiry as instructional strategies, abilities, and ideas to be learned;
3. Activities that investigate and analyze science questions;
4. Investigations over extended periods of time;
5. Process skills in context;
6. Using evidence and strategies for developing or revising an explanation; and
7. Management of ideas and information.

Conclusion

Attention to the Standards among all authors indicates to what degree we have succeeded in finding real exemplars in teaching, professional development, assessment, and content consistent with the NSES recommendations. We now have data regarding a great variety of content, continuing growth and professional development programs, grade levels, discipline samples, and varying geographic regions. The diversity of teachers, schools, and curricular focus is extraordinary. Perhaps we should have anticipated that the most remarkable and successful teachers, classes, and schools would vary greatly from the norm.

All told, the 15 programs described herein illustrate where we are with respect to realizing the visions included in the 1996 Standards—nine years after their publication and acceptance as needed new directions. Our exemplars here have been scored in terms of what the contents of the 15 chapters indicate. The range is a high of 100% of the *More Emphasis* conditions met by one program to a low of 64% by another. When all are considered, the 15 exemplars meet the NSES *More Emphasis* conditions with an average score of 87%.

We hope and expect that the stories told will inspire teachers. There are still areas to explore and to stress more diligently. However, if all teachers and all schools were to develop similar models with similar evidences for their success, we would have achieved much of what the teachers and others involved with the development of the NSES envisioned over four years of debate. At that point we would need to consider new Standards as suggested ways that we could be even more successful creating scientifically literate middle school graduates, such as our society sorely needs.

There is only one year remaining in the decade that the NSES leaders predicted would be needed to make major advances. We hope there will be many more exemplars in the years to come and that NSTA and the profession will continue to support searches for them so that they, too, can continue to light a path to a better tomorrow.

Appendix

The *National Science Education Standards* envision change throughout the system. The **teaching standards** encompass the following changes in emphases:

LESS EMPHASIS ON	MORE EMPHASIS ON
Treating all students alike and responding to the group as a whole	Understanding and responding to individual student's interests, strengths, experiences, and needs
Rigidly following curriculum	Selecting and adapting curriculum
Focusing on student acquisition of information	Focusing on student understanding and use of scientific knowledge, ideas, and inquiry processes
Presenting scientific knowledge through lecture, text, and demonstration	Guiding students in active and extended scientific inquiry
Asking for recitation of acquired knowledge	Providing opportunities for scientific discussion and debate among students
Testing students for factual information at the end of the unit or chapter	Continuously assessing student understanding
Maintaining responsibility and authority	Sharing responsibility for learning with students
Supporting competition	Supporting a classroom community with cooperation, shared responsibility, and respect
Working alone	Working with other teachers to enhance the science program

Reprinted with permission from National Science Education Standards. 1996. National Academy of Sciences, courtesy of the National Academies Press, Washington, DC.

National Science Teachers Association

The *National Science Education Standards* envision change throughout the system. The **professional development** standards encompass the following changes in emphases:

LESS EMPHASIS ON	MORE EMPHASIS ON
Transmission of teaching knowledge and skills by lectures	Inquiry into teaching and learning
Learning science by lecture and reading	Learning science through investigation and inquiry
Separation of science and teaching knowledge	Integration of science and teaching knowledge
Separation of theory and practice	Integration of theory and practice in school settings
Individual learning	Collegial and collaborative learning
Fragmented, one-shot sessions	Long-term coherent plans
Courses and workshops	A variety of professional development activities
Reliance on external expertise	Mix of internal and external expertise
Staff developers as educators	Staff developers as facilitators, consultants, and planners
Teacher as technician	Teacher as intellectual, reflective practitioner
Teacher as consumer of knowledge about teaching	Teacher as producer of knowledge about teaching
Teacher as follower	Teacher as leader
Teacher as an individual based in a classroom	Teacher as a member of a collegial professional community
Teacher as target of change	Teacher as source and facilitator of change

The *National Science Education Standards* envision change throughout the system. The **assessment standards** encompass the following changes in emphases:

LESS EMPHASIS ON	MORE EMPHASIS ON
Assessing what is easily measured	Assessing what is most highly valued
Assessing discrete knowledge	Assessing rich, well-structured knowledge
Assessing scientific knowledge	Assessing scientific understanding and reasoning
Assessing to learn what students do not know	Assessing to learn what students do understand
Assessing only achievement	Assessing achievement and opportunity to learn
End of term assessments by teachers	Students engaged in ongoing assessment of their work and that of others
Development of external assessments by measurement experts alone	Teachers involved in the development of external assessments

The *National Science Education Standards* envision change throughout the system. The science **content and inquiry standards** encompass the following changes in emphases:

LESS EMPHASIS ON	MORE EMPHASIS ON
Knowing scientific facts and information	Understanding scientific concepts and developing abilities of inquiry
Studying subject matter disciplines (physical, life, earth sciences) for their own sake	Learning subject matter disciplines in the context of inquiry, technology, science in personal and social perspectives, and history and nature of science
Separating science knowledge and science process	Integrating all aspects of science content
Covering many science topics	Studying a few fundamental science concepts
Implementing inquiry as a set of processes	Implementing inquiry as instructional strategies, abilities, and ideas to be learned

CHANGING EMPHASES TO PROMOTE INQUIRY

LESS EMPHASIS ON	MORE EMPHASIS ON
Activities that demonstrate and verify science content	Activities that investigate and analyze science questions
Investigations confined to one class period	Investigations over extended periods of time
Process skills out of context	Process skills in context
Emphasis on individual process skills such as observation or inference	Using multiple process skills—manipulation, cognitive, procedural
Getting an answer	Using evidence and strategies for developing or revising an explanation
Science as exploration and experiment	Science as argument and explanation
Providing answers to questions about science content	Communicating science explanations
Individuals and groups of students analyzing and synthesizing data without defending a conclusion	Groups of students often analyzing and synthesizing data after defending conclusions
Doing few investigations in order to leave time to cover large amounts of content	Doing more investigations in order to develop understanding, ability, values of inquiry and knowledge of science content
Concluding inquiries with the result of the experiment	Applying the results of experiments to scientific arguments and explanations

Management of materials and equipment

Private communication of student ideas
and conclusions to teacher

Management of ideas and information

Public communication of student ideas
and work to classmates

The *National Science Education Standards* envision change throughout the system. The **program standards** encompass the following changes in emphases:

LESS EMPHASIS ON	MORE EMPHASIS ON
Developing science programs at different grade levels independently of one another	Coordinating the development of the K–12 science program across grade levels
Using assessments unrelated to curriculum and teaching	Aligning curriculum, teaching, and assessment
Maintaining current resource allocations for books	Allocating resources necessary for hands-on inquiry teaching aligned with the *Standards*
Textbook- and lecture-driven curriculum	Curriculum that supports the *Standards*, and includes a variety of components, such as laboratories emphasizing inquiry and field trips
Broad coverage of unconnected factual information	Curriculum that includes natural phenomena and science-related social issues that students encounter in everyday life
Treating science as a subject isolated from other school subjects	Connecting science to other school subjects, such as mathematics and social studies
Science learning opportunities that favor one group of students	Providing challenging opportunities for all students to learn science
Limiting hiring decisions to the administration	Involving successful teachers of science in the hiring process
Maintaining the isolation of teachers	Treating teachers as professionals whose work requires opportunities for continual learning and networking
Supporting competition	Promoting collegiality among teachers as a team to improve the school
Teachers as followers	Teachers as decision makers

The emphasis charts for **system standards** are organized around shifting the emphases at three levels of organization within the education system—district, state, and federal. The three levels of the system selected for these charts are only representative of the many components of the science education system that need to change to promote the vision of science education described in the *National Science Education Standards.*

FEDERAL SYSTEM

LESS EMPHASIS ON	**MORE EMPHASIS ON**
Financial support for developing new curriculum materials not aligned with the *Standards*	Financial support for developing new curriculum materials aligned with the *Standards*
Support by federal agencies for professional development activities that affect only a few teachers	Support for professional development activities that are aligned with the *Standards* and promote systemwide changes
Agencies working independently on various components of science education	Coordination among agencies responsible for science education
Support for activities and programs that are unrelated to *Standards*-based reform	Support for activities and programs that successfully implement the *Standards* at state and district levels
Federal efforts that are independent of state and local levels	Coordination of reform efforts at federal, state, and local levels
Short-term projects	Long-term commitment of resources to improving science education

STATE SYSTEM

LESS EMPHASIS ON	**MORE EMPHASIS ON**
Independent initiatives to reform components of science education	Partnerships and coordination of reform efforts
Funds for workshops and programs having little connection to the *Standards*	Funds to improve curriculum and instruction based on the *Standards*
Frameworks, textbooks, and materials based on activities only marginally related to the *Standards*	Frameworks, textbooks, and materials adoption criteria aligned with national and state standards
Assessments aligned with the traditional content of science	Assessments aligned with the *Standards* and the expanded education view of science content

Current approaches to teacher education	University/college reform of teacher education to include science-specific pedagogy aligned with the *Standards*
Teacher certification based on formal, historically based requirements	Teacher certification that is based on understanding and abilities in science and science teaching

DISTRICT SYSTEM

LESS EMPHASIS ON	MORE EMPHASIS ON
Technical, short-term, in-service workshops	Ongoing professional development to support teachers
Policies unrelated to *Standards*-based reform	Policies designed to support changes called for in the *Standards*
Purchase of textbooks based on traditional topics	Purchase or adoption of curriculum aligned with the *Standards* and on a conceptual approach to science teaching, including support for hands-on science materials
Standardized tests and assessments unrelated to *Standards*-based program and practices	Assessments aligned with the *Standards*
Administration determining what will be involved in improving science education	Teacher leadership in improvement of science science education
Authority at upper levels of educational system	Authority for decisions at level of implementation
School board ignorance of science education program	School board support of improvements aligned with the *Standards*
Local union contracts that ignore changes in curriculum, instruction,	Local union contracts that support improvements indicated by the *Standards*

Contributors List

Svetlana Beltyukova, coauthor of *Do You See What I See? The Relationship Between a Professional Development Model and Student Achievement,* is an assistant professor of research and measurement at The University of Toledo in Toledo, Ohio.

Jacqueline Grennon Brooks, author of *Teaching Science With Student Thinking in Mind,* is an Associate Professor of Curriculum and Teaching at Hofstra University in Hempstead, New York.

Janice Catledge is coauthor of *ARIES—Science as Discovery and Discovery as Science!,* and a coordinator. At the time of writing, she was a teacher at Alice M. Harte Elementary School in New Orleans, Louisiana.

Charlene M. Czerniak, coauthor of *Do You See What I See? The Relationship Between a Professional Development Model and Student Achievement,* is a professor of science education at The University of Toledo in Toledo, Ohio.

Barbara Kay Foots, coauthor of *Teaching Science With Pictures,* is a science education consultant and retired manager of science, Houston Independent School District in Houston, Texas.

Margaret Foss, author of *Finding out What... and How They Learn,* is a teacher at Hawkins Middle School in Hawkins, Wisconsin.

Chris Gleason, coauthor of *Creating a Classroom Culture of Scientific Practices*, is a seventh/eighth-grade science teacher at Greenhills School in Ann Arbor, Michigan.

Yulonda Hines-Hale, coauthor of *"More Emphasis" on Scientific Explanation: Developing Conceptual Understanding and Science Literacy,* is a middle school science teacher for Detroit Public Schools in Detroit, Michigan.

Jodi J. Haney, coauthor of *Do You See What I See? The Relationship Between a Professional Development Model and Student Achievement,* is an associate professor of science education and environmental science at Bowling Green State University, Bowling Green, Ohio.

Deborah Hanuscin, coauthor of *"Re-Inventing" Science Instruction: Inquiry-Based Instruction in a Fifth/Sixth Grade Classroom,* is an assistant professor in the department of learning, teaching, and curriculum and the department of physics at the University of Missouri-Columbia.

Manisha Hariani, coauthor of *Achieving a Vision of Inquiry through Engaging and Rigorous Curriculum and Instruction,* is the associate director of the Science Education for Public Understanding (SEPUP) at the Lawrence Hall of Science at the University of California, Berkeley.

Tracy Hornyak, coauthor of *Unlocking the National Science Education Standards With IMaST,* is the IMaST team leader at Great Meadows Middle School in Great Meadows, New Jersey.

Hector Ibarra, author of *Teach Them to Fish,* is a middle school science teacher and department chair at West Branch Middle School in West Branch, Iowa.

Joseph S. Krajcik, coauthor of *"More Emphasis" on Scientific Explanation: Developing Conceptual Understanding and Science Literacy* and *Creating a Classroom Culture of Scientific Practices,* is a professor at University of Michigan in Ann Arbor, Michigan.

Franzie L. Loepp, coauthor of *Unlocking the National Science Education Standards With IMaST,* is a distinguished professor emeritus at Illinois State University in Normal, Illinois.

Andrew T. Lumpe, coauthor of *Do You See What I See? The Relationship Between a Professional Development Model and Student Achievement,* is a professor in the department of instruction at Southern Illinois University Carbondale.

Jay Mahoney, coauthor of *Creating a Classroom Culture of Scientific Practices*, is a seventh-grade science teacher at Greenhills School in Ann Arbor, Michigan.

Alyssia Martinez-Wilkinson, author of *Traveling the Inquiry Continuum: Learning Through Teacher Action Research,* is a science teacher at Bryan Middle School in Omaha, Nebraska.

Alycia Meriweather, coauthor of *"More Emphasis" on Scientific Explanation: Developing Conceptual Understanding and Science Literacy,* is a middle school science teacher for Detroit Public Schools in Detroit, Michigan.

Karen Mesmer, author of *Modeling: Naturally Selecting an Effective Teaching Method,* is a seventh-grade teacher at Baraboo Middle School in Baraboo, Wisconsin.

Elizabeth Birr Moje, coauthor of *"More Emphasis" on Scientific Explanation: Developing Conceptual Understanding and Science Literacy,* is a professor at University of Michigan in Ann Arbor, Michigan.

Marilyn K. Morey, coauthor of *Unlocking the National Science Education Standards With IMaST,* is associate director of the Center for Mathematics, Science and Technology and associate professor in curriculum and instruction at Illinois State University in Normal, Illinois.

Barbara Nagle, coauthor of *Achieving a Vision of Inquiry through Engaging and Rigorous Curriculum and Instruction,* is the director of the Science Education for Public Understanding (SEPUP) at the Lawrence Hall of Science at the University of California, Berkeley.

Ann M. Novak, coauthor of *Creating a Classroom Culture of Scientific Practices,* is a seventh/eighth-grade science teacher at Greenhills School in Ann Arbor, Michigan.

Warren Phillips, author of *Adapting the JASON Project—Real Science. Real Time. Real Learning,* is a science and TV technology teacher at Plymouth Community Intermediate School in Plymouth, Massachusetts.

Jim Pilla, coauthor of *Unlocking the National Science Education Standards With IMaST,* is a teacher at Great Meadows Middle School in Great Meadows, New Jersey.

Kathy Price is coauthor of *ARIES—Science as Discovery and Discovery as Science!* At the time of writing, she was a teacher at Naaba Ani Elementary School in Bloomfield, New Mexico.

Mary Reescano, coauthor of *Teaching Science With Pictures,* is a curricula and instructional strategies consultant at VisualRealization.com in Houston, Texas. She is also a retired science teacher and department chairperson, Houston Independent School District.

Melissa Rooney, coauthor of *"Re-Inventing" Science Instruction: Inquiry-Based Instruction in a Fifth/Sixth Grade Classroom,* is a teacher at Arlington Heights Elementary School in Bloomington, Indiana.

Sheryl Rucker, coauthor of *"More Emphasis" on Scientific Explanation: Developing Conceptual Understanding and Science Literacy,* is a middle school science teacher for Detroit Public Schools in Detroit, Michigan.

Paula Sarratt, coauthor of *"More Emphasis" on Scientific Explanation: Developing Conceptual Understanding and Science Literacy,* is a middle school science teacher for Detroit Public Schools in Detroit, Michigan.

Richard E. Satchwell, coauthor of *Unlocking the National Science Education Standards With ImaST,* is a director of the Adventure of the American Mind Project at Illinois State University in Normal, Illinois.

Terry Shaw, author of *What Do We Get to Do Today? The Middle School Full Option Science System Program,* is a coordinator of middle level professional development for the Full Option Science System (FOSS) at Lawrence Hall of Science, University of California, Berkeley.

Marcelle A. Siegel, coauthor of *Achieving a Vision of Inquiry Through Engaging and Rigorous Curriculum and Instruction,* is a science educator at the University of California, San Francisco.

Karl Spencer, coauthor of *Teaching Science With Pictures,* is a technology and pedagogical strategies solutions integrator at VisualRealization.com in Houston, Texas.

Janet Struble, coauthor of *Do You See What I See? The Relationship Between a Professional Development Model and Student Achievement,* is a science education coordinator at The University of Toledo in Toledo, Ohio.

LeeAnn M. Sutherland, coauthor of *"More Emphasis" on Scientific Explanation: Developing Conceptual Understanding and Science Literacy,* is a research scientist at University of Michigan in Ann Arbor, Michigan.

R. Bruce Ward, coauthor of *ARIES—Science as Discovery and Discovery as Science!,* is a science education researcher and curriculum developer at the Harvard-Smithsonian Center for Astrophysics, Harvard University, Cambridge, Massachusetts.

Index

Note: Page numbers in *italics* refer to figures or tables.

A

Achievement tests. *See* Assessment tools

Adiabatic pressure, Big Idea project, 8–9

Air quality project, 101, 108

Amusement parks, science questions about, 2

Anemometer activity, *73*

Artifacts. *See* Student-created products

Assessment Standards, 131

    Changing Emphases, *38–40*, 70, 71, 211–12, *218*

    in guided inquiry teaching, 78–79, *79*

    in IMaST curriculum, 144–45

    See also Changing Emphases; National Science Education Standards (NSES)

Assessment tools

    achievement rubrics, 77, *77*, 109–10, *109, 169*

    Criterion Referenced Test (CRT), 121, 126

    data tables, 122, 123, *129*

    Iowa Test of Basic Skills (ITBS), 81–82, *82*

    Kentucky Core Content Test (KCCT), 191

    Likert Survey, 123, *130*

    Louisiana Education Assessment Program (LEAP), 205

    Morgan-Jinks Student Efficacy Scale, 149

    Oklahoma Priority Academic Student Skills (PASS) Test, 190

    TerraNova Multiple Assessment, 149

    Third International Mathematics and Science Study (TIMSS), 149

Astronomy, Big Idea project example, 5

B

Ballard, Bob, 164, 166, 167, 168

Balloon car rubric, 77, *77*

Banneker CEMS (Community of Excellence in Mathematics and Science), 115–16, 126

Benchmark lessons, 86–87, 89–90, *90*

Best practices for teaching science, 48–49

Big Ideas seminars, 5

Biology. *See* Life science

Bowling Green State University, 15

C

California, Lemon Grove, demographic data, 153

Campus-based learning model, 53

Case studies model, 54

Catledge, Janice, 196, 198, 203, 204

Changing Emphases, 3, 154, *154*, 173–74

    assessment program for, 59-61

    conditions in Discover Lab Concept, 3, 8

    digital imagery technology and, 51–52

    explanatory science writing and, 100, 112

    Project ARIES and, 196–97

    in Project-Based Study, 54, 65–66

    Visual Realization Program goals and, 46

    See also Assessment Standards; Content and Inquiry Standards; National Science Education Standards; Professional Development Standards; Teaching Standards

Chapman, Kathy, 2, 3–4, 5, 10

Chemistry project, 86, 88, 91

Chinook winds, Big Idea project, 8–9

Collaborative learning

    in guided inquiry teaching, 76, 77, 78

    in IMaST curriculum, 147